Henry Maine's *Ancient Law* as an Expression of Victorian Humanism

'To every thing there is a season, and a time to every purpose under the heaven.' –
Ecclesiastes 3.1 (KJV)

Henry Maine's *Ancient Law* as an Expression of Victorian Humanism

Paul J. du Plessis

EDINBURGH
University Press

Edinburgh University Press is one of the leading university presses in the UK. Publishing new research in the arts and humanities, EUP connects people and ideas to inspire creative thinking, open new perspectives and shape the world we live in. For more information, visit www.edinburghuniversitypress.com.

Edinburgh University Press Ltd
13 Infirmary Street, Edinburgh EH1 1LT

Typeset in 10/12 Goudy Old Style by
IDSUK (DataConnection) Ltd, and
Printed and bound in the UK using 100% renewable electricity by
CPI Group (UK) Ltd

A CIP record for this book is available from the British Library

ISBN 978 1 3995 5062 8 (hardback)
ISBN 978 1 3995 5064 2 (webready PDF)
ISBN 978 1 3995 5063 5 (epub)

EU Authorised Representative:
Easy Access System Europe
Mustamäe tee 50, 10621 Tallinn, Estonia
gpsr.requests@easproject.com

MIX
Paper | Supporting responsible forestry
FSC® C013604
FSC www.fsc.org

This book is printed using paper from well-managed forests, recycling and other controlled sources

Contents

Acknowledgements

The majority of the research for this book was carried out in the 2021–2022 academic year while I was privileged to be a visiting fellow at All Souls College, University of Oxford. The outstanding library resources, stimulating discussions with fellow scholars during meals and various social engagements significantly contributed to my work. In recognition of this intellectual support, I dedicate this book to the warden and fellows of All Souls College.

Introduction

I first encountered Henry Maine's *Ancient Law* while researching for a PhD in Roman law. My initial impression of the book was positive, although, like many of Maine's readers, I found the boldness of his assertions and the lack of supporting evidence breathtaking. Despite these shortcomings, the book provided a fresh and thought-provoking narrative that has profoundly influenced my research trajectory. Throughout the years, I have frequently revisited *Ancient Law* for inspiration. Moreover, as my interest in his work increased, I kept up with the growing literature on Henry Maine. This literature spans legal history, sociology, and anthropology.

Given the broad scholarly interest in Maine and his works, it is unsurprising that his intellectual legacy, rather than his actual scholarly contributions, has become the focal point of much of the secondary literature. This is expected from the work of an influential Victorian intellectual who significantly influenced many academic disciplines and their development throughout the twentieth century. And yet, this shift in focus risks creating a disconnect between the interpretations of Maine's scholarly output and its substantive content. This observation inspired the conception of this book.

This study aims to strengthen the connection between Maine's writings and their interpretations. It seeks to accomplish this by revisiting the contents of Maine's seminal work, *Ancient Law*. Rather than examining the book's subsequent intellectual legacies or broader contextualisation within Victorian intellectual concerns such as colonialism or liberalism as its primary focus, the book will re-engage with its sources in the spirit of Victorian Humanism that underpins Maine's work. It will delve into the sources Maine utilised to construct the narratives in *Ancient Law*, thus illuminating his intent with the book and the message he sought to convey. By re-examining these sources, I aim to contribute to ongoing debates concerning Maine, his scholarly output, and his legacies. Given the comparative nature of Maine's endeavour, this book should also be read as a Humanist critique of current global and comparative legal history debates.[1]

This book consists of seven chapters. The first two chapters are designed to give the reader an account of Maine's life and the contexts in which *Ancient Law* was written. These chapters frame the rest of the book, in which the different aspects of Maine's *Ancient Law* are discussed separately. I firmly believe that the arrangement of topics in Maine's book was purposeful. The chapters of Maine's

[1] Duve, 'What is Global Legal History?', for a survey of these debates.

book contain a series of interwoven arguments that can only be understood adequately when the work is assessed using the structure that Maine settled on when writing the book. These are explored in the order in which Maine arranged them in *Ancient Law* in chapters three to seven. The final part is devoted to conclusions and assessing broader themes emerging from this study.

The present study had to impose limits due to Maine's vast influence across various disciplines. It is essential to state these limits explicitly to avoid disappointing potential readers. This book does not offer an intellectual history of Maine's role in the growth and decline of Victorian liberalism, as this topic has been extensively discussed throughout the twentieth century. Additionally, the book will not delve into Maine's colonial legacy in detail, as this has been covered in a recent comprehensive work by Mantena, and insights from it have been used in this book. Lastly, the book does not provide an in-depth analysis of Maine's work from a contemporary sociological or anthropological angle. Again, these angles have been studied comprehensively throughout the twentieth century. While the significance of Maine's *Ancient Law* for developing these disciplines is touched upon in the final part, a full account is not provided, as this would divert the present study's focus.

Ancient Law is a rich and intellectually complex work. It was written by a Victorian intellectual who received the best education, steeped in the traditions of Greece and Rome, that social connections and privilege afforded. As a work in the tradition of Victorian Humanism, it engages subtly and cautiously with important geo-political debates of its own time. It is hardly surprising that this book has had such an important intellectual legacy. As I will show in this monograph, this legacy can be adequately understood only through a careful reading of *Ancient Law*.

Paul J. du Plessis
September 2024

Chapter 1

Institutions and Criticism

Wise or fortunate is the prince who connects his own reputation with the honour and interest of a perpetual order of men.[1]

1. INTRODUCTION

1861 was another successful year for the London-based publisher John Murray III. The publishing house that bore his name, founded by his grandfather in 1768, had by then already established itself as one of the foremost publishers in the United Kingdom and had amassed an impressive book list that included works by Jane Austen, Walter Scott and Lord Byron. Two years earlier, in 1859, Murray had published Charles Darwin's *On the Origin of Species by Means of Natural Selection.* This book, an instant success, revolutionised the natural sciences in the late nineteenth century. Its impact continues today across much of this field and beyond.[2] Murray's next project, in 1861, was the publication of a legal treatise by Henry Maine, a former Regius Professor of Civil Law at Cambridge University. This book, *Ancient Law*, proved to be another best-seller. Much like Darwin's work, it, too, significantly influenced the social sciences during the late nineteenth century.[3] Unlike Darwin's work, however, its contemporary impact has been more modest, though not insignificant.[4] The fact that the two works have such different legacies speaks not only to their respective content but also to broader changes within the realm of social sciences and the study and teaching of English law, specifically. This gives cause for a renewed investigation of the book and its content.[5] This study will focus on the book *Ancient Law*, seeking to understand its historical contexts and the author's message, crucial to its widespread influence in the late 1800s.

1 Gibbon and Fernández-Armesto, *The History of the Decline and Fall of the Roman Empire. Vol. 5, Justinian and the Roman Law*, 249.

2 Geroulanos, *The Invention of Prehistory*, 75–91.

3 The impact of Maine's work is still visible in many legal traditions across Europe and elsewhere. See Lira Gonzalez and Martin, 'Henry S. Maine', generally, for an account of his influence in Spain. For a survey, see Hadjigeorgiou, 'The Legacy of Sir Henry Maine'. For a recent account of his impact in the United States of America, see Adcock, 'Liberalism, Progress, and Comparative Inquiry', generally.

4 Cotterrell, *The Politics of Jurisprudence*, 46–8; Schmidt, 'Henry Maine's "Modern Law" From Status to Contract and Back Again?', generally.

5 Capogrossi Colognesi, *Dalla storia di Roma alle origini della società civile*, 9–14, for an assessment of the continued importance of nineteenth-century legal scholarship such as that of Maine for contemporary debates on the origins of the State and of the law.

Henry James Sumner Maine was born in 1822. He spent most of his childhood in Henley-on-Thames.[6] Although his family was not wealthy, they had connections, and these enabled him to attend Christ's Hospital, a respectable chartered public school founded in the mid-sixteenth century, where he received a robust Victorian education based on Humanist ideals and steeped in the classical traditions of Greece and Rome.[7] After completing his secondary education, he attended Pembroke College, Cambridge, where he excelled in studying classics.[8] There, he was exposed to the latest methodological developments in the field, which profoundly impacted his intellectual formation as a scholar, especially concerning his first book, *Ancient Law*.[9] Upon graduation, he became a tutor in classics at Trinity Hall, Cambridge. Soon after that, in 1847, he was elected Regius Professor of Civil (Roman) Law – a post he occupied until 1854. Even with its prestigious status, the position offered low pay.[10] Maine lacked independent wealth and had to secure supplementary sources of income. He was called to the bar during this period, but found little success.[11] Two years later, he was appointed a Reader in Jurisprudence and Civil Law at Middle Temple, which provided a better salary.[12] This new source of income permitted him to resign from the Cambridge chair in 1854.

From 1854 to 1862, Maine continued lecturing in law while working as an essayist for various publications in London.[13] During this time, he wrote *Ancient Law*, his first book, which likely originated from lectures delivered at Middle Temple and developed previously during his time at Cambridge.[14] The book was written when British colonial rule in India had become politically contentious.[15] In the wake of the Sepoy Mutiny (1857–1859) and the subsequent revocation by Parliament of the authority of the East India Company in 1858, British attitudes towards the nature and purpose of colonial rule there had begun to change. This shift in public opinion came to be reflected in an energetic public debate

[6] Grant Duff, *Sir Henry Maine*, 2; Cocks, *Sir Henry Maine*, 9; Feaver, *From Status to Contract*, 3–5.

[7] Feaver, *From Status to Contract*, 1–7; Feaver, 'The Victorian Values of Sir Henry Maine', 30–4; Kennedy, 'A Sense of Place: Rome, History, and Empire Revisited', generally; Grant Duff, *Sir Henry Maine*, 2; Kumar, 'Greece and Rome', generally.

[8] Feaver, *From Status to Contract*, 8–16; Feaver, 'The Victorian Values of Sir Henry Maine', 28–30; Grant Duff, *Sir Henry Maine*, 3–6.

[9] O'brien, '"Something Older than Law Itself"', 230. As Kuper, 'Civilization, Culture, and Race', 398, has shown, it is also during this period that the discipline of anthropology begins to form. Sera-Shriar, 'Race', generally.

[10] Feaver, *From Status to Contract*, 17–28; Batzel, 'Sir Henry James Sumner Maine', 28.

[11] Cocks, *Sir Henry Maine*, 40–5.

[12] Feaver, *From Status to Contract*, 24; Stein, *Legal Evolution*, 78–9.

[13] Coxall, '"The Use and Misuse of Internal Evidence in Authorship Attributions"'; Feaver, *From Status to Contract*, 29–40; Grant Duff, *Sir Henry Maine*, 11–13.

[14] Kuper, 'Ancestors', 266.

[15] Bell, 'Empire', generally.

concerning the nature of colonial governance and law reform in India.[16] *Ancient Law* should be read, at least on one level, in the context of this more extensive debate.[17]

As a Victorian intellectual in the latter half of the nineteenth century without independent wealth, Maine's career invariably had a colonial orbit. In 1862, having already turned down the offer of employment once before, Maine was appointed as a legal member of the Viceroy's Council in India, positioning him as the head of the colonial apparatus responsible for drafting legislation there.[18] Despite his lifelong complicated relationship with legislation as a legal form, it held considerable sway over his professional life during this period, as is evident from the legislative output under his aegis.[19] Upon his return from India in 1869, he was elected as the inaugural holder of the Corpus Professorship of Historical and Comparative Jurisprudence at Oxford University.[20] Maine published prolifically during this period. In 1877, he was elected Master of Trinity Hall, Cambridge. He occupied this position for the next decade until he was elected Whewell Professor of International Law at Cambridge in 1887. He died in 1888. In the roughly two decades after his return from India, Maine published five books exploring many of the themes raised in *Ancient Law*.[21] These included *Village Communities in East and West* (1871), *The Early History of the Property of Married Women* (1873) and *The Early History of Institutions* (1875). After returning to Cambridge, he published *Early Law and Custom* (1883) and a controversial book about franchise extension, *Popular Government* (1885).[22]

16 Kuper, *The Reinvention of Primitive Society*, 33–4; Mantena, *Alibis of Empire*, 21–2; Bayly, *New Cambridge History*, 106–35; Pitts, 'Jeremy Bentham Legislator of the World?'; Majeed, Schultz, and Varouxakis, 'James Mill's The History of British India: The Question of Utilitarianism and Empire'; Varouxakis, 'Empire, Race, Euro-Centrism', generally.

17 Mantena, *Alibis of Empire*, 149–50, for the opposing views of the participants in this debate concerning the need for legal reform in India. See Landauer, 'From Status to Treaty', 225–6.; Kuper, 'Ancestors', 269–70. Goëtzmann, 'La "Comparative Jurisprudence" de Henry Sumner Maine, Entre École Analytique et École Historique', 102–7, has argued that the intellectual differences between Maine and Bentham should be read through the prism of Burke's influence. While Burke is not cited in *Ancient Law*, he influenced Maine's worldview. See Agnani, 'The Reception of Edmund Burke's Imperial Ideas Relating to India, or Burke, the Brahmin and the Hot-House', for a survey.

18 Kuper, *The Reinvention of Primitive Society*, 41–2; Johnson, 'India and Henry Maine'; Bayly, 'Maine and Change in Nineteenth-Century India', generally; Batzel, 'Sir Henry James Sumner Maine', 67–105.

19 Mantena, *Alibis of Empire*, 96–9, for a recent assessment of Maine's tenure in India and the volume of statute law passed during his term; Cocks, *Sir Henry Maine*, 79–100; Feaver, *From Status to Contract*, 65–73, 74–109; Grant Duff, *Sir Henry Maine*, 24–5.

20 Grant Duff, *Sir Henry Maine*, 36–7.

21 Cocks, *Sir Henry Maine*, 101–40.

22 Viereck, *Conservative Thinkers*, 167. For the influence of Edmund Burke's philosophy on this work, see Agnani, 'The Reception of Edmund Burke's Imperial Ideas Relating to India, or Burke, the Brahmin and the Hot-House', 32–3. See Prochaska, *Eminent Victorians on American Democracy*, 72–95. For historical context, see Landauer, 'From Status to Treaty', 224–5; Maine and Capellán de Miguel, *El gobierno popular*, especially the introduction (9–70); Harrison, *On Jurisprudence and the Conflict of Laws*, 9–36.

2. THE BOOK

Henry Maine's *Ancient Law* is still cited in contemporary scholarship across various disciplines, such as legal history, sociology,[23] and the anthropology of law.[24] In the Anglosphere, these three disciplines were still in their infancy when the book was published, and it had a critical foundational role in their intellectual formation. Even though subsequent scholarly evaluations[25] of the book have raised doubts about the accuracy of a significant portion of its information and the reliability of its approach, it continues to be cited for many reasons, not least because its publication represents a crucial moment in the history of the study of law in Victorian-era England.[26] One of the reasons for its enduring popularity is Maine's aptitude for producing memorable statements, seemingly of considerable breadth and scope, chief among which must be the frequently quoted line about the movement from status to contract. These play an essential role in the book. They also represent one of the often-overlooked aspects of Maine's work. As Cocks has shown, the book was written from a series of lectures designed to be delivered verbally – first, to an audience of law students at Cambridge and subsequently to an audience of aspiring barristers at Middle Temple.[27] It is, in essence, an elaborate piece of rhetorical prose, cleverly deploying elements of classical rhetoric and drawing on his extensive classical education.[28] This is a crucial insight. Every chapter of the book must be read as a freestanding yet interrelated exposition of a specific topic. The core arguments of each chapter rely on the reader accepting several foundational premises, often based on one or two examples only, and being guided through a series of arguments towards accepting generalised conclusions. In the broadest of terms, Maine's *Ancient Law* describes the changes the Roman legal system underwent over time. Still, those readers expecting a blow-by-blow account of how specific rules of law developed will search in vain. Instead, Maine's account offers a thick description – in keeping with the book's origins as a series of lectures. He does not cite many primary or secondary sources and uses only a few well-chosen examples to reinforce his arguments.

[23] Shils, 'Henry Sumner Maine in the Tradition of the Analysis of Society'; Peel, 'Maine as an Ancestor of the Social Sciences'; Nielsen, 'The Sociological Theories of Sir Henry Maine', 184–205.

[24] Cocks, *Sir Henry Maine*, 155–69, for an account of the reception of Maine's work in the fields of sociology and anthropology; Nielsen, *The Sociological Theories of Sir Henry Maine*, 17–32; Macfarlane, 'Some Contributions of Maine to History and Anthropology', generally.

[25] Feaver, *From Status to Contract*, 56–64, 136–48.

[26] Kuper, 'Ancestors', 278–9; Rabban, 'From Maine to Maitland via America', generally. For Maine's impact on the development of anthropology, Orenstein, 'The Ethnological Theories of Henry Sumner Maine'; Cocks, *Sir Henry Maine*, 169–83, 183–95; Abrahams, 'Ancient Law and Modern Field Work'; Yale, 'Further Thoughts on Maine's Historical Jurisprudence', 240.

[27] Cocks, *Sir Henry Maine*, 52–3; Landauer, 'Henry Sumner Maine's Grand Tour', 136–8, referencing Cocks's work, has suggested that more attention should be paid to 'rhetorical strategies' deployed by Maine throughout *Ancient Law* to create an image of himself as a scholar. For the work's underlying message aimed at the legal profession, see Cocks, *Sir Henry Maine*, 64–71.

[28] Landauer, 'Henry Sumner Maine's Grand Tour', 137.

Physically, the volume consists of ten chapters and may be broadly divided into two parts.[29] This division is not absolute since Chapter five is a work of two halves. Books one through four set out the main thrust of the argument, whereas book five concludes the first part with some thoughts on methodology. It also contains a discussion of the family in ancient law. This signals a transition – a rhetorical shift – in the narrative arc. Books six through ten are case studies devoted to specific areas of law where the insights from books one to four are applied. Unlike many textbooks on Roman law of the period, Maine's book does not follow the 'Institutional scheme' set out in the Institutes of Gaius, a textbook of Roman law from the mid-second century rediscovered in palimpsest form by the German scholar Barthold Georg Niebuhr (1776–1831) in the early decades of the 1800s.[30] The case studies in Maine demonstrate a distinct inner logic that can be grasped only after understanding the book's purpose and main message. By contextualising this book within the broader intellectual environment of the mid-1800s, when Maine researched it, this study offers a deeper understanding of the author's intention for writing it.[31] To appreciate the book's significance, it is essential to consider the broader context fully.

3. CONTEXTS

A book is a product of its author's experiences, and *Ancient Law* is no exception.[32] Maine's work was influenced intellectually by several significant legal and political events of the 1850s, both domestically and globally. Domestically, the nineteenth century was a period of significant legal change in England, precipitated and accelerated by the Industrial Revolution. The uncodified common law was increasingly subjected to reform through legislation, and scholarly debates raged between supporters of the English jurist Jeremy Bentham (1748–1832), known as Utilitarians, and their opponents over the uncodified nature and possible future directions of English law.[33] Relatedly, Britain's colonial presence in India and the nature and direction of future law reform there had become contentious nationally and globally.[34] Maine's engagement in *Ancient Law* with these events and associated debates is subtle.[35] This is especially evident in his choice of examples. Although the book is ostensibly devoted to 'ancient law', it contains several references also to contemporaneous legal systems. Still, these references are, at

29 Kuper, 'Ancestors', 271–3.

30 Gooch, *History and Historians in the Nineteenth Century*, 14–23, on Niebuhr.

31 Skinner, 'Meaning and Understanding in the History of Ideas', generally. See also Palti, *Intellectual History*, 9–37, 54–77, 95–112.

32 Feaver, 'The Victorian Values of Sir Henry Maine', 34–7; Batzel, 'Sir Henry James Sumner Maine', 1.

33 Cotterrell, *The Politics of Jurisprudence*, 40; Lerminier, *Introduction générale à l'histoire du droit*, 169–73; Field, *Codification of the Common Law*; Conway, 'Bentham and the Nineteenth-Century Revolution in Government', generally.

34 Steinbach, *Understanding the Victorians. Politics, Culture, and Society in Nineteenth-Century Britain*, 65–83.

35 Kuper, *The Reinvention of Primitive Society*, 33–4; Kuper, 'Ancestors', 265–6.

best, indirect. When he refers to English law, it tends to be a historical reference. Similarly, his references to Hindu law do not focus on contemporaneous issues directly.[36] This suggests that Maine's aim with the book was not to offer an overt critique of contemporaneous law and politics. Instead, the purpose of the book was different, and to understand it, one must closely examine the content.

Maine's *Ancient Law* has been the subject of several book-length studies.[37] These have focused on the book's broader intellectual, cultural and colonial legacies and its impact on emerging Victorian fields of study such as legal history, anthropology and the sociology of law. While these works are essential for informing contemporary understanding of Maine's work, their focus has tended to be on the legacy of the work rather than its content. The aim of this study is different. This book will examine the content of Maine's arguments in *Ancient Law*. This will further expand upon insights by O'brien, who proposed that *Ancient Law* should be contextualised within the Victorian intellectual landscape constructed upon the foundations of early modern Humanism.[38]

Much has been written about the rise of Humanism and its connection to the Renaissance of the early modern period.[39] The term signifies an intellectual agenda, developed first in France, critical of the medieval world, its worldview and its modes of producing knowledge. It was deeply rooted in the desire to rediscover ancient Greece and Rome's intellectual contributions and apply these insights to contemporaneous problems. Fuelled by the renewed availability of texts from Graeco-Roman antiquity dispersed after the fall of the Byzantine Empire in the mid-fifteenth century, Humanist scholars began creating critical editions of texts using manuscript editions by applying the principles of philology. In addition, these scholars were profoundly interested in classical rhetoric and its conventions to convey their intellectual agenda. Such critical editions and the educational agenda built upon them in schools and university curricula would profoundly affect the European and English intellectual landscape in the centuries that followed. While subsequent scholarly assessments of the impact of Humanism have been mixed, recent scholarship has stressed its intellectual significance as a means to criticise political figures and theories of the State indirectly.[40] Victorian Humanism, or neo-Humanism to give it its proper appellation, was built on these foundations, as is evident from Maine's training at Christ's Hospital and Cambridge.[41] It was an

[36] Derrett, *Sir Henry Maine and Law in India, 1858-1958*, 40–3, for criticism of the superficial nature of Maine's references to Hindu law.

[37] Feaver, *From Status to Contract*; Cocks, *Sir Henry Maine*; Piccinini, *Tra legge e contratto*; Cassani, *Diritto, antropologia e storia*; Goëtzmann, 'La "Comparative Jurisprudence" de Henry Sumner Maine, Entre École Analytique et École Historique'; are the primary book-length studies.

[38] O'brien, '"Something Older than Law Itself"', 250; Bevir, 'Historicism and the Human Sciences in Victorian Britain'; Gallagher, 'History/Historicism', generally.

[39] Mack, 'Humanism and the Classical Tradition', for a survey; Carroll, 'Humanism and English Literature', 264–5.

[40] Cairns and du Plessis, 'Introduction', for a survey.

[41] Batzel, 'Sir Henry James Sumner Maine', 3–4.

essential cultural force in Victorian circles, reinforced by school and university curricula focused on Greece and Rome. It permeated nearly all aspects of its intellectual discourse. As Turner has shown, Graeco-Roman antiquity was used critically and reflectively by Victorian intellectuals to comment on more significant social and political problems of the time.[42]

Maine's use of Roman law in *Ancient Law* has not been systematically investigated.[43] The reasons for this are complex and will be unpacked more fully in this book. In a nutshell, they relate to Maine's perceived lack of knowledge of Roman law.[44] The following chapters will challenge this assumption. As shown in this book, the lack of focus on Maine's use of Roman law has obscured much of *Ancient Law*'s message. Roman law formed the backbone of Maine's discussion of *Ancient Law*.[45] As a scholar of the discipline, it provided both an interpretative framework and a convenient narrative source that could be used to make more significant claims throughout. This book will assess Maine's use of sources and explore his intellectual influences to demonstrate their impact on his thinking when writing *Ancient Law*.

Maine's use of Roman law in *Ancient Law* should be viewed against the backdrop of more significant events in his professional life. As a scholar of Roman law, he was passionate about it and staunchly promoted its importance as a didactic tool for studying English law.[46] In 1850, he was invited to give evidence to a Royal Commission created to investigate the poor state of law teaching in England.[47] By this time, he had already attempted, without much success, to practice law, and his negative experiences in this regard, specifically the lack of training and opportunities for aspiring barristers, undoubtedly informed the substance of his evidence at this enquiry. As Regius Professor of Civil Law at Cambridge, as he then was, Maine gave evidence at an inquiry in 1854 on the desirability of teaching English law in a 'scientific manner', separate from legal practice.[48] As Cocks put it:

> He [Maine] thought that there should be an end to the traditional training of lawyers; the modern world demanded an education which could never be obtained through a

42 Turner, 'Antiquity in Victorian Contexts'; Hall and Stead, *People's History of Classics*, 3–44; Gaukroger, 'The Shaping of Character'; Kraemer, 'The Influence of the Classics on English Literature'; Schiavone, *The End of the Past*, 3–15.

43 Cocks, *Sir Henry Maine*, 8, for example, deliberately shifted the focus of his book away from Maine's knowledge of Roman law to explore other issues. The only work in which the Roman law in Maine's text is summarised is Nelson, *An Analysis*, published in Madras in 1899. These are mainly factual summaries with no attempt to analyse Maine's use of Roman law or its purpose within the text.

44 Yale, 'Further Thoughts on Maine's Historical Jurisprudence', 240; Woodard, 'A Wake (or Awakening?) For Historical Jurisprudence', 219.

45 Cocks, *Sir Henry Maine*, 23; Capogrossi Colognesi, *Dalla storia di Roma alle origini della società civile*, 142.

46 Stein, *Legal Evolution*, 86–7; Grant Duff, *Sir Henry Maine*, 17–20.

47 Cocks, *Sir Henry Maine*, 46–51; Baker, *750 Years of Law at Cambridge*, 10–13; Hoeflich, 'The Americanization of British Legal Education in the Nineteenth Century', generally; Feaver, *From Status to Contract*, 20.

48 Cocks, *Sir Henry Maine*, 14–19, for an account of the 'scientific' turn in Victorian jurisprudence; Stein, 'Maine and Legal Education', for a survey.

> practical apprenticeship in the form of a pupillage. Even the idea that pupillage was a desirable supplement to a theoretical course had to go. There would be no need for such an unsound, unscientific form of learning the law; instead, apprenticeship was to be replaced by knowledge learned from books and lectures.[49]

Maine saw great intellectual potential in teaching Roman law to English law students, and he passionately made the case that Roman law should be a foundational subject of an English law degree.[50] He later summarised many of these ideas in a piece written while researching *Ancient Law* and published in the 1856 *Cambridge Essays* concerning the role of Roman law in English legal education.[51] The focus of this piece is broader than his use of Roman law in *Ancient Law*, but the primary arguments are worth revisiting since they also resonate with his treatment of Roman law in the book.

According to Maine, there were two primary reasons why Roman law was pedagogically valuable for English legal education. The first reason was the comparative advantage of studying Roman law. Throughout history, Roman law greatly influenced the formation and development of many European legal systems. Therefore, students of English law could use their knowledge of Roman law as a form of comparative law. Conversely, students who did not study Roman law would miss out on knowledge and engagement with these legal systems and their content. Knowing Roman law provided more than just an understanding of legal systems in continental Europe. Maine believed that the language and categories of Roman law also had a significant impact on the development of disciplines such as moral philosophy and political economy, both in England and on the continent. This is not an unimportant point, as it demonstrates the broader Humanist underpinnings of the book in Maine's mind. Thus, knowledge of Roman law would enrich the intellectual armour of students of English law more broadly.

Maine's second argument concerning Roman law's value focused on its intellectual merits. Roman juristic argumentation and interpretation form the bedrock of the discipline. This approach to law (interpretation and legal reasoning) could enrich students' understanding of English law by exposing them to a different legal culture. More specifically, Roman law's precise, technical terminology, on the one hand, and the use of broad, abstract rules of law that could be applied deductively to new legal problems were quite appealing to him. Maine lamented the imprecise nature of English legal terminology. He argued that it had had a knock-on effect on the reasoning of English lawyers and how court decisions were recorded in law reports. In his view, the study of Roman law would instil in English

49 Cocks, *Sir Henry Maine*, 46.

50 Hoeflich, *Roman and Civil Law and the Development of Anglo-American Jurisprudence in the Nineteenth Century*, 77–84, for a survey.

51 Maine, *Village Communities in the East and West*, 330–83. See also Bryce, *The Academical Study of the Civil Law*, generally, who discusses the value of Roman law for English law students. For context, see Landauer, 'From Status to Treaty', 228; Cotterrell, *The Politics of Jurisprudence*, 44–6; Feaver, *From Status to Contract*, 27–8; Stein, 'Maine and Legal Education'; Twining, 'Maine and Legal Education', generally.

law students a greater appreciation of the benefits of technical vocabulary and precision of expression. Jurisdictions based on Roman law paid greater attention to the teaching of law and training law students. Thus, by teaching Roman law as a component of an English law degree, he wished to make a case for better training for law students.

The extent to which these considerations, written primarily to justify the teaching and study of Roman law in England, also applied to *Ancient Law* as a book is worth considering. In a nutshell, Maine's motivation for using Roman law in *Ancient Law* was that it provided the most complete account of a legal system from the past and of the changes it had undergone over time.[52] It could thus be used as an interpretative tool.[53] It was worth studying since it was a 'progressive' system, according to his definition of the term, and had such an enormous influence on many legal systems historically and contemporaneously.[54] Maine's theory on the slow pace of legal development and its connection to other past and present legal systems via the Indo-European language family made Roman law a crucial frame of reference to be utilised extensively. When the three arguments in favour of the study of Roman law are compared to the use of Roman law in the book, these are clearly at the core of his thinking when writing it.

1.1 Maine's Knowledge of Roman Law

After the book's publication, Maine's knowledge of Roman law soon became a focal point of critique. There is more to this matter than first meets the eye. It is a complex issue based on a disparaging comment made by one of his contemporaries, uncritically repeated in subsequent scholarship since then. Cocks, in a lengthy footnote on the subject, cites as an early example a statement of Alfred Gardiner (1865–1946) who, in his *The Life of Sir William Harcourt*, published in London in 1923, quotes Sir Leslie Stephen (1832–1904), a prominent Victorian writer and editor of the *Dictionary of National Biography*, as saying that Maine could not have had any formal education in Roman law, mainly on account of him having studied classics (not law) and being elected to the chair so young (only a handful of years after finishing his studies).[55] The second piece of evidence provided by Cocks is a quotation from one of Maine's students, Frederic Harrison, recounted in a book published in 1911, which opined that Maine leant more

[52] Scala, 'Henry Sumner Maine's Ancient Law', 48–50, Mantena, *Alibis of Empire*, 99–102, shows that Maine's views on the purpose of teaching Roman law in England were broadly similar to those of Savigny.

[53] Landauer, 'Henry Sumner Maine's Grand Tour', 136, has suggested that while Roman law holds a special significance for Maine in *Ancient Law*, the book itself should be read not as an account of Roman law, but as an account of legal change using Roman law as an example. Although this is an important insight as to the purpose of the work, the central importance of Roman law as the bedrock of the work should not be underestimated.

[54] See Smellie, 'Sir Henry Maine', 66.

[55] Cocks, *Sir Henry Maine*, 23–4.

towards history than law.[56] Aside from these two comments, Cocks also mentions how subsequent scholars of the discipline, such as the English jurist Sir Frederick Pollock (1845–1937) and the Scottish jurist William Alexander Hunter (1844–1898), criticised Maine's use of Roman law in *Ancient Law*.

None of these statements provides a detailed and sustained critique of Maine's use of Roman law.[57] Stephen's comment is wholly based on the fact of Maine's youth and the uneven teaching of Roman law at Cambridge at the time, thus implying that he could not have been taught the subject formally or comprehensively. It does not, however, provide any evidence of Maine's independent study of the subject or his subsequent acquisition of knowledge of it. In addition, the second piece of evidence cited by Cocks relates to a judgement on Maine's approach to law rather than his knowledge of Roman law. Maine's approach, as Cocks has shown, was one identified with Historical Jurisprudence, a movement which famously looked beyond black-letter law.[58] This is the gist of the student's criticism rather than making any specific point concerning his knowledge of Roman law. Finally, negative comments by later scholars such as Pollock and Hunter concerning Maine's use of Roman law should be viewed in context. These were academic disagreements rooted in his lack of citations or that *Ancient Law* did not contain the granular details on Roman law found in contemporaneous textbooks.

Even though the sources of Maine's work are difficult to pin down, there is good evidence that he was well-read on the subject and informed of the debates circulating in many of the most important European works of the time. Before a detailed survey can be undertaken, however, Landauer's assessment of Maine's use of Roman law in *Ancient Law* must be evaluated.[59] Other than Landauer, few works have focused directly on Maine's use of Roman law. Although his treatment of the topic is not a blow-by-blow account of Maine's use of Roman law across the various chapters of *Ancient Law*, Landauer raised several important points of criticism that are worth considering here.

The first point of criticism concerns the title of the book. According to Landauer, the book could have been better named.[60] It primarily discusses Roman law rather than other legal systems of antiquity. It is, therefore, not so much about ancient law as Roman law. Maine did not systematically survey other ancient legal systems in *Ancient Law*, as a cursory reading of the title might suggest. Bearing in mind that the title for this book was settled on in consultation with the publisher (more on this later), this criticism misses the point of the work.[61] It also fails to appreciate his interpretation of the term 'comparative jurisprudence', as Maine later explained in *Village Communities*. Roman law provided the most detailed

[56] See also Feaver, *From Status to Contract*, 26.

[57] Ibid. 18–19.

[58] Cocks, *Sir Henry Maine*, 32; Woodard, 'A Wake (or Awakening?) For Historical Jurisprudence', 223–6.

[59] Landauer, 'Henry Sumner Maine's Grand Tour', generally.

[60] Ibid. 136.

[61] Utz, 'Maine's *Ancient Law* and Legal Theory', 825, also misunderstands Maine's endeavour. The book is not essentially a 'narration of the progress of legal systems from primitive to modern forms'.

exposition of the changes to a legal system across time. It was the proverbial lens through which he viewed other systems included in his project. In this sense, Roman law was emblematic of ancient law. The narrative of legal change that Maine constructed in *Ancient Law* is foundationally dependent upon Roman law. It could not have been built without it. Roman law formed the body of the book, while references to other legal systems, ancient and modern, were included only as and when required. Maine never aimed to produce a work comparing various legal systems from antiquity to highlight similarities and differences. He never aimed to create an 'ancient law' in the abstract consisting of rules and institutions commonly visible from his comparisons.[62]

Landauer's second point of criticism is the lack of clarity in Maine's book concerning the impact of ancient law on modernity.[63] This is an important issue and worth unpacking carefully. The title of Maine's work, *Ancient Law*, contains two essential terms: 'connection' and 'relation'. Although Maine and his publisher collectively developed the title of *Ancient Law*, he approved of its final form, and it thus provides good evidence of his aims with the book. Let us examine these two terms since they represent, in my view, the boundaries of his endeavour. 'Connection', according to Maine, spoke to the issue of the Indo-European language family. Maine, taking his cue most likely from views on law and language held by supporters of Historical Jurisprudence, proposed a connection between different legal systems because of their common roots in the Indo-European language family.[64] This, to him, justified the 'comparative' references to ancient Greek, 'Anglo-Saxon law' and the 'vulgar' Roman laws of the early medieval period.[65] 'Relation', on the other hand, referred to Maine's conception of temporality. *Ancient Law* was never designed to be a linear account of the development of law from Plato to NATO. This is a common misconception associated with the book. Instead, his point was that specific parallels could be drawn across time and space without subscribing to a linear narrative of 'progress'. This allowed him to compare ancient Rome and nineteenth-century India, for example. Temporality played an essential role in Maine's work. *Ancient Law* was never written as a textbook of Roman law. Instead, it was aimed at a broad audience and used Roman law to make larger philosophical and legal claims.[66] This, rather than his discussion of the intricacies of Roman legal doctrine, was the chief function of *Ancient Law*.

62 By the end of the nineteenth century, however, subsequent interpreters of Maine's work had begun constructing an abstract notion of 'ancient law' from his scholarship based on an amalgam of rules and concepts taken from a number of systems. Nowhere is this more visible than in the student text of Evans, *Theories and Criticisms*, 1–5, 8–12.

63 Landauer, 'Henry Sumner Maine's Grand Tour', 137.

64 Kuper, 'Ancestors', 267; Tomalin, 'Language', generally; Demoule, *The Indo-Europeans*, 19–32; Tuori, *Lawyers and Savages*, 37–40; Lerminier, *Introduction générale à l'histoire du droit*, 145–61.

65 Mantena, *Alibis of Empire*, 57, for an account of the popularity of the comparative method in Victorian Britain. See also Jolly, 'Robert Louis Stevenson, Henry Maine, and the Anthropology of Comparative Law', generally.

66 Cocks, *Sir Henry Maine*, 53–6.

1.2 Maine's Sources for *Ancient Law*

Maine's scholarship is commonly associated with Historical Jurisprudence. This intellectual movement, originating in Germany in the early nineteenth century with the work of the celebrated jurist Friedrich C. von Savigny (1779–1861) and his pupils, formed one camp in a well-documented controversy concerning the nature of law and the desirability of codification of the law of the German Empire.[67] The nature of this debate was both jurisprudential and political. The Pandectists, their intellectual opponents, favoured the transformation of the existing uncodified European *ius commune*, based in large part on Roman and canon law, operative in the patchwork of principalities comprising the former Holy Roman Empire, into a civil code for a united Germany. By contrast, supporters of Historical Jurisprudence did not favour codification. They preferred the continued organic, incremental development of law in which its authority was rooted in tradition rather than the legislator's will. Although Maine's aims with *Ancient Law* may be identified generally with this movement, it is essential to appreciate that Historical Jurisprudence was a broad church intellectually. As Kuper has shown, it provided Maine with two key insights when writing *Ancient Law*: the slow, organic development of law and the importance of the comparative method developed in philology.[68] Still, there is more to Maine's work than these two insights. It is much richer intellectually than merely an English engagement with a German debate.[69] Maine's *Ancient Law*, while rooted in a European intellectual discussion, was a uniquely Victorian interpretation of the aims of this movement grounded in Victorian Humanism.

This is an important insight. Earlier literature proposed a close intellectual link between Maine and Savigny but without substantiation.[70] Recent literature has favoured a more nuanced assessment.[71] An analysis of Savigny's works has shown significant intellectual differences from those of Maine on crucial issues, such as the origins of the law in the 'spirit' of the people, the drivers of legal change and the wisdom of codification.[72] Based on these differences, it has been suggested that the intellectual link between Savigny and Maine was more diffuse

67 Reimann, 'Historical Jurisprudence', 397–418; Reimann, 'Nineteenth Century German Legal Science'; Canale, 'The Many Faces of the Codification of Law in Modern Continental Europe'; Becchi, 'German Legal Science'; Freund, 'Historical Jurisprudence in Germany'; Eldridge, 'Gone and Forgotten', generally; Gooch, *History and Historians in the Nineteenth Century*, 43–9; Stein, *Legal Evolution*, 72–8; Rahmatian, 'Friedrich Carl von Savigny's *Beruf* and *Volksgeistlehre*', generally.

68 Kuper, *The Reinvention of Primitive Society*, 34–5; O'brien, '"Something Older than Law Itself"', 241; Kuper, 'Ancestors', 267–8. For a discussion of the influence on Maine of the works of Victorian jurists whose works deployed elements of philology, such as Kemble and Jones, see Cocks, *Sir Henry Maine*, 22–4. See also Jackson, 'Law and Language'; Lyons, 'Linguistics and Law', generally.

69 Cocks, *Sir Henry Maine*, 25.

70 Ibid. 25–6. See, for example, Oldham, *Analysis*, vi.

71 Goëtzmann, 'La "Comparative Jurisprudence" de Henry Sumner Maine, Entre École Analytique et École Historique', generally.

72 Ibid. 227–31.

and likely indirect.[73] If this is the case, the scholarly similarities between Savigny and Maine likely came via their common reliance on the works of an intermediary author such as Barthold Georg Niebuhr, as Goëtzmann has argued.[74] This seems highly likely given the formative influence of Niebuhr's work on Maine during his time as a Cambridge student. Furthermore, given that Niebuhr's work substantially impacted the Victorian intellectual landscape, Maine's engagement with this work acquires new significance.

Earlier scholarship identified Maine as the vanguard of Historical Jurisprudence in England.[75] Recent scholarship has suggested, however, that this assessment needs to be revised and that he should be viewed not as the first but as one in a long tradition of English jurists stretching back to Blackstone, whose focus was historical.[76] From this angle, Maine's engagement with his intellectual opponents in *Ancient Law*, Jeremy Bentham and his pupil, John Austin (1790–1859), takes on a significance deserving of renewed intellectual scrutiny.[77] Thus, the book must be read as a debate concerning the nature of law, its relationship to larger Victorian Humanist ideals such as historicism and comparativism, and the emergence of new fields of knowledge such as sociology and anthropology.[78] As Bock reminds us, the aim of Victorian Humanism was: 'to bring time and space dimensions to humanistic inquiry.'[79] Against this backdrop, his use of sources must be assessed.

Various avenues of investigation may be pursued to determine the sources an author used to write a specific book. Chief among these is the printed text of the book itself and the citations deployed by the author. In the case of *Ancient Law*, this strategy presents two complications. In the printed text, Maine, similar to many of his Victorian peers, used citations very sparingly, whether in footnotes or within the main text, which makes it challenging to pinpoint any particular sources he might have consulted.[80] Maine is not unique in this regard. Many English-language legal treatises of the period employed the same technique. It is also possible that he was emulating the style of Edward Gibbon (1737–1794),

73 Cocks, *Sir Henry Maine*, 27–9.

74 Goëtzmann, 'La "Comparative Jurisprudence" de Henry Sumner Maine, Entre École Analytique et École Historique', 179–204. Compare the impact of Mommsen on the work of Vinogradoff, Maine's intellectual heir, as discussed by O'brien, '"In Vino Veritas"', generally.

75 Cocks, *Sir Henry Maine*, 141–55; Feaver, 'The Victorian Values of Sir Henry Maine', 31.

76 Goëtzmann, 'La "Comparative Jurisprudence" de Henry Sumner Maine, Entre École Analytique et École Historique', 233; Berman, 'The Origins of Historical Jurisprudence', generally.

77 Bock, 'Comparison of Histories', 237–41; Cocks, *Sir Henry Maine*, 71–8; Nielsen, *The Sociological Theories of Sir Henry Maine*, 32–60; Hoeflich, 'John Austin and Joseph Story', generally. See also Maine, *Lectures on the Early History of Institutions by Sir Henry Sumner Maine*, 180–210, (lectures 12 and 13) where Maine engages extensively with the views of Bentham and Austin, specifically also on sovereignty and Empire.

78 Goëtzmann, 'La "Comparative Jurisprudence" de Henry Sumner Maine, Entre École Analytique et École Historique', 144–52, 232–6.

79 Bock, 'Comparison of Histories', 232.

80 Goëtzmann, 'La "Comparative Jurisprudence" de Henry Sumner Maine, Entre École Analytique et École Historique', 232, has argued that Maine's intellectual influences can only be understood by first identifying the nature and purpose of the book itself; Stein, *Legal Evolution*, 97–8.

whose *The History of the Decline and Fall of the Roman Empire*, published in several volumes from 1776 onwards, had a seminal influence on Maine's book. Gibbon's work is famously lacking in many notes. This approach sets Maine apart from many contemporaneous German legal scholars in the tradition of Historical Jurisprudence, whose works tended to have more footnotes.[81] This difference again reinforces contemporary scholarly opinion that Maine's project was not merely an emulation of a German work.

The second complication concerns the manuscript of *Ancient Law*. Traditionally, the manuscript of a book can provide insight into the sources used to construct it. A manuscript may be examined to determine whether the author had cited specific references in the draft that did not find their way into the printed text for various reasons. In the case of *Ancient Law*, however, the manuscript of the work does not exist. The archive of Maine's publisher, John Murray, now housed in the National Library of Scotland, does not hold a copy. This is not unusual for Victorian manuscripts, as the author's legible written submission to the publisher was often destroyed during the production of the printed version. This leaves one further source, namely the author's archive. Yet again, this leads to a dead end. Maine's papers are incomplete, and the remaining ones do not contain a manuscript of *Ancient Law*, nor any notes associated with the book.[82]

Given these complexities, one may question the feasibility of making meaningful assertions about Maine's sources in composing *Ancient Law*. This study will show that it is possible. The techniques employed are contextual and textual. In addressing this matter, three issues need to be unpacked—the first concerns Maine's language skills. As an accomplished scholar of classics, Maine would have had excellent knowledge of Latin and Greek. This is borne out by the evidence of his training and performance as a student at Cambridge and the associated notebooks from the 1840s, in which his critical engagement with the original Greek and Latin texts is visible. It is also here that the influence of the new methodology in the study of classics, which underpinned his training at Cambridge, is evident. His practice here was one of 'source criticism' – line-by-line notes, often philological, on words and phrases from the Latin and Greek texts he studied. As O'brien has shown, Maine's time as a student at Cambridge coincided with the teaching of 'progressive classical studies', a new methodology imported from German scholarship.[83] This method, popularised by the work of Niebuhr, an acquaintance of Savigny, had two essential aspects.[84] First, this method emphasised the importance of

81 Vinogradoff, *The Teaching of Sir Henry Maine; an Inaugural Lecture Delivered in Corpus Christi College Hall on March 1, 1904*, 3, 14, for an assessment of the differences in approach between Maine and the legal scholarship of the period in Germany and France.

82 Feaver, *From Status to Contract*, xviii.

83 O'brien, '"Something Older than Law Itself"', 234.

84 Ibid. 237. Goëtzmann, 'La "Comparative Jurisprudence" de Henry Sumner Maine, Entre École Analytique et École Historique', 159–78, has shown that Maine's comparative methodology has more in common intellectually with that of Bentham and Austin than Savigny. For a general account, see Hoeflich, 'Savigny and His Anglo-American Disciples'; Capogrossi Colognesi, 'Niebuhr and Bachofen', generally.

historical contextualisation and a healthy dose of 'scientific' scepticism towards the accuracy of the information presented in the sources. It considered a broader range of material culture in reconstructing historical narratives than had been done previously. In addition, as in the case of Niebuhr's work, a comparative element could be introduced, often with contemporaneous relevance, to make more significant claims. As O'brien labelled it, it was 'philosophical history' with a storied intellectual pedigree.[85] The second aspect of this method emphasised the role of institutions, particularly law, in reconstructing the past. This approach underscored the importance of understanding how legal frameworks and institutional structures have shaped historical events and narratives.

In addition to Latin and Greek, Maine's knowledge of modern European languages also deserves comment. The Victorian curriculum of classics at Cambridge presupposed a reading knowledge of French since many of the translations of and commentaries on Latin and Greek works were produced by French scholars during the eighteenth and nineteenth centuries. It is safe to assume that Maine also had a working knowledge of French. His knowledge of German is equally significant for this project, given his relationship to the German movement of Historical Jurisprudence. From his comments across various works, one may deduce that Maine also had a working knowledge of this language. Evidence of this can be seen, for example, in his discussion in *Village Communities* of the work of Erwin Nasse (1829–1890), published in German, on immovable property in England in lecture five on feudalisation as well as Appendix 2 to this work where he lists recent works on village communities – mainly in German.[86] This is not an insignificant point, especially given the proverbial deluge of works on Roman law in Germany during the first half of the 1800s. In addition, his knowledge of German should be viewed in the context of his education in classics at Cambridge. As O'brien has shown, at the time of Maine's studies at Cambridge, the teaching of the subject was dominated by Niebuhr's *Römische Geschichte* and its methodology. This work, published in German in three volumes from 1811 onwards, had already been translated into English by two Cambridge scholars, Thirlwall and Hare, between 1828 and 1832. Niebuhr, an associate of Savigny and a supporter of his methodology, was a prominent scholar widely known in Roman law circles for discovering the palimpsest of the Gaius manuscript in Verona.[87]

Specific comments on sources are required to understand Maine's use of other works when writing *Ancient Law*. Since neither the manuscript nor any notebooks relating to the work exist, the only viable alternative is to identify Maine's use of themes or points of view visible in academic works to which he likely had access.[88] Two types of themes may be identified in this regard. At various points

[85] O'brien, '"Something Older than Law Itself"', 241; Mantena, *Alibis of Empire*, 62; Evans-Pritchard, *A History of Anthropological Thought; Edited by André Singer; with an Introduction by Ernest Gellner*, 7; Gooch, *History and Historians in the Nineteenth Century.*, 18; Feaver, *From Status to Contract*, xvi.

[86] Maine, *Village Communities in the East and West*, 398.

[87] O'brien, '"Something Older than Law Itself"', 238.

[88] Skinner, 'Meaning and Understanding in the History of Ideas', generally.

in *Ancient Law*, Maine mentions individuals, such as Bentham or Charles de Secondat, Baron de Montesquieu (1689–1755), by name. It is generally possible to trace the source of his engagement with an individual to a specific viewpoint and, in some cases, the particular work in question. The second type is more difficult to pin down. These are instances where Maine appears to have been influenced by the scholarly work of a specific individual, such as Edmund Burke (1729–1797) or Auguste Comte (1798–1857), but does not cite them by name.[89] In such cases, little more can be done than to suggest a possible work by such an author as a potential influence. Owing to the limitations of this method, no attempt has been made to link these themes to specific editions of specific works. In this regard, two issues deserve comment. First, given the book's genesis as a series of lectures, Maine likely used a limited range of books to compile his narrative. This study bears this out. Second, Maine was an original thinker. *Ancient Law* is not primarily a work of compilation. Thus, not every thought or idea can be traced to an earlier work.

As subsequent chapters will show, his primary source for information about events in Roman history appears to have been Niebuhr's *Römische Geschichte*, published in three volumes (1811–1812) and by then already translated into English. It is hard to overstate the importance of Niebuhr's work for Maine's endeavour.[90] It provided Maine with a methodology rooted in source criticism. It also demonstrated the importance of comparison since Niebuhr refers to comparative examples from India to substantiate some of his more speculative claims. However, it is more difficult to pinpoint his sources of Roman law. These appear to have been mainly the celebrated chapter 44 of Edward Gibbon's *The History of the Decline and Fall of the Roman Empire*,[91] published in six volumes (1776–1789), and on specific points of legal doctrine, Savigny's *System des heutigen römischen Rechts*, published in eight volumes (1840–1849), as well as the works of Joseph Ortolan (1802–1873), *Explication historique des institutes de Justinien* (1827) and *Histoire de la legislation romaine* (1828). Both Ortolan's works cite Niebuhr extensively. One notable absence from this list of possible sources is the work by Rudolf von Jhering (1818–1892), *Geist des römischen Rechts auf den verschiedenen Stufen seiner Entwicklung*, published in three volumes (1852–1865). Although two volumes of this work were newly published when Maine was undertaking his research for *Ancient Law*, there is little evidence of any of the themes contained in them having influenced him.[92] As Capogrossi Colognesi has shown, the similarities between

[89] Conniff, *The Useful Cobbler*, 37–48, 215–49; Whatmore, *The End of Enlightenment*, 161–90.

[90] O'brien, '"Something Older than Law Itself"', 245.

[91] Hoeflich, 'Edward Gibbon, Roman Lawyer', for an account of his significance in the nineteenth century; Whatmore, *The End of Enlightenment*, 135–60.

[92] Smith, 'Four German Jurists. III', 23–6; Cocks, *Sir Henry Maine*, 26–7; Hofmann, 'From Jhering to Radbruch', as well as Stein, *Legal Evolution*, 65–8. As Capogrossi Colognesi, *Dalla storia di Roma alle origini della società civile*, 77–102, has shown, there are many similarities between Jhering's work and that of Maine, ranging from their views on the family and its role in the formation of the State, to their opinions on etymology. Capogrossi Colognesi, *Modelli di stato e di famiglia nella storiografia dell'800*, 1–42. See also Pollock and Maine, *Introduction and Notes*, x.

the ideas of Jhering and Maine are likely the result of a shared general intellectual atmosphere rather than direct influence.[93]

As for Maine's references to other legal systems, such as ancient Greek or Hindu law, the likely sources of his information will be mentioned in context. His primary reference for archaic Greek law was *A History of Greece*, a twelve-volume work published by John Murray from 1846 to 1856, authored by the English politician and classicist George Grote (1794–1871). This is not an unimportant point. With respect to scholarly reputation, Grote's contributions to Greek history can be likened to those of Niebuhr in relation to Roman history.[94] Their works shared a common methodology in source criticism and comparative references.

1.3 The Methodology of *Ancient Law*

The incomplete set of Maine's notebooks, housed in the special collections section of the London School of Economics and Political Science library (The British Library of Political and Economic Science), contains working notes for some of Maine's books but none for *Ancient Law*.[95] The earliest extant notebook associated with one of Maine's monographs dates from the period after his return from India in the late 1860s, thus a considerable period after the publication of *Ancient Law*. Accepting that the collection is incomplete, it is possible that Maine did make similar notes, now lost, for *Ancient Law*. Then again, his note-taking practice is inconsistent. He did not make notes for all the monographs written after *Ancient Law*; thus, it is equally possible that notes were not made for *Ancient Law*. It was, after all, his first monograph, and his research method was still developing. Since the writing of *Ancient Law* is commonly linked to Maine's lectures at Middle Temple, it seems reasonable to infer that his lecture notes, either from Cambridge or Middle Temple, might provide some insights into his sources. Frustratingly, the extant notebooks containing texts of lectures (notebooks 20–24) also date from later in Maine's life, and none of the college libraries at Cambridge associated with Maine hold copies of his lecture notes. Only the printed summaries of his earlier lectures at Middle Temple are extant. They show some themes appearing in *Ancient Law*, lending significant weight to the likely origins of the book in a series of lectures.[96] Still, this does not mean all is lost in this regard. As we will presently see, a contextual approach can shed considerable light on Maine's method.

The methodology of *Ancient Law* can only be understood by first focusing on two issues, namely the book's overall structure and the contours of each chapter. As far as the first issue is concerned, chapters six through ten of *Ancient Law*, which is devoted to an exposition of different areas of Roman private and criminal law, does not follow the established Institutional scheme of the two most famous textbooks of Roman law preserved from antiquity, namely the Institutes of Gaius

[93] Capogrossi Colognesi, *Dalla storia di Roma alle origini della società civile*, 145–6.

[94] Gooch, *History and Historians in the Nineteenth Century*, 291–7; Stein, *Legal Evolution*, 77–8.

[95] These may be consulted in the archive of this library under the shelfmark: COLL MISC 247.

[96] Cocks, *Sir Henry Maine*, 29–30.

and Justinian respectively.[97] Instead, the order in which the topics are discussed is as follows: succession (chapters six and seven), property (chapter eight), contract (chapter nine), delict and crime (chapter ten). To the extent that there is an arc in the narrative of *Ancient Law*, the family (discussed in the latter half of chapter five) is at the beginning, and the individual, or more specifically, the individualised legal obligation, originating from contract or delict in Roman law, forms the end of that arc. Or, as Maine famously phrased it at the end of chapter five, there has been a gradual movement in the law of 'progressive societies' from status to contract.[98] This indicates that Maine's arrangement of the chapters was purposive. The same conclusion presents itself when the contours of each chapter are examined. Given the book's origins as a series of lectures, rhetorical elements are present in the printed text. Maine structured each chapter around major and minor claims. In each case, the significant claims contain textual references for support, while the minor claims generally do not. This suggests that the minor claims only provided additional support for the central claims.

Although chapter five of *Ancient Law* is commonly said to contain the most explicit account of Maine's method, his subsequent works provide crucial additional information. In chapter five, Maine proposed to examine 'ancient law'. The term was used descriptively to refer to a chosen number of past legal systems. It was by no means a technical term. Additionally, he never aimed to compare different legal systems on the same issues. Instead, he focused on one legal system, Roman law, owing to its extensive influence on legal development in subsequent periods of European legal history. The focus on Roman law presented Maine with a scope problem since he also wanted to include India in his book. Drawing insights from comparative philology and no doubt inspired by the example of Niebuhr[99]– and more generally by Montesquieu[100]– he proposed a link between specific legal systems based on their common Indo-European heritage. This permitted Maine to label the legal systems he chose to focus on as 'progressive'. As shown in the next chapter, this word had a precise meaning in the context of Maine's project. For all the apparent clarity of Maine's prose in chapter five, however, it left much concerning his methodology unclear.[101]

Only after his return from India and with the publication of *Village Communities* in 1871 did he find an opportunity to clarify his methodology further.[102] This work consists of several lectures delivered during his tenure as Corpus Professor of Historical and Comparative Jurisprudence at Oxford. One lecture, entitled

97 For a different view, see O'brien, '"Something Older than Law Itself"', 240.

98 Smellie, 'Sir Henry Maine', 74; Nielsen, *The Sociological Theories of Sir Henry Maine*, 61–116.

99 O'brien, '"Something Older than Law Itself"', 242; Jackson, 'Law and Language', generally.

100 Evans-Pritchard, A *History of Anthropological Thought; Edited by André Singer; with an Introduction by Ernest Gellner*, 5; Lerminier, *Introduction générale à l'histoire du droit*, 125–33; Stein, *Legal Evolution*, 15–19.

101 Capogrossi Colognesi, *Dalla storia di Roma alle origini della società civile*, 155–9; Capogrossi Colognesi, *Modelli di stato e di famiglia nella storiografia dell'800*, 43–98, 141–64.

102 Capogrossi Colognesi, *Dalla storia di Roma alle origini della società civile*, 175–98; Cocks, *Sir Henry Maine*, 79–100.

'The East, and the Study of Jurisprudence', addressed the matter squarely. In this wide-ranging lecture, three crucial points of clarification regarding his methodology in *Ancient Law* were made. The first concerned the classification of Maine's endeavour as 'comparative jurisprudence'.[103] As he pointed out, his method was 'comparative' only in a limited and specific sense. It did not share much in terms of method with the works of those legal scholars of 'comparative jurisprudence', whose aim was to compare different legal systems on a specific point of law to improve (usually) statute law in one or more of these systems. These investigations tended to be ahistorical – an anathema to Maine's entire project. By contrast, Maine's method, thoroughly rooted in history, was 'comparative' in the sense employed by scholars of comparative philology. As such, he opined that it was functionally equivalent to the historical method. He phrased it as follows:

> We shall examine a number of parallel phenomena with the view of establishing, if possible, that some of them are related to one another in the order of historical succession.[104]

> We take a number of contemporary facts, ideas, and customs, and we infer the past form of those facts, ideas, and customs not only from historical records of that past form, but from examples of it which have not yet died out of the world, and are still to be found in it.[105]

These two statements summarise Maine's method in *Ancient Law*. His methodology comprises several steps. First, certain phenomena are identified in Roman law, his archetypal 'ancient law' system. Next, in some instances, parallel phenomena are isolated in the legal systems from the past or present on which he chose to focus. Given the connection between these systems through the Indo-European language family, these parallel phenomena are assumed to be intellectually comparable. The third step involves an assessment of the temporal order of these parallel phenomena or, to phrase it differently, whether one appears to be an earlier and the other a later incarnation of it. This was the purpose of the 'comparative' element of Maine's methodology. These temporal points on the trajectory of a legal phenomenon permit reconstruction of its earlier or later form in his archetypal system, Roman law. This point is often overlooked in *Ancient Law*. Maine's aim was never to construct a system of 'ancient law' in the abstract as, for example, in the *Vorgeschichte der Indoeuropäer*, published posthumously in 1894 under the name of Rudolph von Jhering, and edited by Victor Ehrenberg (1851–1929). His was a book of specifics, mainly aimed at reconstructing the developmental trajectories of phenomena in Roman law using comparative evidence to fill in the gaps. When read in the round, the two statements quoted above demonstrate the fundamental historical nature of his method as well as the purpose of the comparative

103 Kuper, *The Reinvention of Primitive Society*, 40–1; Cassani, *Diritto, antropologia e storia*, 1–19. See also Cocks, *Maine* (Dictionary Entry), 206.

104 Maine, *Village Communities in the East and West*, 6.

105 Ibid. 6–7.

element.[106] In Maine's discussion surrounding these quotations, he observed that 'parallel phenomena' had to be carefully assessed to establish their comparability before an investigation of this kind was undertaken.[107] Although he does not provide any insight into how this should be done, his reference to German legal historical scholarship, such as that of Georg Ludwig von Maurer (1790–1872), suggests that 'scientific' rigour was required.[108]

The other point of clarification concerned issues of temporality. As the second quotation above shows, the comparison of 'parallel phenomena' was not limited to past examples but also included extant contemporaneous ones. This enabled Maine to deploy temporality creatively. Appreciating why this approach was necessary for Maine's work is essential. On one level, it was an apparent critique of the stadial theories of 'progress' found in, among others, the works of legal scholars of the Scottish Enlightenment.[109] Legal systems are not the same. They do not 'progress' through defined stages of development, nor can they be positioned on a civilisational scale compared to one another.[110] As Maine observed, this becomes evident only once when the investigation parameters are expanded beyond the conventional (European) focus. Then:

> [W]e find it to be not wholly a conceit or a paradox to say that the distinction between the Present and the Past disappears. Sometimes the Past *is* the Present; much more often it is removed from it by varying distances, which, however, cannot be estimated or expressed chronologically.[111]

If Maine's readers needed any further evidence that he did not subscribe to a stadial theory of 'progress', the final sentence of this quotation is definitive proof of his position.[112] It also links up with his additional comments relating to his method.[113] Two points are worth noting. Readers of *Ancient Law* may have noted that Maine suggested the existence of 'epochs' in the rise and fall of legal systems.[114] Maine does not define this term, but in context, it is perhaps best described as periods in which more significant intellectual shifts occurred within a legal system. These shifts were not universally positive or unidirectional in line with Maine's broader views on 'progress'. Thus, while the Roman encounter with natural law was viewed positively in the book's narrative, the rise of feudalism was viewed negatively. Furthermore, and in line with the Humanist underpinnings of *Ancient*

106 Adcock, 'Liberalism, Progress, and Comparative Inquiry', 106–7.

107 Maine, *Village Communities in the East and West*, 7–9; Bock, 'Comparison of Histories', 243.

108 Maine, *Village Communities in the East and West*, 9; see also Vinogradoff, *The Teaching of Sir Henry Maine; an Inaugural Lecture Delivered in Corpus Christi College Hall on March 1, 1904*, 15–16; Kelley, *Faces of History*, 188–216.

109 Marcos, 'Conceptual Aspects of Legal Enlightenment in Europe', generally. Mantena, *Alibis of Empire*, 22, for a survey. See also Piccinini, *Tra Legge e Contratto*, 65.

110 Smellie, 'Sir Henry Maine', 80; Mantena, *Alibis of Empire*, 25–30.

111 Maine, *Village Communities in the East and West*, 7.

112 DiMatteo, 'Unframing Legal Reasoning', generally.

113 Bock, 'Comparison of Histories', 244–5.

114 Ibid. 250.

Law, using contemporaneous examples enabled Maine to critique perceived problems in these legal systems.

4. CONCLUSIONS

Recent academic studies have greatly improved our understanding of the intellectual significance of Maine's *Ancient Law*. Authored in the mid-nineteenth century, this work focuses on local concerns about teaching English law and addresses global political issues related to Britain's colonial role in India. While this type of scholarly analysis is essential for grasping the later impact of Maine's contributions, the book's content has been notably overlooked – an oversight that needs to be addressed.

Understanding the extent to which *Ancient Law* was rooted in Maine's knowledge of Roman law is essential to comprehending its narrative. This insight shows that the work was multifaceted, operating on various levels. Exploring the content of *Ancient Law* allows the reader to assess Maine's expertise in the subject and its role within the work. *Ancient Law* was much more than a law textbook focused on the ancient world. Instead, it was a sophisticated piece of rhetoric that aligned with the intellectual traditions established in the early modern period and beyond, aiming to critically engage with natural law scholarship and Victorian intellectual debates on 'progress'.

Chapter 2

Conceptions of 'Progress'

I enter with just diffidence on the subject of civil law, which has exhausted so many learned lives, and clothed the walls of such spacious libraries.[1]

1. INTRODUCTION

Of all of Maine's '*aperçus*', as Stein called them, none is more frequently repeated than his statement on status and contract.[2] It is worth quoting in full. '[T]he movement of the progressive societies has hitherto been a movement from Status to Contract.'[3] This famous line, located at the end of chapter five of *Ancient Law*, provides a convenient starting point for a chapter on the concept of 'progress' and its meaning in this work. The abstract noun 'progress' does not frequently occur in *Ancient Law*. Instead, the adjective 'progressive' is the more frequently used term, usually in the phrase 'progressive society', but the two words are etymologically related and will thus be discussed together. Maine's statement contains three crucial words, namely, 'progressive', 'movement' and 'hitherto'. An analysis of these words will form the core of this chapter since they collectively reveal Maine's understanding of the concept of 'progress' in *Ancient Law* and beyond. Still, some background is required before undertaking an analysis of this kind. Contemporary debates concerning Maine's understanding of the word 'progress' are inextricably linked to the broader intellectual environment of the mid-1800s in which the book was written and the differing opinions of contemporary scholars on the nature and purpose of *Ancient Law*.[4] To those who read this book as an (unsuccessful) attempt by Maine to offer a predictive theory of legal change (or progress), the absence of any demonstrable definition of the term in question is viewed as a substantial shortcoming of its method.[5]

This is an incorrect perspective on the matter. While it is true that the book is devoted to the issue of legal change in a broad sense, Maine did not set out to provide any abstract theory of legal change (a 'law of progress') that could be

1 Gibbon and Fernández-Armesto, *The History of the Decline and Fall of the Roman Empire. Vol. 5, Justinian and the Roman Law*, 250.

2 Stein, *Legal Evolution*, 98.

3 Maine, *Ancient Law*, 170.

4 Burrow, 'Henry Maine and Mid-Victorian Ideas of Progress', generally; Batzel, 'Sir Henry James Sumner Maine', 107–90, 194–250; Cassani, *Diritto, antropologia e storia*, 19–55; Piccinini, *Tra legge e contratto*, 69–137; Woodard, 'A Wake (or Awakening?) For Historical Jurisprudence', 221–3.

5 Cocks, *Sir Henry Maine*, 57: '[H]e never claimed that he had fully explained the occurrence of progress; he never arrived at a final, all-inclusive generalisation.' See also Ibid. 57–64.

replicated and applied in a predictive fashion to all other societies in other periods.[6] It is, therefore, incorrect to state, as Feaver did in 1969, that *Ancient Law* was a book 'tracing the historical development of law in the ancient world'.[7] This is too general. Instead, Maine's aims with *Ancient Law* were specific. Since this work has often been associated with a theory of legal change, it is legitimate to ask why *Ancient Law* has come to be interpreted in this manner. A large part of the answer lies in the fact that *Ancient Law* was published in 1861 by the same publisher, John Murray III, and shortly after Darwin's *On The Origin of Species* in 1859. It thus came to be read within the rapidly growing intellectual environment of Darwinism in the mid-to-late nineteenth century.[8] The fact that it can be read in a Darwinian manner – that a legal system is a living organism which 'evolves' over time through natural selection – has caused many problems with interpretation, even in Maine's lifetime. It has also affected how subsequent generations have viewed Maine's project and its limitations.[9] It is crucial to determine whether this Darwinian reading of Maine's work reflects the author's aims.

Before exploring the meaning of 'progress' in *Ancient Law*, it is worth noting that the term serves two distinct yet related functions in the book. Both are linked to the meaning of the term. The first function is that of an instrument of critique. Maine opposed the meaning that the term 'progress' had acquired in the Victorian intellectual discourse. Thus, on one level, his comments about the term are designed to critique this nineteenth-century meaning of 'progress' and its philosophical implications. The second function is constitutive. Maine proposed that the term had an older sense, based on Greek philosophy, that needed to be uncovered and that tied into his argument about 'progressive' legal systems. This connection allowed him to explore issues of time and connection in philosophical terms.

Let us start with matters of definition.

2. ISSUES OF DEFINITION

Maine's use of the term 'progress' in *Ancient Law* can only be understood fully once it is appreciated that, by the mid-nineteenth century, the term itself had already acquired a substantial intellectual history dating back to the early modern period.[10] *En route*, it had become linked with ideas such as 'history', 'modernity'

6 Cocks, 'Maine, Progress and Theory'; Smith, 'Maine's Concept of Progress', generally.

7 Feaver, *From Status to Contract*, 41.

8 Ibid 43, 44. See Oldham, *Analysis*, v–vi, citing the views of Vinogradoff and Pollock, who proposed a close intellectual connection between the works of Darwin and Maine. See also Pollock and Maine, *Introduction and Notes*, viii.

9 Bock, 'Comparison of Histories', 232; Kumar, 'Maine and the Theory of Progress', 85. See also Feaver, 'The Victorian Values of Sir Henry Maine', 42; Landauer, 'From Status to Treaty', 219–20; Cotterrell, *The Politics of Jurisprudence*, 42–4; Newman, *Law and Economic Organization*, 6–49.

10 Woodard, 'A Wake (or Awakening?) For Historical Jurisprudence', 221–3; Gibbins, 'J.S. Mill, Liberalism, and Progress', for a survey.

and even 'civilisation'.[11] Schiavone, in a recent book devoted to the history of the idea of 'progress', summarised its nineteenth-century meaning as follows:

> It [Modernity] was based on the conviction that the ceaseless activity of human beings – the productivity of their effort, their intelligence, their daily labor [sic] – was creating the foundation for a continual change for the better in our modes of life, at least in the part of the world that Europeans inhabited; a privileged region (it was thought), called on to build a civilization without equal that would elaborate standards and rules to be imposed in the four corners of the earth.[12]

'Progress', defined by Schiavone in its nineteenth-century meaning as 'a continual change for the better', had impressive intellectual roots. It was anchored in two fundamental notions derived from interpretations of (among others) Biblical sources.[13] These early modern interpretations, distinct from the medieval understanding of the same issues, held that time operated linearly from the past to the present and that the future would inevitably be better. Collectively, these two interpretations had given the term 'progress' a critical function in the political and legal discourse of the eighteenth century, specifically concerning matters such as the origins of society and the relationship between rulers and subjects. By the start of the nineteenth century, 'progress' had become an important intellectual concept which, as Schiavone's quotation demonstrates, was linked to broader notions of 'modernity' and 'civilisation'.[14] It took on a particular significance in the context of the works of defenders of the British colonial presence in India, such as James Mill, who championed the 'civilising' influence of Empire.[15] It is against this wider intellectual environment that Maine's use of the term must be investigated.

When assessing the importance of the lack of a definition of 'progress' in *Ancient Law*, one must first examine the issue of definition in this work more generally. It cannot be said that Maine did not, as a rule, employ definitions in *Ancient Law*. He is quite fond of them. Thus, he resorts to established Roman-law definitions of terms such as *occupatio* or *obligatio* when required, and he even creates definitions, such as 'legal fiction', for example. This suggests that if he had wanted to define the term 'progress' (and thus also 'progressive society') in *Ancient Law*, he could have done so. This would suggest, in turn, that the lack of a definition is likely a choice. And it is this authorial choice that deserves closer scrutiny. If one assumes he did not see the need to define this term, two plausible reasons for such a decision may be offered. First, he was confident that his audience would understand what he

[11] Kuper, 'Civilization, Culture, and Race', 398–9; Cassani, *Diritto, antropologia e storia*, 141–202; Bordoni, *Hubris and Progress*, 1–31.

[12] Schiavone and Goldstein, *What is Progress*, 16–17.

[13] Ibid. 17–19.

[14] Mantena, *Alibis of Empire*, 30–9, for an account of the prominence of this line of thought in the work of John Stuart Mill. See also Kuper, 'Civilization, Culture, and Race', 399, for an account of the Utilitarians' support of 'progress' and the Burkeans' opposition to it.

[15] Gibbins, 'J.S. Mill, Liberalism, and Progress', generally.

meant by this term. And second, that an absence of a definition of it would not harm the broader thesis of this book.

Let us explore these two plausible reasons. The first concerns his audience's understanding of this term. As Cocks pointed out in his 1988 book on Maine, it is essential to consider the target audience of the work.[16] *Ancient Law* was written as a book for both specialists and a general audience. This suggests that Maine's use of 'progress' in *Ancient Law* tended towards a meaning both readerships would understand. Consequently, if one were to examine an authoritative account of the general sense of these words, it would likely provide some clues as to the meaning Maine had intended to convey to his readers. In the *Oxford English Dictionary* entry for the term 'progress', which sets out the history of the word in the English language from the early modern period onwards, two broad meanings are offered: '(1.) The course or process of a series of actions, events, etc., through time; advancement through such a course. (2.) The action or act of journeying or moving onward in space.'[17] The two core elements contained in these definitions are movement and temporality. Having surveyed Maine's use of this term throughout *Ancient Law*, this is the sense in which he used it, as one can see, for example, in the following statement concerning the state of Roman law after the enactment of the Twelve Tables: 'The authors of the new jurisprudence during the whole progress of its formation professed the most sedulous respect for the letter of the Code.'[18]

There is another indication of Maine's understanding of 'progress'. In a book written towards the end of his life, *Popular Government*, Maine used one of the four essays comprising the book to comment on 'the age of progress'.[19] The title of this essay suggests that it was an essential intellectual theme in his work, as indeed it was. In this essay, which contains a rather complex argument about human nature, Maine defined the term 'progress' as follows:

> [I]f Progress be understood with its only intelligible meaning, that is, as the continued production of new ideas, [then] scientific invention and scientific discovery are the great and perennial sources of these ideas.[20]

There is, of course, a gap in time between *Ancient Law* and *Popular Government*. Although it has been noted in contemporary scholarship that Maine became more sceptical about his thesis in *Ancient Law* towards the end of his life, there seems to be no evidence of a radical shift in his understanding of 'progress' between the statements in *Ancient Law* and his definition in *Popular Government*.[21] The definition

[16] Cocks, *Sir Henry Maine*, 53, 54–5.

[17] *Oxford English Dictionary*, s.v. 'progress (n.),' June 2024, https://doi.org/10.1093/OED/3034306464.

[18] Maine, *Ancient Law*, 34.

[19] Feaver, *From Status to Contract*, 60–1.

[20] Maine, *Popular Government*, 145.

[21] Kumar, 'Maine and the Theory of Progress', 80. As Lippincott, *Victorian Critics of Democracy*, 167–206, has shown, Maine's critique of progress in his later works was also a critique of democracy as the inevitable result of progress. See Collini, 'Democracy and Excitement: Maine's Political Pessimism', generally.

of the term in *Popular Government* would function equally well in the context of *Ancient Law*. Thus, taken cumulatively, it seems reasonable to infer that Maine's understanding of 'progress' was general – the continued production of new (legal) ideas through time, driven by 'scientific invention' and 'discovery'.[22] In addition, given this general meaning, the term 'progressive societies' did not require any further circumscription since the term merely referred to those societies in which 'progress' occurs.[23]

The second plausible reason for the absence of definitions of 'progress' or 'progressive society' offered above relates to the function of these terms within Maine's broader argument in *Ancient Law*. By the nineteenth century, the idea of 'progress' (and its two underlying assumptions about the linearity of time and the optimism for the future) had taken on a central role in many aspects of the Victorian intellectual discourse.[24] In *Ancient Law*, there is good evidence to suggest that this meaning of 'progress', or rather a critique of the general understanding of the term in Victorian intellectual circles, was the focus of Maine's thesis. He thus did not need to define these terms as it would have been clear to his audience what he meant. One may go as far as to assert that the overarching message in *Ancient Law* was Maine's attempt to decentre the idea that 'progress' was universal in at least two crucial respects.[25] First, he argued that 'progress' was not, in fact, universal across all societies and all periods as earlier natural law scholarship had assumed. This can be seen from a variety of statements in the work, but nowhere as clearly as in the following quotation: 'It is only with the progressive societies that we are concerned, and nothing is more remarkable than their extreme fewness.'[26]

Thus, to Maine, 'progress' and its corollary, 'progressive society', were not the norm but the exception.[27] These exceptional cases formed the focus of his book. He did not believe that the Victorian idea of 'progress', and legal progress more specifically, was endemic to all societies in all periods. One further piece of evidence supports this claim. The book's title, *Ancient Law*, was one of several titles Maine had suggested in a letter of 6 July 1860 to his publisher.[28] In this letter, three possible titles are mentioned. Tellingly, Maine does not use 'progress' in the three potential titles. Instead, he uses the words 'relation' and 'connection'. Later correspondence shows that his publisher chose one of these three titles, with which Maine agreed.[29] None of them, not even the final title chosen, contained the words 'progress' or 'progressive'.

The second way Maine decentralised the Victorian meaning of 'progress' within *Ancient Law* was to argue against the prevailing idea that 'progress' necessarily

22 Kumar, 'Maine and the Theory of Progress', 83.
23 Cocks, 'Maine, Progress and Theory', 70–1; Nielsen, *The Sociological Theories of Sir Henry Maine*, 154–83.
24 On perceptions regarding the linearity of time, see DiMatteo, 'Unframing Legal Reasoning', generally.
25 Bock, 'Comparison of Histories', 261–2; Scala, 'Henry Sumner Maine's Ancient Law', 47.
26 Maine, *Ancient Law*, 22, 24.
27 Collini, 'Democracy and Excitement: Maine's Political Pessimism', generally.
28 Feaver, *From Status to Contract*, 41–2.
29 Ibid. 42.

involved unidirectional improvement. Or, as Schiavone had summarised it: 'a continual change for the better'. Maine was sceptical of this, as one can see from the following statement:

> The tendency to look not to the past but to the future for types of perfection, was brought into the world by Christianity. Ancient literature gives few or no hints of a belief that the progress of society is necessarily from worse to better.[30]

As this quotation shows, Maine was aware of the intellectual associations between the term 'progress' and the notion of providential history ('perfection') based on an analysis of Biblical sources. It was not a new idea, of course, as Auguste Comte (1798–1857), for example, had previously established the link between 'progress' and Christianity.[31] And it is this connection between 'progress' and betterment to which he objected. As will become apparent below, this association played an important role in debates about a Darwinian reading of Maine's project. It is also within this context that specific observations concerning the relationship between 'progress' and 'evolution' are required. Maine's *Ancient Law* was published by the same publisher shortly after Darwin's *On the Origin of Species* had appeared. According to Burrow, the ideas on which Maine's book is based were likely formed between 1843 and 1853.[32] Although Darwin's ideas had been publicly debated before the publication of his work and would therefore have been familiar to Maine, there is little evidence of any demonstrable influence between these two works other than the fact that *Ancient Law* can be read in light of Darwin's work.[33] Maine's aims in *Ancient Law* were very different from those of Darwin's in *The Origin*, and the critical point of difference relates to the distinction between the terms 'progress' and 'evolution'. As Conlin pointed out:

> Many who came before and after Darwin saw 'evolution' (which literally means 'unfolding') as the gradual unravelling or revealing of a divine plan. Even those who did not believe in a divine Creator often assumed that evolutionary mechanisms like natural selection were engines moving along a preordained, progressive track (e.g. from 'lower' to 'higher' forms of life). The vast majority of Victorians were 'teleological' in that they saw evolution as a process directed towards a certain goal.[34]
>
> 'Evolution' and 'the theory of natural selection' were not synonymous. Natural selection as proposed in *The Origin* was just one mechanism by which species change was explained.[35]

[30] Maine, *Ancient Law*, 74.

[31] Evans-Pritchard, *A History of Anthropological Thought; Edited by André Singer; with an Introduction by Ernest Gellner*, 50.

[32] Burrow, *Evolution and Society*, 140.

[33] Ibid. 139–40; Feaver, *From Status to Contract*, 46; Landman, 'Primitive Law, Evolution, and Sir Henry Sumner Maine', generally; Bock, 'Comparison of Histories', 232, 236–7.

[34] Conlin, *Evolution and the Victorians*, 5.

[35] Ibid. 5.

As these two quotations demonstrate, 'progress' and 'evolution', while superficially similar, were quite different intellectually. For Maine, 'progress' was the continuous production of new legal ideas over time. 'New' was not the same as 'better', however. This was vastly different from 'evolution', a term used by Darwin to describe the evolution of various species of plants and animals through processes such as natural selection.[36] Natural selection essentially implied improvement, since it permitted some species of plants and animals to overcome environmental challenges through incremental adaptation.[37] Thus, while Darwin's was an abstract theory that could be applied with predictive effect to all living creatures, Maine did not intend to create any similar abstract theory of legal change in *Ancient Law*, nor did he advocate that legal change occurred because of any process like natural selection. Maine does not use the term 'evolution' in *Ancient Law*, again suggesting that his endeavour differed. It is worth bearing in mind that in the Victorian intellectual discourse, 'progress' as 'improvement' refers to intellectual progress and moral progress. The relationship between 'progress' and morality is also addressed in *Ancient Law*. The topics are not unrelated since Victorian ideals of improvement often also implied the presence of a more refined form of morality. This will be discussed towards the end of the next section.

To preserve the logic of this discussion, I will now examine Maine's method in *Ancient Law*. This investigation aims to demonstrate Maine's use of the term 'progress' in the book and its role in his broader thesis.

3. MAINE'S METHODOLOGY AND 'PROGRESS'

Modern scholarship on Maine's method encompasses a wide range opinions. At the more negative end of the spectrum, the work has been variously described as being 'not systematic',[38] 'not . . . a work of logic'[39] and 'riddled with inconsistencies'.[40] These more critical comments tend to be linked to the differing views held by contemporary scholars as to the nature and purpose of *Ancient Law*. Thus, those scholars who interpret the book as providing (or failing to provide) a general theory of legal change tend to be more critical of Maine's methodology than those who do not. Maine did not intend to set out such a generalised theory of legal change. Rather, he aimed to describe the 'progress', in the general sense in which he understood this term, of a select few legal systems (and one in particular) found

36 Ibid. 7–12.

37 Bock, 'Comparison of Histories', 237.

38 Burrow, *Evolution and Society*, 156.

39 Cocks, *Sir Henry Maine*, 52.

40 Kuper, 'Ancestors', 277. Evans, *Theories and Criticisms*, v, a compiler of one of the student texts based on Maine's work, wrote towards the end of the nineteenth century: '[i]n these works there is a great deal of writing that is absolutely useless to the student for examination purposes, and page after page has to be waded through in the search for a criticism or a theory.' For a survey of continental criticisms of Maine's book, see Pollock and Maine, *Introduction and Notes*, vi–vii. One of Maine's fiercest critics was the English legal historian, Frederic Maitland. For a survey of his criticisms of Maine's work, see Rabban, 'Maitland', 383–422.

in 'progressive societies' which had 'hitherto' occurred. To prove his general thesis, Maine looked beyond the surface level of the legal system. He set it out as follows:

> If by any means we can determine the early forms of jural concepts, they will be invaluable to us. These rudimentary ideas are to the jurist what the primary crusts of the Earth are to the geologist. They contain, potentially, all forms in which law has subsequently exhibited itself.[41]

The mention here of the popular Victorian science of geology is telling and ties into the 'scientific' ideals of Historical Jurisprudence, a movement with which Maine has come to be associated.[42] One might also point out that the image of geological sediment layers provides a visual aid to Maine's understanding of 'progress' as the continuous production of new legal ideas over time.[43] We must now turn to these ideals of Historical Jurisprudence.

Historical Jurisprudence has a historical and scientific component.[44] As Bock has argued, these two elements were intertwined, each acting as a corrective to the other.[45] As far as history is concerned, the broader intellectual environment of the nineteenth century, particularly in European scholarship, was one in which the methodologies of studying history were vigorously debated, especially concerning the 'scientific' method. Although Maine does not make any overt statements about this issue in *Ancient Law*, other than to criticise natural law scholars for their lack of historical understanding in general terms, in a speech to the students at the University of Calcutta in 1865 – four years after the publication of the book – he addressed the issue squarely in his comments to the arts graduates of that year:[46]

> Why should history be studied? The only answer, I suppose, which could be given is, Because it is true: because it is a portion of the truth to which it is the object of all study to attain. It is, however, an undoubted fact that the quality of the truth expected from history has always been changing and cannot be said to be even now settled.[47]

[41] Maine, *Ancient Law*, 3.

[42] Cocks, *Sir Henry Maine*, 71. For a possible source of Maine's interest in geology, see Stein, *Legal Evolution*, 88.

[43] Kuper, 'Civilization, Culture, and Race', 403–4, has shown that the popularisation of 'geological time' occurred as a result of the work of the Scottish geologist Charles Lyell, whose *Principles of Geology*, published by John Murray from 1830 onwards, ran through multiple editions. This growing interest in geology and the concept of time contributed to the Victorian perspective that 'civilisation' was a recent development preceded by an era referred to as 'prehistory'. For the history of the concept of 'progress' in Victorian anthropology, see Ibid. 409–10.

[44] Burrow, *Evolution and Society*, 144–5. It is important to remember that proponents of Historical Jurisprudence, while influenced by the German Historical School, did not share all their intellectual preoccupations. As Reimann, 'Historical Jurisprudence', has shown, it was a broad movement. See also Bock, 'Comparison of Histories', 232; Piccinini, *Tra legge e contratto*, 175–258.

[45] Bock, 'Comparison of Histories', 243.

[46] Cocks, 'Maine, Progress and Theory', 71–3.

[47] Maine, *Village Communities in the East and West*, 264.

> It is now affirmed, and was felt long before it was affirmed, that the truth of history, if it exists, cannot differ from any other form of truth. If it be truth at all, it must be scientific truth. There can be no essential difference between the truths of the Astronomer, of the Physiologist, and of the Historian. The great principle which underlies all our knowledge of the physical world, that Nature is ever consistent with herself, must also be true, of human nature and human society which is made up of human nature.[48]

These two quotations suggest that Maine was well informed about the debates in German intellectual circles regarding the aims and methods of historical enquiry. He had no doubt been confronted with these during his studies at Cambridge. The connection between history and truth seems to echo the famous dictum of the contemporaneous German historian, Leopold von Ranke, that it was the function of history to use primary sources to demonstrate 'Wie es eigentlich gewesen ist'. History fulfilled an essential role in Maine's thesis in *Ancient Law*, and as will be shown in subsequent chapters, one of his main criticisms of the likes of Bentham and Austin was their lack of historical understanding.[49] However, it was not only the lack of historical knowledge that caused Maine to object. He also rejected the non-scientific 'idealised' versions of the past employed by earlier natural-law scholarship.[50] Thus, in his address to the students at the University of Calcutta in 1866, he commented:

> Although there is much in common between the Present and the Past, there is never so much in common as to make life tolerable to the men of the Present if they could step back into the Past. There is no one in this room to whom the life of a hundred years since would not be acute suffering, if it could be lived over again.[51]

> [O]ur modern trick of constructing, by means of works of fiction, an imaginary Past out of the Present, taking from the Past its externals, its outward furniture, but building in the sympathies, the susceptibilities, and even (for it sometimes comes to that) the knowledge of the present time.[52]

As these quotations show, the historical component of Maine's method was rooted in a 'scientific' view of history in which primary sources had to be evaluated critically. The spectre of Niebuhr and his 'source criticism' looms large in this

48 Ibid. 265–6.

49 Bock, 'Comparison of Histories', 237–8, Feaver, *From Status to Contract*, 45; Cocks, *Sir Henry Maine*, 64. Goëtzmann, 'La "Comparative Jurisprudence" de Henry Sumner Maine, Entre École Analytique et École Historique', 72–108, 109–54, in an assessment of the similarities and differences between the positions of Maine and Bentham, as well as Austin, has called for a more nuanced interpretation of their intellectual relationship. Per Goëtzmann (233–4), apart from their differences over the nature of law as a command, Maine stressed the differences between his historical methodology and those of Bentham and Austin while at the same time acknowledging their influence on him.

50 Bock, 'Comparison of Histories', 233–4; Cocks, *Sir Henry Maine*, 71–2.

51 Maine, *Village Communities in the East and West*, 289–90.

52 Ibid. 290–1.

quotation. This 'scientific' attitude towards interpreting sources also extended to Maine's choice of subject matter. In chapter five of *Ancient Law*, where Maine sets out the main thrust of his thesis, he comments on the issue as follows:

> The rudiments of the social state, so far as they are known to us all, are known through the testimony of three sorts – accounts by contemporary observers of civilisations less advanced than their own, the records which particular races have preserved concerning their primitive history, and ancient law.[53]

In the subsequent pages, he proceeded to argue that the first two types of source material were too unreliable to be used for the task at hand, hence his focus on ancient law:

> Much of the old law which has descended to us was preserved merely because it was old. Those who practised and obeyed it did not pretend to understand it; and in some cases they even ridiculed and despised it. They offered no account of it except that it had come down to them from their ancestors. If we confine our attention, then, to those fragments of ancient institutions which cannot reasonably be supposed to have been tampered with, we are able to gain a clear conception of certain great characteristics of the society to which they originally belonged. . . . [I]f the materials for this process are sufficient, and if the comparisons be accurately executed, the methods followed are as little objectionable as those which have led to such surprising results in comparative philology.[54]

Thus, according to Maine, ancient law provided more reliable evidence for his endeavour than any other available source material on the past. In addition, as we shall presently see, the reference to 'comparative philology' in the final sentence of this quotation is telling.

There was more to Maine's method than merely providing an account of how his chosen legal system from the past produced new ideas through the critical use of primary sources. The technique he describes in the quotation above, namely 'determining the early forms of jural concepts', was influenced by his interest in comparative philology through the work of the Oxford philologist Friedrich Max Müller (1823–1900), among others.[55] Burrow has shown that the late publication and uneven dissemination of Max Müller's work are problematic when attempting to pinpoint the extent to which he was an essential source for Maine's ideas in *Ancient Law*.[56] Nevertheless, despite these issues, he was almost certainly influenced

[53] Maine, *Ancient Law*, 120.

[54] Ibid. 121–2.

[55] Kuper, 'Civilization, Culture, and Race', 404, shows the popularity of the comparative method also in emergent works of anthropology at this time. See also Bock, 'Comparison of Histories', 241; Cocks, *Sir Henry Maine*, 20–2; Cassani, *Diritto, antropologia e storia*, 57–108; Feaver, 'The Victorian Values of Sir Henry Maine', 39–40.

[56] Burrow, *Evolution and Society*, 148–53.

by Max Müller and possibly, more generally, by German philological scholarship of the period.[57]

Since the former provides a tangible link, it is worth pointing out what Max Müller believed one could gain from studying the 'science of language', as he called it. In his *Three Lectures on the Science of Language*, published in 1890, Max Müller, having devoted a lifetime to the study of comparative philology, summarised the 'lessons' one could learn from such an investigation. As a scholar of Sanskrit, he was primarily concerned with the linguistic connections between different Indo-European languages. From his research, he deduced three crucial 'lessons'. First, the possession of language is what separates humans from other creatures on earth.[58] Second, people share 'a linguistic bond thicker than blood' by being part of a joint Indo-European language family, and this bond transcends any subsequent divisions and animosities between societies that may have arisen in the meantime.[59] Finally, the sheer diversity of the Indo-European language family led him to appreciate that there were other languages, not just Greek and Latin, worth studying.[60]

But how does this apply to Maine? Taking his cue from Savigny, or perhaps the German Historical School more generally, who saw law as an element of culture like language, Maine applied Max Müller's insights to his research of ancient law.[61] Thus, if one were to describe Maine's methodology, it would be as follows. Several legal systems from the past are intellectually related owing to their shared linguistic heritage in the Indo-European language family. These systems are exceptional because they are 'progressive' and continuously produce new legal ideas over time. Within this group, one legal system, Roman law, provided the most complete account of how new legal ideas are produced.[62] It, therefore, could be used as the model for his investigation. As Bock pointed out in 1974, Maine realised that to apply the principles of comparative philology to his investigation of law, he had to narrow the scope of his inquiry and find a commonality between

[57] Ibid. 150–3; Stein, *Legal Evolution*, 91–2.

[58] Müller, *Three Lectures*, 6, 9.

[59] Ibid. 40.

[60] Ibid. 42.

[61] Burrow, *Evolution and Society*, 142–4; Bock, 'Comparison of Histories', 241, 243. Burrow shows in the quoted pages that it is difficult to pinpoint the extent of Savigny's influence upon Maine. See Feaver, *From Status to Contract*, 46; Stein, *Legal Evolution*, 89–92. Goëtzmann, 'La "Comparative Jurisprudence" de Henry Sumner Maine, Entre École Analytique et École Historique', 179–204, in a comprehensive comparison of the methodologies of Maine and Savigny, has shown that the latter's influence on the former was both direct and indirect, likely owing to their shared reliance on the work of Niebuhr. In certain places within the book, Maine overtly engages with Savigny's views on possession, for example.

[62] Bock, 'Comparison of Histories', 242. Burrow, *Evolution and Society*, 161, 164, criticises Maine's use of this common link. Kuper, 'Civilization, Culture, and Race', 405–6, has shown that in anthropological terms, the Indo-European hypothesis opposed the 'common descent' hypothesis, also popular in Victorian scholarship.

the systems he had chosen to discuss.[63] To him, this common link lay in the concept of the Indo-European (or 'Aryan') language family.[64]

There was a further element to this method, namely the linguistic idea of common roots, which Max Müller had discussed at the start of his second lecture. Here, he explained it as follows:

> You take a word, remove from it all that can be accounted for, that is, all that can be proved to be purely formative and derivative; and what cannot be accounted for, what cannot be further analyzed, you accept as an element, as an ultimate fact, or as scholars are in the habit of calling it, as a root.[65]

The link is clear when Max Müller's statement is compared to the above quotation from Maine's *Ancient Law*. For Maine, 'early forms of jural concepts' were to a legal system what 'roots' were to a language.

Contemporary scholars such as Burrow have been dismissive of this methodology. Thus, in his 1966 book, Burrow commented that:

> The theory of an 'Aryan' past, including both India and Europe, had some curious, but for Maine highly convenient, results. It permitted him to make, within its limits, the dashing comparisons, the equation of the past institutions of one society with the present ones of another so characteristic of the Comparative Method and of his own writing.[66]

> The Aryan hypothesis was a façade hiding from Maine and his opponents the requirements of his method.[67]

While hindsight is revealing, especially given the eventual fortunes of Historical Jurisprudence, this is perhaps too cynical a reading of Maine's method. There is no evidence that Maine used his insights from the work of, among others, Max Müller as 'a façade' or merely to make 'dashing comparisons'. If the other works produced by Maine during his lifetime are an indication, he never wavered in his belief that Historical Jurisprudence could be a useful intellectual tool.

To appreciate what Maine wanted to achieve in this regard, we must return to our initial observations concerning the meaning of 'progress'. Maine's argument here was broadly that the nineteenth-century meaning of the term, based on underlying notions of universality and unidirectionality, did not accurately take account of its earlier sense. But what was this earlier sense? To answer this question, Maine's later statements in the Rede lecture must be cited:

> Not one of those intellectual excellencies which we regard as characteristic of the great progressive races of the world . . . would apparently have come into existence if those races had been left to themselves. To one small people, covering in its original seat no

[63] Bock, 'Comparison of Histories', 243–5.

[64] Maine, *Village Communities in the East and West*, 230, for a link to Maine's understanding of the concept of 'civilisation'; Burrow, 'Henry Maine and Mid-Victorian Ideas of Progress', 61.

[65] Müller, *Three Lectures*, 29.

[66] Burrow, *Evolution and Society*, 161.

[67] Ibid. 164.

> more than a handsbreadth of territory, it was given to create the principle of Progress, of movement onwards and not backwards or downwards, of destruction tending to construction. That people was the Greek.[68]

To Maine, as this quotation shows, the earlier sense of the term was rooted in Greek philosophy. The consequence of this association was that Maine could use it to critique the universality associated with the nineteenth-century meaning of the term 'progress'. Still, there was more to this Greek association than first meets the eye. To appreciate its deeper meaning, one must focus on Maine's statement towards the end of the quotation, where 'progress' is described as 'destruction tending towards construction'. Earlier in the Rede lecture, one finds the following statement: '[c]ivilisation is nothing more than a name for the old Aryan world, dissolved but perpetually re-constituting itself under a vast variety of solvent influences.'[69]

To anyone in his audience with a passing knowledge of Greek philosophy, these two statements would have triggered an association with, for example, Plato's discussion of cycles of government in *The Republic* or the cyclical theories of time discussed in Greek philosophy more generally.[70] This is what lay behind these statements. To Maine, 'progress' in the older sense of the term, and when restricted to the legal systems connected via the Indo-European language family, was not linear; it was cyclical.

Limiting the concept of 'progress' in the Greek philosophical sense to a few legal systems was purposive and not a value-neutral choice. To understand his motives for employing this approach, one must look again at Max Müller's work. One key element of Max Müller's account of the science of language deserves closer attention. When read collectively, the three lectures on this topic mentioned above were written as a dialogue between Max Müller and contemporaneous Victorian debates on race and ethnicity, specifically, those scholars (both in Germany and Britain) who were progressively attempting to transpose discussions concerning the Indo-European language family – a linguistic category – into a racial category.[71] Max Müller was vehemently opposed to this idea. This is, for example, visible in the following quotation from the third lecture:

> It is language that makes man. Language is surely more of the essence of man than his skin, or his color, or his skull or his hair. Blood, flesh, and bone are not of our true

[68] Maine, *Village Communities in the East and West*, 238.

[69] Ibid. 230.

[70] Martin, 'The Golden Age and the ΚΥΚΛΟΣ ΓΕΝΕΣΕΩΝ (Cyclical Theory) in Greek and Latin Literature', for a survey. Piccinini, *Tra legge e contratto*, 34–40, has suggested that the cyclical theory of history proposed by the Italian historian Giambattista Vico (1668–1744) may also have influenced Maine's views here. Vico's work is known to have influenced Maine during his formative years.

[71] Kuper, 'Civilization, Culture, and Race', 406–7; Lyons, 'Linguistics and Law', generally; Pereltsvaig, *The Indo-European Controversy*, 19–38. Demoule, *The Indo-Europeans*, 33–95, has shown that this was the eventual fate of research in this field. See Demoule, 'The Canonical Indo-European Model and Its Underlying Assumptions', for a survey.; Majeed, 'Comparativism and References to Rome in British Imperial Attitudes to India', 98–100; Jones, 'The Early Utilitarians, Race, and Empire', generally; Tuori, *Lawyers and Savages*, 58–9.

> essence. They are in constant flux, and change with every year, till at last they return to the dust. Our body is our uniform, very tight sometimes, very painful to don, very painful to doff, but still our uniform only. It matters very little whether it is black or white. Language, on the contrary, is the very embodiment of our true self.[72]

The message is clear. The scientific study of the roots of languages intellectually connected through the paradigm of the Indo-European language family could unite rather than divide people. Max Müller was not unique in his opposition to the transposition of the Indo-European language family as a linguistic category into a racial category. There is strong evidence, from an address delivered to the students at the University of Calcutta in 1864, that Maine shared a similar idea and saw it as applicable to his own work:

> [T]he equality which results from intellectual cultivation is always and at once possible. Be sure that it is real equality. No man ever yet genuinely despised, however he might hate, his intellectual equal. In Europe, the only community, which, so far as I can see, is absolutely undivided by barriers of race, of nationality, of prejudice, of birth and wealth, is the community of men of letters and of science. The citizens of that Republic have before now corresponded with each other and retained their friendships, while the deadliest wars were separating their fellow-countrymen.[73]

Despite the Eurocentrism underlying this statement, to Maine, setting out a position quite similar to that of Max Müller, the study of ancient law had a potentially unifying rather than a divisive purpose. As he phrased it rather eloquently in his discussion of joint ownership in *Village Communities*, comparative investigations of ancient law demonstrated that 'all men are brothers, and all men are equal'.[74] Nowhere is this more visible than in the closing words of the Rede lecture, where he commented as follows:

> It is this principle of progress which we Englishmen are communicating to India. We did not create it. We deserve no special credit for it. It came to us filtered through many different media. But we have received it; and as we have received it, so we pass it on. There is no reason why, if it has time to work, it should not develop in India effects as wonderful as in any other of the societies of mankind.[75]

There is much to unpack in this quotation. It summarises Maine's objections to the nineteenth-century meaning of the term and the intellectual associations implicit within it. 'Progress', in the Greek sense, was something far rarer. It was neither universal nor unidirectional. This was the fundamental lesson. This insight could be shared based on the intellectual connection between England and India via the Indo-European language family.

[72] Müller, *Three Lectures*, 53.
[73] Maine, *Village Communities in the East and West*, 254.
[74] Ibid. 225–6.
[75] Ibid. 238–9.

To understand the full implications of this statement, a detailed investigation into the specifics of Maine's method in *Ancient Law* is required. This discussion has two aspects: the English context of *Ancient Law* and his approach to the prevailing Victorian notions concerning the linearity of time implicit in the nineteenth-century understanding of the term. First, let us consider Maine's treatment of his primary source material since it illuminates the English context of *Ancient Law*. Having justified his focus on ancient law and his purpose, Maine also commented on how he approached this material. Contemporary scholars on Maine have shown that his approach to primary sources, while broadly in line with the aims of Historical Jurisprudence, was quite different from, say, Savigny. Unlike similar works of the period in Germany, Maine's *Ancient Law* does not contain the same detailed exegetic analysis characteristic of such works. While some scholars seized upon this difference to emphasise Maine's perceived lack of knowledge of Roman law, the reality is far more nuanced. Bearing in mind Cocks' point, namely that *Ancient Law* was written not only for specialists but also for a general audience, it stands to reason that his treatment of the source material would reflect this broader aim. In his address to students at the University of Calcutta in 1865, Maine's comments show evidence of this. There, specific comments were directly aimed at the graduating class of law students. First, he pointed out that law as a field of study was attractive because it combined scholarly and practical pursuits. The technicalities of the law formed an essential part of it, but they should not be overemphasised:

> Technicalities are absolutely indispensable to lawyers, just as the ideas of form, and proportion, and colour have to be thrown into a technical shape before they can give birth to painting or sculpture. A lawyer cannot do without technical rules, any more than a sculptor or a painter; but still, it is universally true that a disposition to overrate technicalities, or to value them for their own sake, is the characteristic mark of the journeyman, as distinguished from the artists.[76]

The technicalities of law should not be used to hinder the basic underlying idea that 'law is common sense'. To that end, Maine cautioned the graduating class with the following:

> [T]he grand criterion of legal soundness is common sense, and if you are inclined to employ an argument, or to draw an inference, or to give an opinion which does not satisfy the test, which is out of harmony with experience and with the practical facts of life, I do not say, reject it absolutely, but strongly suspect it, and be sure that the presumption is heavily against it.[77]

This advice offered to law students at the University of Calcutta also reflects Maine's approach to using primary source material in *Ancient Law*. Law consists

[76] Ibid. 259.
[77] Ibid. 260.

of technicalities, which should never be disregarded when studying it. At the same time, legal technicalities were not the ultimate focus of the law. Rather, attention to technicalities should be tempered by an understanding of the basic underlying notion: 'law is common sense' and should strive to be in 'harmony with experience and with the practical facts of life'. These insights formed the core of his engagement with the primary sources in *Ancient Law*.

When all these insights are combined, Maine's methodology in *Ancient Law* becomes clearer. It was not written as an attempt to provide an abstract theory of legal change which could be replicated linearly across space and time with predictive results.[78] Instead, *Ancient Law* described how Roman law, one of the best-preserved examples of a 'progressive' legal system, continuously generated new legal ideas. Since Roman law is intellectually linked to other legal systems of the past and the present through a common linguistic bond rooted in the Indo-European language family, comparative insights from these systems can be used to enhance the understanding of the trajectory of legal phenomena identified in Roman law. Maine's aim with *Ancient Law* was never one of comparative law in the sense that it would be understood today. It was an account of the generation of new legal ideas in Roman law with selected insights from other legal systems intellectually linked to it.

Maine's notion of 'progress' had two elements: movement and temporality. According to Maine, evidence of movement could be seen from the production of new legal ideas. Equally, as far as temporality is concerned, Maine did not seem to assign a meaning to it beyond a general one, namely the passage of time. Since the aim of *Ancient Law* was not to show the relentless onward march of a legal system into modernity, where everything was better, he could deal with temporality more circumspectly. Evidence for this can be seen from the following quotation:

> The tendency to look not to the past but to the future for types of perfection, was brought into the world by Christianity. Ancient literature gives few or no hints of a belief that the progress of society is necessarily from worse to better.[79]

More than any other, this quotation shows that Maine's aim with *Ancient Law* was not to chart the linear progress of law in the abstract. His was a different project, namely, to identify and study basic legal notions in Roman law with comparative evidence from a few legal systems intellectually connected through their common linguistic roots.[80] It did not matter whether these legal systems existed at different times (Rome vs India) or in various locations (Ancient Greece vs nineteenth-century England). His aim was never to argue that Hindu law would necessarily follow the same developmental route as the Roman legal system or that it was at the same developmental stage where the latter once was regarding legal ideas.

[78] Kumar, 'Maine and the Theory of Progress', 76–7.
[79] Maine, *Ancient Law*, 74.
[80] Bock, 'Comparison of Histories', 236.

Instead, it was to show the developmental trajectory of specific basic jural ideas using Roman law as his model.[81]

Evidence for this non-linear approach to time is also visible in Maine's 1856 Cambridge Essay on 'Roman Law and Legal Education'. In this essay, Maine observed:

> It is not because our own jurisprudence and that of Rome were once alike that they ought to be studied together, - it is because they will be alike. It is because all laws, however dissimilar in their infancy, tend to resemble each other in their maturity.[82]

According to Stein, this comment indicates that, to Maine, Roman law had to be studied because '[t]hey were technically ahead of us, and we should recognise that fact'.[83] While it is, without doubt, possible to read this statement in this manner, Stein's interpretation should be read with caution, given the arguments made above concerning linearity in *Ancient Law*. To that end, some context is required. Maine's 1856 essay was written when his ideas for *Ancient Law* had already been formed. Given that he was to use Roman law in *Ancient Law* to argue against the linear notion of progress a few years later, it seems unlikely that he would have used it in the 1856 essay to make a point about linearity. It seems more likely that the statement above should be read in the context of Maine's participation, not long before, in a government enquiry concerning the state of law teaching in England, where he had argued that Roman law should be taught comprehensively in the English law degree to counteract the ahistorical approaches espoused by Bentham and his followers.[84] When read against this background, Maine's comment becomes capable of a different reading. His point was precisely the opposite of Stein's interpretation. Roman law should be taught not because the common law had some connections to European ideas in the past. It had to be taught because it had contemporary value as an interpretative tool. In a cyclical sense, it could well be that the future of English law might resemble Roman law in terms of its 'scientific' approach, but it was by no means its destiny.

So, what was Maine's approach to time? To answer this question, a distinction must be drawn between the passage of time across each legal system and the relative passage of time between those systems on which he chose to focus. The latter issue can be dealt with swiftly. Since Maine never attempted to plot the development of different legal systems on a 'civilisational' scale concerning one another, any attempt to interpret his project in this manner is doomed to fail. The chief purpose of Maine's project was to use Roman law as a model. In some instances, past and present legal systems could provide additional information that could be used to conjecture the earlier or later history of basic legal ideas visible in Roman law, but that did not mean that predictive conclusions concerning their

81 Majeed, 'Bathos, Architecture and Knowing India', generally.
82 Maine, *Village Communities in the East and West*, 332; Stein, *Legal Evolution*, 86.
83 Stein, *Legal Evolution*, 86.
84 Scala, 'Henry Sumner Maine's Ancient Law', 47.

future trajectories could be drawn. As for the first issue, it is, of course, true that time passes. As it passes, legal systems change in response to new social concerns. At the same time, these changes are not always for the better. This was Maine's central point. If anything, change across time tended to be cyclical, as Plato and Aristotle had maintained. No doubt, this insight from Greek antiquity lay behind the famous opening lines of *Ancient Law*: '[t]he most celebrated system of jurisprudence known to the world begins, as it ends, with a Code.'[85] This sentence eloquently expresses Maine's view on the cyclical nature of legal change. The cycle of change in Roman law began as it ended – with a code.

One final aspect of Maine's method in *Ancient Law* deserves specific comment. Although this work did not propose an abstract theory of legal progress, it can be read as a commentary on 'moral progress'.[86] The Victorian intellectual discourse concerning 'progress' in the sense of betterment also extended to the issue of morality. Thus, both Burrow and Collini have argued that in *Ancient Law*, Maine engaged with the idea of moral progress.[87] As both authors show, this reading of Maine relies upon a contextualisation of Maine's writing within broader themes such as the Whig interpretation of history and his acknowledged conservatism. At the same time, however, it is crucial to focus on the content of Maine's book to understand his views. For the moment, I wish to focus on Maine's references to morality in *Ancient Law*.[88] It is important to situate his discussion of morality in context. The relationship between law and morality formed part of a more extensive discussion in European legal literature, traced in Montesquieu's *De L'Esprit*, who argued for a separation between law and morality, and in the works of Bentham, whose position is somewhat more complex, though broadly similar.[89] There can be little doubt that Maine was drawing his audience's attention to this debate. At the same time, however, his engagement with the issue is primarily restricted to his discussion of the law of contract, where, as will be discussed in greater detail below, he uses it to critique the linear nature of 'progress'. It is essential to survey his use of the term across the book. References to morality appear throughout *Ancient Law*, but it is not easy to form a coherent picture of Maine's view on the subject. Thus, for example, he observes, when discussing the transition to written law, that law should have begun the long process of separating from religion and morality at this point. At the same time, the effect of morality on law forms an essential part of his discussions concerning 'equity' as a mechanism of legal

85 Maine, *Ancient Law*, 1; Woodard, 'A Wake (or Awakening?) For Historical Jurisprudence', 228–37.

86 Burrow, 'Henry Maine and Mid-Victorian Ideas of Progress', 57–9.

87 Collini, 'Democracy and Excitement: Maine's Political Pessimism', 88–9 for a survey of the debate. Goodlad, 'Moral Character', generally. See also Cocks, *Sir Henry Maine*, 56–7; Piccinini, *Tra Legge e Contratto*, 223.

88 Cocks, *Sir Henry Maine*, 56–64.

89 de Champs, 'Utility, Morality, and Reform', 194–6. See also Larrère and Ning Seah, 'Montesquieu and the Classical World', 78; Hendrickson, 'Ordinary Passions', 1–11; Kodama, 'Bentham's Distinction between Law and Morality', for a survey. Bentham, Dumont and Hildreth, *Theory of Legislation*, 79–86.

change. Collectively, Maine's *Ancient Law* contains four important statements concerning morality.

> The movement of the collective opinion of a whole society is too palpable to be ignored, and is generally too visibly for the better to be decried; but there is the greatest disinclination to accept it as a primary phenomenon, and it is commonly explained as the recovery of a lost perfection – the gradual return to a state from which the race has lapsed.[90]

> Everywhere a new morality has displaced the canons of conduct and the reasons of acquiescence which were in unison with the ancient usages, because in fact they were born of them.[91]

> [I]n the interval between their days and ours, morality has advanced from a very rude to a highly refined conception.[92]

> The mistake of judging the men of other periods by the morality of our own day has its parallel in the mistake of supposing that every wheel or bolt in the modern social machine had its counterpart in more rudimentary societies.[93]

If one were to take these four statements cumulatively as indicative of Maine's position on morality in *Ancient Law*, the following conclusions may be drawn. First, morality played a role in developing a legal system and, thus, in legal change. Second, different legal systems approached morality differently. Maine, for example, referred to the Romans' 'imperfect morality'. Third, to avoid the idea of a linear progress of legal systems, it was incorrect to assume that ancient legal systems, like that of the Romans, had a more refined conception of morality than those of the present day. This would be a perpetuation of the 'golden age' fallacy. Instead, the point was that morality is contingent, and that it was scientifically incorrect to interpret the laws of others through the lens of present-day morality.[94]

4. MAINE'S INSIGHTS

Although Maine did not set out to produce an abstract theory of legal change that could be replicated across space and time, his investigation of Roman law, his primary focus, led him to draw various conclusions. These conclusions were not meant to be read as abstract generalisations. They were inductive conclusions reached by Maine from his investigations into changes in Roman law. To

[90] Maine, *Ancient Law*, 71.
[91] Ibid. 168.
[92] Ibid. 307.
[93] Ibid. 310–11.
[94] Bock, 'The Moral Philosophy of Sir Henry Summer Maine', 153–4. Moral decline is a central theme of Montesquieu's *Considérations sur les causes de la grandeur des Romains et de leur decadence*, first published in 1734 and widely regarded as having significantly impacted Gibbon's *Decline and Fall*.

Maine, the transition from unwritten to written law in the Roman legal order was pivotal and functioned as the start of his narrative in *Ancient Law*. He described what came before, but the treatment of the subject matter shows that he was not greatly interested in pre-written law. Instead, it was used primarily to demonstrate the advantage of written law. According to Maine, writing down the law, like the Twelve Tables, had one prime advantage: publicity. Only once the law had been reduced to writing and thus rendered public did the distinction between progressive and stationary societies begin to manifest itself more clearly.[95] Maine drew two additional conclusions on the transition from unwritten to written law in the Roman legal experience.[96] First, the transition to written law occurred relatively early in the history of the Roman legal system. Second, the progress of a legal system was aided by the separation between law and religion which began at this point. Failure to do so could hamper the 'progress' of a legal system. Still, the transition from unwritten to written law did not guarantee that a legal system would continue producing new ideas. As Maine demonstrated, there was every possibility that progress might still stall. Much depended on how a legal system coped with social impulses. This is where Maine's insights are sharpest.

Once written law had been introduced, a legal system had to manage the relationship between the law and societal impulses. He explains it as follows:

> [S]ocial necessities and social opinions are always more or less in advance of Law. We may come indefinitely near to the closing of the gap between them, but it has a perpetual tendency to reopen. Law is stable; the societies we are speaking of are progressive. The greater or less happiness of a people depends on the degree of promptitude with which the gulf is narrowed.[97]

Acknowledging the gap between societal impulses and the legal system is undoubtedly one of Maine's most critical conclusions. In addition, he proposed three 'instrumentalities', as he called them, to narrow the ever-widening gap between law and social impulses: legal fictions, equity and legislation. It is to these that we now turn.

When Maine refers to these three mechanisms as 'instrumentalities', it is essential to consider what this means in the context of his book. They were, in short, mechanisms of legal change – three different ways in which the Roman legal order produced new ideas across time. Their function, collectively, was to ensure that the gap between the written law and the evolving societal impulses remained as narrow as possible. Two aspects of Maine's identification of these three mechanisms of legal change require specific comment. The first relates to the order in which Maine has arranged them in his work. He comments on the matter as follows:

95 Nielsen, *The Sociological Theories of Sir Henry Maine*, 154–5; Stein, 'Maine and Legal Education', 205, for speculation as to the origins of this distinction; Twining, 'Maine and Legal Education', generally.

96 Nielsen, *The Sociological Theories of Sir Henry Maine*, 157–8.

97 Maine, *Ancient Law*, 24.

> Their historical order is that in which I have placed them. Sometimes two of them will be seen operating together, and there are legal systems which have escaped the influence of one or other of them. But I know of no instance in which the order of their appearance has been changed or inverted.[98]

As is evident from this carefully worded statement, the order in which Maine discussed these mechanisms of legal change was driven by the order in which they had occurred in the history of Roman law. He was by no means wedded to this order, however. Hence, he cautiously worded that, when writing *Ancient Law*, he had not encountered a legal system in which these mechanisms had occurred in a different order. It is also essential to read this statement considering the metaphor of geological sediment layers mentioned above. Within the sedimentary layers comprising the Roman legal system, different legal mechanisms gave rise to new legal ideas. Occasionally, these mechanisms operated collectively, thus indicating that he did not see them as representing a linear progression of mechanisms.

5. CONCLUSIONS

In 1991, Yale pointed out that the 'residual value [of Maine's work] lies in his method'.[99] This, at first, seems a strange statement, considering the perceived lack of clarity concerning this issue. As this chapter has shown, Maine's work does not suffer from a lack of method. Rather, the perceived problems with method have arisen because the work's message has been incorporated into nineteenth-century intellectual narratives concerned with Darwinian evolution and applying this general theory of adaptation through natural selection. This was never Maine's aim with *Ancient Law*, nor did he subscribe to a Darwinian interpretation of legal change through natural selection. His was a different project altogether, the purpose of which can only be understood through a contextual reading of *Ancient Law*. To understand the purpose of the work and its crucial message, attention must be paid to the meaning of terms such as 'progress' and 'progressive' and their function within Maine's book. In addition, the intellectual environment in which the book was created must be studied to understand the purpose of *Ancient Law*.

98 Ibid. 25.

99 Yale, 'Further Thoughts on Maine's Historical Jurisprudence', 238.

Chapter 3

Ancient Law and Legal Change

The laws of a nation form the most instructive portion of its history.[1]

1. INTRODUCTION

Maine wrote *Ancient Law* to critique natural law scholarship on the State's formation and the role of law in that process.[2] In his view, natural law scholars had paid insufficient attention to historical realities when canvassing these topics in their works.[3] These ahistorical speculations had nonetheless acquired significant traction due to the widespread influence of natural law on legal scholarship in the early modern period and beyond, especially in the wake of the French Revolution of 1789. *Ancient Law* was written, therefore, to engage with these speculations critically and to offer an alternative narrative. The alternative that Maine proposed was a historically informed account of 'ancient law'. The term was deployed conceptually in his work. It did not refer to all legal orders from antiquity. Instead, Maine used it in a specific manner and for particular reasons. This chapter will examine the concept's nature and the reasons for its use. Three issues will be explored in detail. First, the meaning of the term and its boundaries will be sketched. Second, the importance of the term for Maine's broader argument in the book will be set out. Finally, the agents of legal change and their impact on ancient law will be discussed.

2. THE MEANING AND BOUNDARIES OF THE CONCEPT OF 'ANCIENT LAW'

'Ancient law', the focus of Maine's book, was a conceptual rather than descriptive term. It did not refer to law in the ancient world in a general, abstract sense, nor was the book designed to account for the growth of such law over time. Rather, the term had a specific meaning rooted in Maine's authorial choices when he began conceptualising the project. The first of these choices was one of focus.

1 Gibbon and Fernández-Armesto, *The History of the Decline and Fall of the Roman Empire. Vol. 5, Justinian and the Roman Law*, 250.

2 Maine, *Ancient Law*, 113–14. Kuper, *The Reinvention of Primitive Society*, 35; Kuper, 'Ancestors', 273–4; Goëtzmann, 'La "Comparative Jurisprudence" de Henry Sumner Maine, Entre École Analytique et École Historique', 47–71; Scattola, '*Scientia Iuris* and *Ius Naturae*', generally; Hart, *Essays on Bentham*, 79–104, for an account of Bentham's opposition to the notion of 'natural rights'.

3 Cocks, *Sir Henry Maine*, 32–5; Stein, *Legal Evolution*, 87.

Since *Ancient Law* was written as a critique of natural law scholarship in the European legal tradition, the law of Graeco-Roman antiquity had to be placed centre stage. It was, after all, the insights drawn from this body of knowledge on which natural law scholars in the European tradition had relied heavily in constructing theories of the origin of the State and the law. Since a large part of Maine's argument was that these scholars had neglected the historical realities of law in the Graeco-Roman world, a historically informed account of this law thus needed to form the backbone of Maine's account. However, his treatment of law in Graeco-Roman antiquity was rather uneven. The careful reader of Maine's book will note little focus on ancient Greek law, even if Greek philosophy is prominent concerning 'progress' and natural law.[4] The reasons for this are twofold. First, in the history of European legal education since the late medieval period, Roman law played a much more significant role intellectually than Greek law. Second, and conveniently for Maine, it was the focus of his chair at Cambridge. This necessarily makes the focus of his work Eurocentric.

Still, there was more to using the law from Graeco-Roman antiquity, specifically Roman law, than merely its intellectual legacy or Maine's knowledge. This brings us to his use of the terminology of 'progressive' legal orders. As pointed out in the previous chapter, the term was used in its ordinary sense of 'involving progress'. Thus, according to Maine, a 'progressive' legal system kept innovating (or had the potential to keep innovating) by producing new solutions to problems. The term had no moral connotation, especially not in the 'civilisational' sense. No evidence suggests that Maine used this term to create two distinct binary categories. Thus, nowhere in *Ancient Law* will the reader find a page listing all the 'progressive' legal orders and a corresponding 'stationary' category. Maine's use of these terms was descriptive rather than classificatory. Nowhere is this more evident than in the two examples of 'stationary' legal orders Maine lists in *Ancient Law*, namely 'Brahminical' India and China. The careful reader will note that his criticism of these two legal systems is not directed at their content. Phrased differently, he does not regard them as inherently 'stationary'. Instead, his criticism of India here, and thus also of Hindu law, relates to the potential peril inherent in the continued use of customary law combined with the domination by a religious elite. Similarly, his criticism of China focuses on its failure to continue 'progressing'. If anything, these two examples indicate Maine's dislike for stadial 'progress' theories. Neither of these legal systems was inherently 'stationary', but they risked becoming so owing to factors that could affect their 'progressiveness'.

Once the term's meaning is understood, asking why it was used becomes necessary. Given Maine's views on 'progress', there is every reason to suspect that his use of the term was purposive and aimed at critiquing Victorian conceptions of it. Maine did not believe in universal 'progress' of all aspects of society, including law, towards a perfect future, as was the mainstream meaning of the term in Victorian thought. This lack of belief formed part of a broader assessment of the impact of

[4] Burrow, 'Henry Maine and Mid-Victorian Ideas of Progress', 64–5.

natural law and its meaning in the early modern period and beyond. Since it was clear to Maine that some legal systems from the past had dealt with legal change better than others, a theory (or at least an explanation) had to be created to link them and to account for their uniqueness. This was achieved using insights from Victorian linguists such as Max Müller to forge a link between these legal systems via their common Indo-European heritage. On a conceptual level, restricting the scope of his enquiry also gave it a surer footing intellectually, at least in his view.

The second of Maine's choices may be described as the narrative's entry point. *Ancient Law* contains little discussion of the 'prehistory' of law. This vital aspect of this book is commonly misinterpreted. Although the term 'primitive' occurs quite frequently, Maine did not use it in the sense of a civilisational phase. Rather, he uses it more generally to mean 'early', especially when comparing early and later Roman law.[5] *Ancient Law*'s narrative starts at a specific point, namely when the law is first reduced to writing, as in the case of the enactment of the Twelve Tables in Roman law. At this point, the State is already in existence, and there is law. Maine's choice to start his narrative here deserves comment for two reasons. First, it foregrounded his point about the significance of writing down the law. Before this point, legal development was unpredictable, whereas recording law into an early code set it on a different trajectory. From then on, legal change becomes 'deliberate and from without'.[6] Thus, writing down the law was a moment of transition. According to Maine, it was also at this point that the 'progressiveness' of legal orders began to manifest. The second reason was related to the significance of early codes of law. These codes played an essential role in Maine's narrative, and he used them to make three critical points.[7] First, the aim of early codes was not the same as that of the civil codes of modernity. This was undoubtedly a veiled criticism of Bentham's predilection for codes of law.[8] Their original purpose was publicity.[9] In this, Maine was likely influenced by Livy's discussion of the early history of Rome surrounding the enactment of the Twelve Tables.[10] The second point concerned the content of these codes. It is worth quoting Maine here:

> [T]hey mingled up religious, civil, and merely moral ordinances without any regard to differences in their essential character; and this is consistent with all we know of early thought from other sources, the severance of law from morality, and of religion from law, belonging very distinctly to the later stages of mental progress.[11]

5 Maine, *Ancient Law*, 48, 135, for examples. His critics frequently misunderstood his use of the term; see Feaver, *From Status to Contract*, 56–7.

6 Maine, *Ancient Law*, 21.

7 Landauer, 'Henry Sumner Maine's Grand Tour', 135–6.

8 Piccinini, *Tra legge e contratto*, 1–68; Schofield, 'Jeremy Bentham (1748–1832)', for a recent account.

9 Maine, *Ancient Law*, 14–15.

10 Cornell, *The Beginnings of Rome*, 272–8, for an overview of Livy's account; see also Niebuhr, *Niebuhr's History of Rome, Epitomised from the Larger Work, and Adapted to the Use of Schools and Colleges by Travers Twiss; with Chronological Tables and an Appendix*, 57.

11 Maine, *Ancient Law*, 16.

The point is made succinctly. Ancient law is different from contemporary law. Specifically, in its earliest written manifestations, one cannot expect to find the same clear separation between law and religion, or law and morality, as in contemporary legal systems.[12] Maine also makes a more subtle point here. 'Simplicity and symmetry' had become the war cry of natural law scholars when it came to the first attempts at codification in modern Europe. This point also spoke to Maine's views on the historical contingency of classifications in ancient law. According to Maine, these ideals of 'simplicity and symmetry' belonged to a later period, and their origins should not be sought in earlier periods. The third point is more challenging to formulate succinctly. It is best introduced by Maine himself. The type of law (whether written or customary) adopted by any society is:

> [G]enerally, those which are on the whole best suited to promote its physical and moral well-being; and if they are retained in their integrity until new social wants have taught new practices, the upward march of society is almost certain.[13]

The spectre of Montesquieu looms large in this statement. As the latter part shows, the type of law a society adopts initially can never remain static. As 'social wants' begin to influence a legal order, the law must change to respond to these new impulses. Conversely, the failure to do so will likely have negative consequences. It is in this context that Maine criticised contemporaneous Hindu law most strongly. Using the caste system as an example, the crux of his criticism concerned the continued use of customary law.[14] Maine's criticism was twofold. First, he implies that customary law, as a type of law, had outlived its utility in Hindu law. Second, because of the continued use of customary law, when it was no longer functional, it had become a corrupting rather than 'progressive' influence. The source of the corruption, in Maine's view, was the religious elite, which, in his scheme, was functionally equivalent in legal developmental terms to the Roman aristocracy as a repository of customary law before the enactment of the Twelve Tables. The instrument of corruption, somewhat unexpectedly, was identified by our author as the analogy. This is not an unimportant point. As demonstrated below, Maine believed that the agents of legal change depended on the context. Thus, analogy was not an appropriate agent of legal change in this

[12] Landauer, 'Henry Sumner Maine's Grand Tour', 144; Cornell, *The Beginnings of Rome*, 278–80. For criticisms of Maine's extrapolation of this insight to Hindu law, see Derrett, *Sir Henry Maine and Law in India, 1858–1958*, 50. Similarly, Diamond, *Primitive Law*, 45–169, devotes much of his book to dismissing Maine's position as without foundation when applied generally and in the abstract as a feature of 'ancient law'. See also Kirkby, 'Law Evolves', for a survey. For an overview of criticisms, see Feaver, *From Status to Contract*, 57.

[13] Maine, *Ancient Law*, 19.

[14] Mantena, *Alibis of Empire*, 159–60, shows that Maine's focus on customary law should be viewed in the context of the treatment of this form of law in European legal scholarship of the eighteenth century and beyond. For criticisms of Maine's understanding of caste, see Derrett, *Sir Henry Maine and Law in India, 1858-1958*, 47.

context because it tended to 'generate unreasonable usage'.[15] The caste system was a prime example to him.[16] As he put it, 'irrational imitation has engrafted in it an immense apparatus of cruel absurdities'.[17] Maine's treatment of Hindu law is generally favourable since it 'proved' many of his broader claims, especially about the 'early jural concepts' he sought to identify in Roman law. Still, in this instance, as well as in his treatment of certain aspects of inheritance, he offers stringent criticism. This is aimed not so much at the content of the specific legal system itself but at the continued use of customary law.

3. THE INTELLECTUAL CONTEXT OF THE CONCEPT OF 'ANCIENT LAW'

Since the purpose of *Ancient Law* was to critique natural law scholarship for its poor use of history, Maine's comments on specific intellectuals who were representative of this approach should be examined.[18] He does not discuss these authors in one specific place in the book but rather through a series of pointed comments interspersed throughout. When these are combined, a fuller picture emerges. In his discussion of the origins of the State, Maine criticised Locke's and Hobbes's theories on this issue specifically.[19] The focus of his critique may be summarised as follows. Their theories focused on the 'non-historic, unverifiable, condition of the race'.[20] Phrased differently, they were grounded in speculation rather than historical reality. These theories conjectured the existence of 'primitive man' without any evidence. In addition, and given the influence of natural law on them, they took a broad-brush approach to the matter rather than focusing on the details.

Maine used a similar argument in chapter four of *Ancient Law*, where he provided a potted history of equity. Here, his criticism focused on Rousseau, who he referred to as a man of 'few virtues, and with no strength of character'.[21] The essence of his criticism was twofold. First, much like Locke and Hobbes, Rousseau's 'state of nature' theory was speculative and devoid of any historical foundation.[22] Also, owing to the intellectual influence of Rousseau's works after

15 Maine, *Ancient Law*, 18–20. See also Austin, *Province*, 26–8 on customary law. Clark, *Practical Jurisprudence*, 273–81, 324–39.

16 Mantena, *Alibis of Empire*, 156–9, shows that despite Maine's criticism of caste in this context, it would become an important component of his reconstruction of 'traditional society' in later works. For Edmund Burke's discussion of caste, a likely influence on Maine, see O'Neill, 'Rethinking Burke and India', 506–7. See also Bayly, *Caste*, 97–143.

17 Maine, *Ancient Law*, 20.

18 Batzel, 'Sir Henry James Sumner Maine', 300–67.

19 Maine, *Ancient Law*, 114.

20 Ibid. 114.

21 Ibid. 87; Conniff, *The Useful Cobbler*, 67, for a similar view held by Edmund Burke.

22 Kuper, *The Reinvention of Primitive Society*, 36; Landauer, 'Henry Sumner Maine's Grand Tour', 139; Goëtzmann, 'La Comparative Jurisprudence de Henry Sumner Maine, Entre Critique et Approfondissement de La Théorie Impérativiste Du Droit', generally; Wood, *Liberty and Property*, 189–204; Feaver, *From Status to Contract*, 59.

the French Revolution of 1789, this speculative, broad-brush approach influenced other scholars (such as Bentham) in the debate.[23] The nature and contours of this debate provided Maine with a point of connection to two further perspectives, namely those of Montesquieu and Bentham.

His assessment of Montesquieu's efforts is far more positive than his judgement of other French jurists such as Rousseau. Still, he did not support Montesquieu's proposition that 'the nature of man is entirely plastic'.[24] According to Maine, this crucial oversight caused Montesquieu to look to too many external factors to explain why laws differed from place to place and the causes of legal change. As he put it, Montesquieu sought these answers in 'the fruit of any causes except those which appear to operate with tolerable constancy'.[25] This criticism speaks to Maine's view on 'causal' factors of legal change as articulated in the instrumentalities. Maine's position differed considerably from that of Montesquieu. While he admitted that external factors may influence legal change, in his view, they played a more limited role.[26]

The criticism of Bentham was primarily directed at his statements concerning the nature of law.[27] As is well known, Bentham's conception of law was restricted principally to written law expressing the lawgiver's will.[28] He preferred statute as a form of law over unwritten law. Maine's critique focused on these two issues. First, *Ancient Law* aimed to show that there was more to law than merely the command of the lawgiver. In his account of the earliest phases of society, he emphatically refused to classify the word of the patriarch as law. The second point of critique focused on Bentham's preference for statute law, precisely the 'elegance and simplicity' implicit within it. As Maine pointed out, these ideals were developed from natural law scholarship of the recent past rather than being a feature of ancient law.

When these comments are combined, a clear picture of the purpose of *Ancient Law* emerges. It was written to critique the ahistorical, lofty speculation, treated as fact by natural law scholars, about the State's formation and the role of law role in that process. Maine wanted to highlight that these speculative accounts lacked detail and projected contemporary sentiments and developments onto this imaginary past. Owing to the substantial influence of natural law scholarship on this issue, discussion of past law had since become bound to larger conceptual

23 See Schofield, 'Jeremy Bentham, the French Revolution and Political Radicalism', 383, 396.

24 Maine, *Ancient Law*, 115–16. See Vinogradoff, *The Teaching of Sir Henry Maine; an Inaugural Lecture Delivered in Corpus Christi College Hall on March 1, 1904*, 10; Landauer, 'Henry Sumner Maine's Grand Tour', 149–50; Carrithers, 'Montesquieu's Philosophy of History'; Krause, 'History and the Human Soul in Montesquieu', generally. See also Watson, *The French Mind*, 117–18.

25 Maine, *Ancient Law*, 116.

26 Landauer, 'Henry Sumner Maine's Grand Tour', 140–1.

27 Maine, *Ancient Law*, 117. Landauer, 'Henry Sumner Maine's Grand Tour', 143; Cassani, *Diritto, antropologia e storia*, 109–39.

28 Goëtzmann, 'La "Comparative Jurisprudence" de Henry Sumner Maine, Entre École Analytique et École Historique', 233.

notions of 'progress'. This connection and its implications for the Victorian intellectual discourse lay at the heart of the book. These were the issues that Maine set out to address.

One further matter that requires explanation is his decision to focus on ancient law and his reasons for doing so. There can be no doubt that his choice was rooted in an element of convenience. Maine's chair at Cambridge focused on Roman law, a discipline close to his heart throughout his life. But there was more to his choice than this. Maine, a student of classics, maintained that ancient law provided more reliable evidence than, say, the more general descriptions of other peoples found in literature from Graeco-Roman antiquity. This was because the latter tended to be coloured by prejudices of judgment, whereas ancient law was less prone to this as a type of evidence. This belief was undoubtedly drawn from works such as those of Montesquieu, Gibbon, and Niebuhr, who gave prominence to law as an institution in their scholarship.[29] As Maine phrased it, ancient law had an element of objectivity, 'because it was old [,] it was preserved'.[30]

Considering this, Maine's purpose in focusing on ancient law was fourfold. First, he wanted to highlight that ancient law tended to be substantially different, both in content and coverage, from contemporary law. This reinforced his critique of natural law scholarship in which contemporaneous sentiments were read back into ancient law, often without sufficient attention to historical fact. Second, he wanted to demonstrate that ancient law could provide the 'germs' of ideas that would, in time, significantly impact the development of law. At the same time, however, Maine was at pains to stress that not all legal developments had their origins in the past and, when they did, that those original ideas might, in time, be used in very different ways and for very different reasons than they were initially devised. His third point concerned human nature. It is a complex point, and his position is worth quoting in full:

> The stable part of our mental, moral, and physical constitution is the largest part of it, and the resistance it opposes to change is such that, though the variations of human society in a portion of the world are plain enough, they are neither so rapid nor so extensive that their amount, character, and general direction cannot be ascertained.[31]

As will be recalled, one of Maine's criticisms of Montesquieu's position was his failure to factor the stability of human nature into his account of legal change. Maine considered the stability of human nature, specifically its resistance to change, fundamental.[32] While it is possible to read this statement in light of Maine's conservatism, it is worth noting that it likely also reflected a more general philosophical position

[29] It is also broadly compatible with the theory of positivism proposed by the French sociologist Auguste Comte (1798–1857). 'Ancient law' could be treated as a form of empirical evidence in contrast to the speculative theories of natural law.

[30] Maine, *Ancient Law*, 121.

[31] Ibid, 117.

[32] Weston, 'Edmund Burke's View of History', generally.

founded in Stoicism, familiar to Maine due to his study of classics.[33] This element, which segues nicely into his description of legal change in 'progressive' legal orders as being 'deliberate and from without', motivated Maine to make a comparison. Human nature tended to be stable. Thus, as the final part of the quotation shows, this enabled comparison, not just between contemporary legal systems but also across time. The careful reader will have noticed an unresolved intellectual tension in Maine's argument here. If human nature were stable (i.e. universal), then, in theory, all past and present legal systems, as expressions of this nature, would be comparable. Given his aversion towards this line of thought and its associations with natural law, an argument had to be found to limit the scope of his investigation. The Indo-European connection, founded in research on comparative philology, provided it.

His final and perhaps most significant point concerned stadial 'progress'. Enlightenment scholarship had settled on a series of stages through which every society 'progressed'. Each of these represented a stage of 'progress' and was also, in time, associated with forms of law. Maine was staunchly opposed to this idea. As he phrased it, 'societies do not advance concurrently, but at different rates of progress'.[34] This statement is problematic; care should be taken when interpreting it. Maine did not believe in a civilisational table in which the state of development of each society and its legal system could be mapped, like the ranking of horses at the end of a race. Instead, he advocated that each legal system had to be examined on its own merits and based on how it responded to change by creating solutions to new problems – hence the term 'progressive'.

4. AGENTS OF LEGAL CHANGE

Maine's discussion of legal change should be viewed within the context of the Roman legal system, which provided most of the ideas for the book. Since, in his view, it contained the best evidence of how a 'progressive' legal system had continuously innovated, he surmised that insights drawn from an analysis of the 'instrumentalities', as he called them, or agents which had caused the legal change in Roman law could help lend support to his broader endeavour.[35] It was an example of 'ancient law' *par excellence*. As he put it, Roman law continued to innovate when 'all the rest of human thought and action materially slackened, and repeatedly threatened to settle down into stagnation'.[36] This problematic statement demonstrates the extent to which Maine held Roman law in high regard. Still, Roman law could not support this narrative at all points. This was because the information was lacking, especially for the earlier periods, or because subsequent jurisprudence on natural law had distorted Roman law. In these instances, he gathered information from other legal systems linked through the theory of

33 Annas, 'The Stoics', for a survey; Passmore, *The Perfectibility of Man*, 58–95.

34 Maine, *Ancient Law*, 120.

35 Diamond, 'Fictions, Equity and Legislation: Maine's Three Agencies of Legal Change', for a survey.

36 Maine, *Ancient Law*, 24.

a shared Indo-European connection to fill the information gaps. It is crucial to appreciate how he viewed these supporting legal systems. His understanding of 'progressive' must be revisited to understand the grounds for such a comparison. Maine used this term descriptively rather than conceptually. The 'progressive' label was contingent since innovation was an ongoing process driven by specific 'instrumentalities'. In several of Maine's comments regarding supporting legal systems, the underlying critique was that they had once had 'progressive' potential but had stopped innovating owing to some broader causal issue.

It cannot be denied that using Roman law as his prime focus, in hindsight, caused one significant intellectual problem. It allowed Maine to make a case for European exceptionalism:

> Except in a small section of the world, there has been nothing like the gradual amelioration of a legal system. There has been material civilisation, but instead of the civilisation expanding the law, the law has limited the civilisation.[37]

> It is most difficult for a citizen of western Europe to bring thoroughly home to himself the truth that the civilisation which surrounds him is a rare exception in the history of the world.[38]

When these two quotations are read without context, they appear problematic.[39] This is why context is essential. As explained above, given the book's aim to critique natural law scholarship in the European tradition, a focus on Roman law was inevitable. In addition, given the nature of his chair at Cambridge, it was the legal order he knew best. It is also true that since the Middle Ages, Roman law has played a significant role in the development of law in Europe. While Maine's approach is thus necessarily Eurocentric, it was not exclusionary, however, as his use of the term 'progressive' shows. This is not an unimportant point. Maine never set out to divide the world's legal systems, past or present, into two categories (progressive vs stationary). Nor did he claim that once a legal system had begun to show signs of progressiveness, it would inevitably continue to innovate unabated. His point was one of the potential of progressiveness rooted in a shared Indo-European heritage. Even those past or present legal systems that had shown signs of progressiveness could still stagnate. Initial progressiveness was not a guaranteed ticket to the sunlit uplands of perfection. Indeed, throughout the various chapters of *Ancient Law*, the comparisons are drawn chiefly to flag issues that might negatively affect the continued progressiveness of specific legal systems.

Maine's examination of Roman law allowed him to identify three critical aspects of his broader thesis. First, he argued that 'progressiveness' was a contingent

[37] Ibid. 23.

[38] Ibid. 22.

[39] Bryce, *The Ancient Roman Empire and the British Empire in India*, 5–8, for a much more overt expression of the colonial agenda.

concept. It manifested only under certain circumstances and, more importantly, could still fail in future. There was no guarantee that a legal system that exhibited 'progressiveness' at a certain point would continue to innovate. Second, legal change in a progressive legal order occurred because of 'instrumentalities' or mechanisms. In the Roman experience, three 'instrumentalities' were identified.[40] These were: legal fictions, Praetorian equity and legislation. An analysis of these three instrumentalities, illuminated by specific examples drawn mainly from Roman law, formed the core of Maine's book. Third, especially in the earliest stages of Roman law, the Roman legal order consisted of 'jural phenomena'. Although Maine never lists them, the family was the prime example of such an early jural phenomenon. This relationship and the instrumentalities' impact on it should be studied since it contained 'all potential forms' of law. It is crucial to acknowledge Maine's metaphor here. He posited that it should be studied 'like a geologist'.[41] This is telling. To Maine, a progressive legal system exhibited stratigraphic levels within which these early jural relations could be unearthed.

Before an analysis of this early jural phenomenon and the impact of instrumentalities upon it can be undertaken, the limitations of Maine's model, for want of a better word, must be acknowledged. First, it is retrospective rather than predictive. Based on his knowledge of Roman law, Maine had identified an early jural phenomenon and the instrumentalities that had affected it. There is no indication that Maine ever intended this model to be one which could be applied predictively, especially given the contingent nature of the concept of 'progressiveness'. At best, the developments in Roman law over time could be used to identify (earlier or later manifestations of) these phenomena in other legal systems, whether historical or contemporaneous, linked to Roman law intellectually. Second, it is also relatively weak on periodisation compared to contemporaneous textbooks on Roman law. Based on his knowledge of Gibbon's account and Niebuhr's work, it must be assumed that Maine was aware of the different phases of the development of Roman law. At the same time, he prefers phrases such as 'the infancy of law/archaic law' or 'developed law' to refer to them. These can be difficult to pin down, but it must be noted that at some points in his narrative, for example where he discusses the law of inheritance, 'developed law' clearly refers to classical Roman law, as the Justinianic position is mentioned separately. Two reasons may be offered for Maine's choice regarding periodisation here. First, as subsequent scholarship has shown, Gibbon's work essentially inspired the narrative, and his periodisation likely influenced that of Maine.[42] Second, given Maine's negative views on the relentless march of 'progress', it is likely purposive.

40 Landauer, 'Henry Sumner Maine's Grand Tour', 145, has pointed out that the notion of mechanisms of legal change, while less developed, already appears in Gibbon's famous chapter on Roman law. See also Thomas, *Legal Artifices*, 107–43.

41 Maine, *Ancient Law*, 3.

42 Landauer, 'Henry Sumner Maine's Grand Tour', 150–1.

Maine's discussion of 'the infancy' of law remains to be considered. Three points are worth noting concerning his treatment of the matter. First, Roman law could not provide Maine with the required narrative here, due primarily to the absence of information. What little could be gleaned from the extant sources concerning the legislative activities of the Roman Kings was too paltry. He therefore had to rely on another legal order from antiquity, namely early Greek law, to fill in the gaps. He obtained most of his information on this issue from George Grote's *History of Greece*, published from 1846 onwards in several volumes, and was candid about his teleological use of early Greek law. He chose Homeric literature here primarily because, in his view, it presented information that had not yet been distorted through 'conscious observation', even if the events described were to some extent idealised.[43] Had he not had access to information concerning early Greek society and law readily to hand in an accessible form through Grote's work, Hindu law could have served the same purpose, Maine tells us.[44]

Second, the 'infancy' of law plays a relatively minor role in Maine's broader thesis. The point at which he becomes interested in law is when it is first reduced to writing. This occurred in the Roman legal experience when the Law of the Twelve Tables was enacted c 450 BCE. There is a specific reason why he focused on the advent of writing as a moment of transition in the development of ancient law. According to Maine's broader thesis, 'progressiveness' began to emerge at this point. This is, consequently, where his discussion begins.

The third point is that his views on the earliest phases of law before it is first reduced to writing are decidedly mixed. He describes the state of the law here as 'unpredictable' and open to abuse by some sectors of society, such as the aristocracy, as was the case in the early stages of Roman law.[45] By contrast, once the law is written down, legal change can occur in a predictable and 'deliberate' fashion through the abovementioned instrumentalities. The importance of this final point should not be underestimated. In the context of Maine's broader narrative in this section of the book, it acted as a veiled criticism of the views of Jeremy Bentham. Bentham and his pupil John Austin are commonly associated with the command theory of law.[46] Maine's point is that according to Bentham and Austin, the early phases of law, whether derived from a Royal command seemingly based on divine inspiration or from custom guarded by an aristocracy, would all be classified as

[43] Jenkyns, *The Victorians and Ancient Greece*, 192–226, for an account of the significance of Homer in Victorian culture.

[44] Maine, *Ancient Law*, 2.

[45] Ibid. 21–2.

[46] Rumble, 'John Austin and His Nineteenth Century Critics', 127 shows that Maine and Austin held similar views on many core issues but that the aims of the works differed. See also Landauer, 'Henry Sumner Maine's Grand Tour', 148–9; Goëtzmann, 'La "Comparative Jurisprudence" de Henry Sumner Maine, Entre École Analytique et École Historique', 234. For a nuanced account of Bentham's views on the issue of 'law as command', see Hart, *Essays on Bentham*, 21–39.

'law-making'. According to Maine, this is too generic, as it masked the situation's complexity, especially surrounding the authorship of early law.

Having arrived at the point where Maine's narrative begins, a few contextual remarks are required. In his view, the main advantage of written law lies in its publicity.

> Inscribed tablets were seen to be a better depositary [sic] of law, and a better security for its accurate preservation, than the memory of a number of persons however strengthened by habitual exercise.[47]

Given the well-documented episodes of civil strife between the plebeians and patricians, which resulted in enacting the Law of the Twelve Tables, as recounted by Livy, this conclusion on the actual value of the Twelve Tables was inevitable. In addition, Maine postulated that written law not only improved knowledge of the law but also ensured that every member of society, whether plebeian or patrician, was equally bound.[48] This can be seen from the definition of law that he provides:

> A true law enjoins on all the citizens indifferently a number of acts similar in class or kind; and this is exactly the feature of a law which has most deeply impressed itself on the popular mind, causing the term 'law' to be applied to mere uniformities, successions, and similitudes.[49]

The use of the term 'true law' speaks volumes here. As Maine correctly observed, these early codes differed significantly in content and arrangement from contemporaneous codifications. The rules were arranged using their internal logic, including 'religious . . . and merely moral ordinances'. The separation between law and religion or morality, while only starting at the time when the law of the Twelve Tables was enacted, would become an essential theme throughout the book.

Before moving on to the issue of legal change, Maine's comments on customary law require consideration.[50] There is little evidence in his statements that he was engaging with the vast European intellectual history of customary law or the debate between Savigny and Jhering concerning its nature.[51] Instead, his account of customary law appears to be drawn mainly from Roman legal sources.[52] According to Maine, customary law was the only actual unwritten law. Based on his interpretation of the Roman evidence, likely taken from Gibbon, he surmised that customary law commonly dominated in the 'infancy' of law when divinely

47 Maine, *Ancient Law*, 15.

48 Cotterrell, *The Politics of Jurisprudence*, 42.

49 Maine, *Ancient Law*, 9.

50 Ibid. 5–7. Yale, 'Further Thoughts on Maine's Historical Jurisprudence', 240.

51 Iurlaro, *The Invention of Custom*, 206–12., for a survey of the debate between Savigny and Jhering. Beiser, *The German Historicist Tradition*, 214–52. Clark, *Practical Jurisprudence*, 273–81.

52 Iurlaro, *The Invention of Custom*, 21–3; Watson, *The Evolution of Law*, 43–63.

inspired Royal judgements on individual issues had ceased to be the main form of law. Again, based on the same evidence, Maine drew a link between custom and an aristocracy as the keeper of tradition. This, according to our author, was the primary advantage of the situation over the earlier Royal judgements:

> Custom or observances now exist as a substantive aggregate, and are assumed to be precisely known to the aristocratic order or caste.[53]

The equation of the Roman aristocracy with the Hindu concept of caste was likely inspired by Burke's works, in which a similar connection is made.[54] According to Maine, while the benefit of customary law was that it could accumulate through actual practice and thus become less ad hoc, the drawback was that knowledge of it remained the preserve of a specific population sector, leaving it open to abuse. In the Roman example, this was one of the main drivers behind enacting the Law of the Twelve Tables, as Livy's narrative reveals. Since Roman law, Maine's archetypal example of a 'progressive' legal order, had replaced customary law with written law early, Maine viewed this development as beneficial even if, at the point of the enactment of the Law of the Twelve Tables, Roman law had not fully separated law from religion or morality. This insight permitted Maine to critique the state of Hindu law in his time. It is important to note how Maine uses Hindu law here. He used it as a point of comparison as a legal order based mainly on customary law and with a strong religious element. Thus, unlike the Roman scenario where the aristocracy dominated knowledge of customary law, in Hindu law, according to Maine, 'the religious element in the East tended to get the better of the military and the political'.[55] This observation also allowed for further reflection. Maine believed that the Hindu law of his time, largely customary and controlled by a religious sector of society, was in danger of stagnation. When customary law remains dominant for too long and is controlled by a religious group, they extend the existing legal rules by analogy to other areas of life. Maine opined that this 'generates usage which is unreasonable'.[56] The effect of this was to burden the existing customary law with an 'apparatus of cruel absurdities'.[57]

This discussion provides the background to Maine's most astute insights concerning legal change. The purpose of legal change was 'a conscious desire for improvement'. Based on his knowledge of Roman law, he concluded that society, as a dynamic force, usually ran ahead of the law. Legal change, therefore, had to occur to narrow the gap between law and society. The narrower the gap between law and society, the more content its members will be.[58] To that end, legal change brought about by the instrumentalities outlined above continuously worked to

[53] Maine, *Ancient Law*, 12.
[54] O'Neill, 'Rethinking Burke and India', generally, for a discussion.
[55] Maine, *Ancient Law*, 11.
[56] Ibid. 19.
[57] Ibid. 20.
[58] Ibid. 24–5.

narrow the gap. It is vital to address the order in which Maine arranged these instrumentalities. He did not view them as stages in the development of a legal system. Instead, he emphasised that they could occur concurrently.[59] Based on his knowledge of Roman law, however, where these instrumentalities had occurred broadly in this order, he chose to discuss them as such. That being said, as Kuper has shown, the order in which they appear in Maine's work is purposive.[60] It is designed to invert the Benthamite position, which placed legislation first.

4.1 Legal Fictions

There can be little doubt that Niebuhr's rediscovery of the Gaius palimpsest in Verona during the first two decades of the nineteenth century had cast new light on the use of legal fictions in Roman law. Although Gaius's discussion of legal fictions is incomplete, owing to the state of the manuscript, his discussion and examples in his Institutes are extensive.[61] According to Maine's narrative, legal fictions were helpful as an instrumentality of legal change because they permitted it to occur covertly, especially where society was uncomfortable with overt legal change.[62] Thus, they created the impression of continuity of the existing law. This was done primarily in the Roman experience in the context of legal procedure, although recent scholarship has shown that they were used in other contexts, too.[63] In procedural terms, they extended jurisdiction over an issue or an individual where the legal order would not have traditionally had jurisdiction. At some point, however, their utility declines. Reading between the lines, one may deduce that this occurs when they begin to conflict with other developments in a legal order. Thus, the utility of fictions was contingent. This is not an unimportant point. Recent scholarship has shown that legal fictions were not limited to Republican Roman law. They continued to be employed in classical Roman law and beyond.[64] They may be helpful in specific contexts and unhelpful in others. This point is similar to his comments on analogy as an instrumentality of legal change in legal orders dominated by customary law.

Maine's treatment of legal fictions should be read in the context of his subsequent chapters, where he uses them to make several specific points about legal change. As subsequent scholarship has shown, it also serves as a critique of Bentham's

[59] Diamond, *Primitive Law*, 206, misses this point in his critique of Maine's account of the instrumentalities of legal change.

[60] Kuper, *The Reinvention of Primitive Society*, 38–9. See Fuller, *Legal Fictions*, 6, 39, 56. Ando, 'Fact, Fiction, and Social Reality in Roman Law', generally, has demonstrated the widespread use of legal fictions in Roman law.

[61] Ando, 'Fact, Fiction, and Social Reality in Roman Law', 295–9.

[62] Maine, *Ancient Law*, 25–7; See Smellie, 'Sir Henry Maine', 70–1; Mantena, *Alibis of Empire*, 105–6. For criticism of legal fictions, see Austin, *Province*, 27.

[63] Ando, 'Fact, Fiction, and Social Reality in Roman Law', 302–10, for procedural fictions. See also Pottage, 'Law after Anthropology', 155.

[64] Ando, 'Fact, Fiction, and Social Reality in Roman Law', generally.

disdain for fictions.[65] Within each chapter devoted to a specific branch of Roman law, he returned to legal fictions on several occasions to reinforce the point about their utility in context. It is also essential to appreciate that Maine's discussion of legal fictions spoke to contemporaneous circumstances. Jeremy Bentham, his primary intellectual opponent in *Ancient Law*, was famously opposed to the widespread use of legal fictions in English law. While Maine was sympathetic to Bentham's position, he tried to show that legal fictions were helpful in certain contexts.[66]

Maine deployed two examples to demonstrate the function of legal fictions, one drawn from contemporaneous English law, the other from Roman law. The example drawn from English law is the lesser of the two in terms of the volume of the discussion but is nonetheless essential.[67] He summarised it as follows:

> We do not admit that our tribunals legislate; we imply that they have never legislated; and yet we maintain that the rules of the English common law, with some assistance from the Court of Chancery and from Parliament, are coextensive with the complicated interests of modern society.[68]

It is an established principle of English law that courts do not produce new law but rather discover the law from existing principles when confronted by a new set of facts. According to Maine, this is a classic example of a legal fiction since the judgment of a court creates 'a new language and a new train of thought' that effectively changes the existing law.[69] Thus, in this instance, the function of the legal fiction is to bring about legal change while simultaneously masking it. It is essential to reflect on the implications of Maine's use of English law as an example here. Did Maine regard the English law of his day as a potentially progressive legal system? The answer seems to be yes. At the same time, though, his use of differing temporalities deserves comment. That a legal fiction of this kind existed in English law of his time could not be used to comment on the state of development of English law *qua* Roman law. There is no evidence that this was the point of his comparison. It was a parallel phenomenon that needed to be studied and nothing more.

The discussion of English case law allowed Maine to segue into Roman law, specifically into the Roman version of 'case law', namely juristic literature.[70] To our author, the work of the jurists also represented a type of legal fiction. While, in theory, they did not have the authority to change the law, they did so covertly through their juristic activities. The discussion of Roman juristic literature shows

65 Landauer, 'Henry Sumner Maine's Grand Tour', 145; Feaver, *From Status to Contract*, 48.

66 For a survey of the role of legal fictions, see Del Mar, 'Legal Fictions and Legal Change in the Common Law Tradition', 225; Del Mar, 'Legal Fictions and Legal Change', 442. See now also Schauer, 'Legal Fictions Revisited', 123, and generally, for a defence of the continued utility of legal fictions.

67 Lobban, 'Legal Fictions before the Age of Reform', for a good account of the extent of the use of legal fictions in English law before the reforms of the nineteenth century. See also Shmilovits, *Legal Fictions*, 5–47.

68 Maine, *Ancient Law*, 33. See Oldham, *Analysis*, 4–5; Pollock and Maine, *Introduction and Notes*, 8–9.

69 Ibid. 31.

70 Cocks, *Sir Henry Maine*, 64–71. Clark, *Practical Jurisprudence*, 282–99.

his command of the material. Roman juristic writing primarily comprised commentaries on written law, such as individual statutes or the Praetorian edict. While the jurists did not possess the authority to change these overtly, they could change their interpretation and, through their connections to Roman legal practice, facilitated legal change. As Maine put it:

> Yet in point of fact, Books of Responses bearing the names of leading jurisconsults obtained an authority at least equal to that of our reported cases, and constantly modified, extended, limited or practically overruled the provisions of the Decemviral law. The authors of the new jurisprudence during the whole progress of its formation professed the most sedulous respect for the letter of the Code.[71]

Having established that the activities of the Roman jurists could be viewed as a type of legal fiction, Maine devoted the remainder of his discussion to the source of their authority. Before the creation of the *ius publice respondendi*, the authority of the Roman jurists was based entirely on their professional reputations through their engagement with matters of legal practice. 'Not the bench, but the bar' gave the Roman jurists their authority.[72]

Our author's treatment of the Roman jurists as a phenomenon that drove legal change in the Roman legal order is filled with insights.[73] In broad terms, Maine's discussion focuses on the emerging knowledge community among the Roman jurists. Tying back to his argument concerning the contingent nature of progressiveness, Maine enquires why, in the absence of any official regulation of the Roman juristic profession during the Republic, the Roman legal order did not suffer the same fate as Greek law, namely a failure to develop a core body of legal rules distinct from other fields of knowledge such as philosophy. In his view, Roman law had escaped this fate due to several factors. These included 'its early wealth of principles'.[74] Because there was no single 'author' of law in its early phases, this created healthy competition among different potential lawgivers. In addition, since the Roman juristic profession was not regulated during the Republic, they could establish conventions regarding their treatment of legal issues, whether real or hypothetical, and could influence how this impacted the development of the law. As with all instrumentalities of legal change, Roman juristic writing flourished only up to a certain point. Maine attributes the decline to two factors: first, a shift in perception regarding the utility of legislation is a vehicle of legal change.[75] This change is attributed to the widespread legislative reforms introduced by Sulla and continued by Augustus. Second, the nature of juristic activity changed with the advent of the Empire, when the locus of legal power increasingly consolidated around the Roman Emperor.

71 Maine, *Ancient Law*, 34.

72 Ibid. 35.

73 Maine, *Dissertations on Early Law and Custom*, 26–39, for a later discussion of the rise of the class of jurists.

74 Maine, *Ancient Law*, 40, 75–6.

75 Ibid. 41.

4.2 Equity

There are two notable differences between Maine's discussion of the previous instrumentality and this one; namely, first, he mentions the source of authority of equity as the 'superior sanctity inherent in those principles'.[76] Equity also tends to operate where society is more receptive to legal change. As with all three instrumentalities discussed in *Ancient Law*, reference is made to English law in the context of this discussion as well. In this case, however, his treatment of English equity is relatively slight.[77] As Maine noted, even though there may be historical points of contact between English equity and the civilian tradition via canon law, this falls outside the scope of his treatment in the book.

Before discussing Maine's treatment of equity as an instrumentality of legal change, the significance of natural law in Maine's broader thesis within the book must be examined. It may be stated, without exaggeration, that a critique of natural law scholarship formed a core part of Maine's book. As will be recalled, Maine objected to the poor use of history employed by natural law scholars and the speculative versions of the past, based on little concrete fact, they had created. Given Maine's position regarding empirical observation as a more reliable source of history, it stands to reason that his discussion of natural law took the different layers in the historical development of this concept in Roman law as its starting point. To that end, a text from the start of Justinian's Institutes must be cited:

> I. 1, 2, 1
> Ius autem civile vel gentium ita dividitur: omnes populi, qui legibus et moribus reguntur, partim suo proprio, partim communi omnium hominum iure utuntur: nam quod quisque populus ipse sibi ius constituit, id ipsius proprium civitatis est vocaturque ius civile, quasi ius proprium ipsius civitatis: quod vero naturalis ratio inter omnes homines constituit, id apud omnes populos peraeque custoditur vocaturque ius gentium, quasi quo iure omnes gentes utuntur. et populus itaque Romanus partim suo proprio, partim communi omnium hominum iure utitur. quae singula qualia sunt, suis locis proponemus.
>
> The civil law (*ius civile*), or the law of nations (*ius gentium*), is divided as follows. All peoples, governed by laws and *mores*, use laws that are partly their own and partly common to all. The laws that each population creates for itself, in other words, the law peculiar to that population, is called civil law as if it were the laws of that specific population. What natural reason (*naturalis ratio*) establishes among all men, however, i.e. the law observed similarly among all peoples, is called the law of nations, as if it were the law all nations use. And the Roman people use partly their own law, partly the common law of all men. We will now discuss each one in its proper place. [Own translation]

This text is at the heart of Maine's discussion of the twofold division of law, even though he does not cite it explicitly. Justinian's compilers tell us that all law may be divided into civil law or the law of nations. Civil law is the law peculiar to a

[76] Ibid. 28; Smellie, 'Sir Henry Maine', 71–2; Mantena, *Alibis of Empire*, 106.

[77] Council of Legal Education, A *Century of Law Reform*, 177–202, for a survey of nineteenth-century changes. See also Cornish et al., *Law and Society in England, 1750-1950*, 43–4.

particular people, whereas the law of nations is that which has been established among all people, *ratio naturalis*. It is this connection between the law of nations and the significance of this term that Maine chose to explore first.

In contemporary Roman law scholarship, the relationship between the law of nations (*ius gentium*) and the law of nature (*ius naturale*) remains a live issue.[78] The reason for this is the ambiguity of the source material. Some scholars treat these two notions as functional equivalents, while others, relying on a particular definition from the Digest, view the law of nations as applicable only to human beings, while the law of nature has a broader application.[79] Maine viewed *naturalis ratio* as equivalent to natural law (*ius naturale*). In addition, as will be shown in this chapter, he also regarded the terms *ius gentium* and *ius naturale* as functionally equivalent but representing different perspectives on the same issue.

The early history of Rome, featured in Niebuhr's work, provided abundant evidence for his narrative.[80] Since its founding in the eighth century BCE, Rome had been an city of asylum with a diverse population. As Maine observed:

> The foreign element in the commonwealth determined the whole course of its history, which, at all stages, is little more than a narrative of conflicts between stubborn nationality and an alien population.[81]

As Livy's narrative of the early history of Rome shows, much of the city's early history involved skirmishes with neighbouring peoples and the occasional population surge. One of these resonated with the development of Roman law, namely the influx of foreigners following the Punic Wars – a series of wars between Rome and Carthage between the mid-third and the mid-second centuries BCE. In most textbooks on Roman law, this event is identified as having precipitated legal change by leading to the creation of a second praetorship, later called the peregrine praetor, who had jurisdiction over lawsuits involving foreigners.[82] This series of events requires further explanation.

As the text from the Institutes of Justinian cited above shows, the Romans referred to the law endemic to their society as civil law (*ius civile*). It was their creation, and since Roman law was not a territorially based legal system at this point, it only applied to those with Roman citizenship. This would have excluded all foreigners without Roman citizenship from using civil law or the courts that enforced it. The Romans circumvented this problem through the instrumentality of legal

[78] Waerdt, 'Philosophical Influence on Roman Jurisprudence?', for a survey. See also Humfress, 'Natural Law and Casuistic Reasoning in Roman Jurisprudence', for an account.

[79] Mackeldey and Dropsie, *Handbook of the Roman Law . . . Translated and Edited by M.A. Dropsie from the Fourteenth German Edition*, 118.

[80] Maine, *Ancient Law*, 47–9; Niebuhr, *Niebuhr's History of Rome, Epitomised from the Larger Work, and Adapted to the Use of Schools and Colleges by Travers Twiss; with Chronological Tables and an Appendix*, 3.

[81] Maine, *Ancient Law*, 47.

[82] Mackeldey and Dropsie, *Handbook of the Roman Law . . . Translated and Edited by M.A. Dropsie from the Fourteenth German Edition*, 19–20.

change known as equity. This involved the creation of a body of law 'common to Rome and to the different Italian communities in which the immigrants were born'.[83] This body of law, created through observation according to Maine, was known as the law of nations (*ius gentium*). He gives simple delivery (*traditio*) as an example of the acquisition of ownership common throughout the Mediterranean.[84]

Two aspects of Maine's discussion here deserve mention. First, his treatment of the issue reflects his awareness of the debates in Roman law. Maine's position here is similar to that of Savigny.[85] Second, setting up the *ius gentium* in this manner permitted him to critique attitudes towards legal concepts of this kind in natural-law scholarship of the early modern period and beyond. Maine's view was essentially this:

> We, at the present day, should probably take a very different view of the jus gentium, if we were performing the operation which was effected by the Roman jurisconsults. We should attach some vague superiority or precedence to the element which we had thus discerned underlying and pervading so great a variety of usage. We should have a sort of respect for rules and principles so universal.[86]

The final two sentences of this quotation are particularly telling. This goes to the heart of his views on the Roman conception of the law of nations. It was not a 'superior' or 'universal' type of law. Rather, it was a practical invention borne from 'political necessity' and driven by the Romans' reluctance to open their legal system to foreigners.

This, then, was the bedrock of Roman equity. In time, however, this pragmatic notion of a law common to all nations would be influenced by the 'Greek theory of a law of nature'.[87] This development would give rise to the law of nature (*ius naturale*), which, according to Maine, was 'simply the jus gentium or a law of nations seen in the light of a peculiar theory'.[88] Our author makes three critical points in his treatment of the Greek theory of the law of nature.[89] First, it was inspired by the concept of nature being governed by general laws that could be identified. In time, however, Greek philosophical discussions also include the relationship of human

83 Maine, *Ancient Law*, 49.

84 Ibid. 49–50.

85 Savigny, *System of the Modern Roman Law, Translated from the German . . . by W. Holloway. Vol. I*, 336–42; Clark, *Practical Jurisprudence*, 340–63. Nelson, *An Analysis*, 36 suggests Maine's reliance on Savigny. Austin, *Province*, xii–xiii covers similar ground to Maine. There is little evidence that Moritz Voigt's work on this matter influenced Maine. His work on the *ius naturale* and *ius gentium* was published in several volumes from 1856 onwards. See Voigt and Seeliger, *Das jus naturale, aequum et bonum, und jus gentium der Römer*, generally. See also Pollock and Maine, *Introduction and Notes*, 10–14.

86 Maine, *Ancient Law*, 50–1.

87 Ibid. 52.

88 Ibid. 52.

89 See Smellie, 'Sir Henry Maine', 68–9; Waerdt, 'Philosophical Influence on Roman Jurisprudence?', for a survey.

beings to nature and, under the influence of Stoicism, whether they should strive to live according to these general laws. Second, this led to a change in the understanding of the term's original meaning. It now signified 'a lost code of nature' that had to be recovered in subsequent law-making.[90] These two points are not unimportant. Maine used them to explain two crucial elements of his general thesis in *Ancient Law*. When the change in the meaning of the term 'law of nature' occurs, it has both structural and moral consequences. Structurally: 'simplicity, symmetry, and intelligibility came, therefore, to be regarded as the characteristics of a good legal system,' whereas morally, the *ius gentium* came to signify a golden past in which, under the influence of Stoicism, legal systems had observed a greater level of morality than in his time.[91]

The change in the meaning of the term 'law of nature' also significantly impacted the term *aequitas*, which Roman jurists used to signify the operation of equity. It originally merely signified 'levelling' in the context of the aims of the law of nations – the equal application of legal rules to citizens and foreigners alike.[92] In time, however, in its guise as the *ius naturale*, it acquired a moral element as well, possibly under the influence of Stoic thought, as is evident in the works of Cicero.

Towards the end of chapter three, Maine summarised his views on equity as an instrumentality of legal change. In the Roman legal system, the praetors and the jurists used equity to effect legal change.[93] Praetors, through the ever-expanding edict, gave a 'new and symmetrical order' to Roman law, while the jurists used equity, as influenced by Greek philosophy, to develop it further:

> It [equity] supplied the jurist with all his materials for generalisation, with all his methods of interpretation, with his elucidation of first principles, and with that great mass of limiting rules which are rarely interfered with by the legislator, but which seriously control the application of every legislative act.[94]

Much like his discussion of legal fictions, Maine concluded that equity as an instrumentality of legal change was also contingent. In time, it lost its utility, especially after the consolidation of the Praetorian edict during the reign of Emperor Hadrian. However, this was not the end of his discussion on the matter. In the final pages of this chapter, Maine briefly addresses an issue that would become significant in his treatment of individual areas of law – namely, morality. He does this by referencing English equity. Again, Maine's point is that morality is a contingent concept. The Roman conception of morality was 'imperfect' compared to nineteenth-century England. The idea that ancient law possessed

[90] Maine, *Ancient Law*, 52, 74. See also McMahon, *Equality*, 93–114.

[91] Ibid. 57; Van Nuffelen and Van Hoof, 'Posidonius and the Golden Age', for a survey.

[92] Maine, *Ancient Law*, 58–60. Austin, *Province*, xiv–xv covers the same ground. Clark, *Practical Jurisprudence*, 366, notes that the common source is Cicero's *Topica*.

[93] Buckland, *Equity in Roman Law*, 5–14; Zwalve, 'The Equity of the Law', for a survey; Beneduzi, *Equity in the Civil Law Tradition*, 21–60.

[94] Maine, *Ancient Law*, 68.

a higher form of morality or that a perfect form of it existed in the natural state of man is a fallacy.

4.2.1 *An excursus on the subsequent fate of the law of nature*

The discussion of instrumentalities of legal change formed part of a larger metacritique offered by Maine throughout the book. It is in the chapter on the modern notions of the law of nature that this critique comes through most significantly. Before examining the details, explaining why Maine offered this critique is essential. The answer is twofold. First, an account of the subsequent history of the law of nature allowed Maine to present various arguments concerning the historical contingency of law.[95] Second, he could raise a more oblique critique of nineteenth-century English law, focusing on Jeremy Bentham's work. The latter point is minor in his overall discussion of natural law, but it is not unimportant. Maine judged Bentham's works, especially those published by Dumont, as having been heavily influenced by the more recent concept of natural law in its French guise post-1789. Owing to his influence, Bentham's works also spread the problems associated with this more recent concept of natural law to English law.[96]

In keeping with Maine's thesis concerning the historical contingency of legal concepts, chapter four continued its account of the Roman idea of the law of nature. Thus, according to Maine, the law of nations in Roman law initially referred to a pragmatic principle born from 'political necessity'.[97] In time, this principle came to be viewed through the prism of Greek philosophy. This change in perspective led to an association with the law of nature, and these two concepts were then seen as functionally equivalent. As a result, the meaning of the original term changed to one which embodied 'simplicity and harmony' in solutions to legal problems. Over time, it also became associated with morality. These developments led to a vagueness at the heart of the law of nature. The concept now exhibited, according to Maine, 'no claim to philosophical precision'.[98] This lack of clarity and precision had given rise to two mistaken points of view, both connected to the influence of Christianity, overlaying the earlier Stoic influence. The first, influenced by the Biblical Old Testament creation myth, regarded natural law as part of a golden past now lost. The second, influenced by the notion of the resurrection as explained in the New Testament, regarded natural law as part of the gradual unfolding of a golden future.[99] It was this latter interpretation,

95 Landauer, 'From Status to Treaty', provides a good comparative account of Maine's use of this method in his later work, *International Law*, based on a series of lectures delivered at Cambridge, published by John Murray in 1888. See also Kustermans, 'Henry Maine and the Modern Invention of Peace', generally. Pollock and Maine, *Introduction and Notes*, 16–22, calls this part of Maine's discussion 'confused', but it misses the point about the layering of earlier and later ideas of natural law.

96 Maine, *Ancient Law*, 78–80. See also McMahon, *Equality*, 195–236.

97 Ibid. 52.

98 Ibid. 73.

99 Passmore, *The Perfectibility of Man*, 202–25.

especially as it related to the French legal philosophy of the eighteenth century and beyond, that Maine focused on in the remainder of the chapter.

> The theory of natural law is the source of almost all of the special ideas as to law, politics, and society which France during the last hundred years has been the instrument of diffusing over the western world.[100]

Given the extensive influence of French legal scholarship on natural law—particularly following the French Revolution—even extending to the United States, this focus appeared warranted to him.

Maine's account of the history of French law from its origins in the medieval *ius commune* is brief but makes two essential points.[101] The first point concerns the historical contingency of law. The development of French law from the late medieval period to the seventeenth century is in no way 'typical'.[102] Rather, it was formed in the context of a divide within the territory of France between 'written law' in the south and 'unwritten law' in the north. At the same time, the early modern French jurists, known throughout Europe for their erudition, were confronted with a peculiar situation. As Maine phrased it: 'the system of laws which they had to administer stood in striking contrast with the habits of mind which they had cultivated.'[103] And it is here that natural law became central to their treatment of French law because it could be used conceptually to smooth over (i.e. level) divisions between written and unwritten law on specific points of law. This gave the concept a particular prominence, and it became, in the words of our author: 'not so much a theory guiding practice as an article of speculative faith'.[104]

The discussion above provided the background for Maine's treatment of eighteenth-century French law. He chose two figures to contrast, namely Montesquieu and Rousseau. While Maine's assessment of the former was essentially (although not unequivocally) positive, his treatment of the latter was openly hostile.

Appreciating these two individuals' roles in Maine's narrative is essential. Montesquieu's most famous work, *De L'Esprit*, published in 1748, forms part of a natural law discourse in European legal thought.[105] As will be recalled, the gist of Montesquieu's book was that the best type of law is made when considering the

[100] Maine, *Ancient Law*, 80. Oldham, *Analysis*, 10–11. See Bentham, Dumont and Hildreth, *Theory of Legislation*, 104–10.

[101] Maine, *Ancient Law*, 80–6.

[102] Evans-Pritchard, *A History of Anthropological Thought; Edited by André Singer; with an Introduction by Ernest Gellner*, 52, shows that in Auguste Comte's *Système*, France is given a special place as the pinnacle of 'civilisation' development. It is impossible to determine whether this statement is at the back of Maine's mind here, but it makes for a curious correlation. Maine likely took his discussion of the historical development of law in France from Savigny, *The History of the Roman Law during the Middle Ages, Translated from the Original German of Carl von Savigny by E. Cathcart. Vol. I*, 165–6, though one can also find a narrative of this kind in the works of Ortolan, see Nelson, *An Analysis*, 60–70.

[103] Maine, *Ancient Law*, 83.

[104] Ibid. 86.

[105] Wood, *Liberty and Property*, 174–7; MacDonald, 'Problems with Principles', for a survey.

social context of a specific society – its spirit. Maine was positively disposed to this notion, even though he criticised Montesquieu for not fully considering human nature's importance in creating good law elsewhere in *Ancient Law*. However, his most significant criticism of the work was not reserved for the content itself but for the political events that overtook it.[106] Had Montesquieu's thesis been given more time to influence the natural law debate in France, Maine opined, its impact may have been more significant. Unfortunately, as he observed:

> The counter-hypothesis which it seemed destined to destroy passed suddenly from the forum to the street, and became the key-note of controversies far more exciting than are ever agitated in the courts or the schools.[107]

There is much to unpack in this quotation. Maine blamed the lack of influence of Montesquieu's work to a change in both the nature of the debate and its location. Natural law changed from a juristic concept developed to cope with a specific complexity in the French legal tradition to a popular trope used with devastating effect by supporters of the French Revolution of 1789. He blamed one individual and his influence for this development – Jean-Jacques Rousseau. Apart from being critical of him personally, Maine was also quite scathing of his misunderstanding of Roman law on the law of nature. The nature of Rousseau's misunderstanding was as follows:

> It is not the law of nature, but the state of nature, which is now the primary subject of contemplation. The Roman had conceived that by careful observation of existing institutions parts of them could be singled out which either exhibited already, or could by judicious purification be made to exhibit, the vestiges of that reign of nature whose reality he faintly affirmed.[108]

> Rousseau's belief was that a perfect social order could be evolved from the unassisted considerations of the natural state, a social order wholly irrespective of the actual condition of the world and wholly unlike it.[109]

The essence of Maine's critique was twofold. First, the focus was incorrect. Second, the consequence of this shift in focus was removing discussions of the state of nature from all empirical reality. The golden future that Rousseau and his supporters advocated had no grounding in fact, let alone history. This is an important point, given Maine's identification with Historical Jurisprudence.

The argument set out in *Ancient Law* concerning the lack of Rousseau's historical knowledge and that of his supporters, and its concomitant effect on their conception of the state of nature, may be divided into two separate issues.[110] The

[106] Maine, *Ancient Law*, 86–7.
[107] Ibid. 87.
[108] Ibid. 88.
[109] Ibid. 88–9.
[110] Ibid. 87–9.

first concerns the reasons for this lack of knowledge. In Maine's view, this could be traced back to their disdain for religion generally and to their scepticism towards the Old Testament:

> One of the few characteristics which the school of Rousseau had in common with the school of Voltaire was an utter disdain of all religious antiquities; and, more than all, of those of the Hebrew race.[111]

The sceptical attitude of Rousseau and his supporters towards the information contained in the Old Testament and its veracity had given rise to an abstract notion of the state of nature that bore no resemblance to any historical reality.[112] It is crucial, at this point, to qualify Maine's point. In his discussion of the transition from unwritten to written law, the point was made that in a 'progressive' system such as Roman law, the first written law, the Law of the Twelve Tables, was enacted in a period where Roman law was still in the process of separating from religion. Maine believed the gradual separation of law from religion had to start early. On the other hand, the value of the information in the Old Testament, as used by Maine in his argument here, is a different matter. As he mentioned in his discussion of the value of ancient law, it was a good source of information since it predated any attempts at interpretation, hence its utility here.

The final part of Maine's discussion used two tangential examples to demonstrate the dangers of an intellectual approach that neglected history. The first concerns the principle of equality, and the second is territorial sovereignty in international law. At first sight, it seems difficult to link these examples to the preceding discussion. Still, upon reflection, the connection lies in what Maine identified as the idea of a golden future rooted in the state of nature, as Rousseau and his followers advocated. Thus, these two examples were deployed to demonstrate the intellectual fallacy of such a position. Let us take these in turn. Regarding the principle that all men are equal, Maine observed: '[t]here cannot, I conceive, be any question that to the assumptions of a law natural we owe the doctrine of the fundamental equality of human beings.'[113]

The notion of equality was one of the chief intellectual outcomes of the French Revolution of 1789. It was expressly articulated in The Declaration of the Rights of Man and the Citizen. As Maine observed, it transformed the idea of equality from a legal concept to a 'political proposition' – an aspiration for the future. He was sceptical of this interpretation of an essentially Roman law principle. In his view, the principle of the equality of man had a different meaning in Roman law, where it was a pragmatic idea introduced to overcome regional diversity by applying law across the Empire. It was not viewed, according to Maine, as a political aspiration, and the Romans did not view the lack of such a principle as a deficiency in their legal order. To that end, an investigation into the change in the meaning

[111] Ibid. 90.
[112] Ibid. 91–2.
[113] Ibid. 92.

of the term had to be undertaken. The significance of this change in meaning for the legal discourse of the nineteenth century cannot not be understated:

> The peculiar Roman idea that natural law coexisted with civil law and gradually absorbed it, had evidently been lost sight of, or had become unintelligible, and the words which had at most conveyed a theory concerning the origin, composition, and development of human institutions, were beginning to express the sense of a great standing wrong suffered by mankind.[114]

The latter part of this quotation is telling. According to Maine, two historical factors contributed to the modern understanding of equality. The first was the notion of feudalism, which, in the French context, influenced debates on the equality of man since the fourteenth century.[115] The second was a more recent influence—the effect of eighteenth-century French legal scholarship across the globe, especially in the context of the founding of the United States of America.

Maine's second example focused on an aspect of international law.[116] More specifically, it addressed Roman law's contribution to the formation of international law, with a specific focus on the notion of territorial sovereignty.[117] According to Maine, international law of the nineteenth century bore little direct impact from Roman law, especially when it concerned the term 'natural law'. The two essential features of modern international law, namely that it had a definite content and was binding upon States, did not come from an interpretation of Roman law but from more recent scholarship such as those of Grotius and Ayala.[118] When their views of natural law are compared to the Roman legal concept bearing the same name, it becomes clear that the two had little in common. Having made this fundamental point, Maine moved on to the consequences of this apparent confusion and its impact on the development of international law. This argument about consequences is somewhat convoluted but attains clarity towards the end. Once it is accepted that natural law has a definite content binding upon States and forms part of a golden future, it triggers a process 'of engrafting on the international system rules which are supposed to have been evolved from the unassisted contemplation of the conception of nature'.[119] One such idea is to treat states similarly to individuals and to give them the same rights over ownerless property as one would afford a Roman owner. This, in turn, leads to the development of the concept of territorial sovereignty, the basis of which is the idea that the ruler of a state has ownership of its territories like that of a Roman owner. As Maine shows through his historical investigation of the principle of territorial sovereignty, while it may

[114] Ibid. 93–4. Desautels-Stein, *The Right to Exclude*, 147–8, discusses a similar critique of this notion in a later work by Jhering.

[115] Maine, *Ancient Law*, 92–6. See Bentham, Dumont and Hildreth, *Theory of Legislation*, 62, 123.

[116] Maine, *Ancient Law*, 86–111.

[117] Mantena, *Alibis of Empire*, 113–18.

[118] Maine, *Ancient Law*, 100.

[119] Ibid. 100.

be based on Roman ideas of ownership, it bears little resemblance to Roman law. It is a product of the late medieval period, further developed through feudalism in the early modern period, and then awarded mainstream support through the work of Grotius.[120]

4.3 Legislation

For all the importance Maine attached to Bentham's position on legislation, the discussion of it as an instrumentality of legal change is slight at best.[121] It occupies roughly two pages in Maine's book. This cannot be accidental. It is a deliberate inversion of sorts. Not only was it treated at the end of the discussion rather than the beginning, but the space devoted to it was limited. Since Maine's position, following that of Historical Jurisprudence, was that a legal order consisted of more forms of law than merely statute law, it seems likely that such a short treatment of the subject was purposive. The essence of his account here is twofold, namely the source of authority of statute and its contingency. The first issue spoke directly to Maine's critique of Bentham's position on statute law. Since statute law drew its authority from an 'external body or person' deemed to represent the citizenry, it was deemed law even if its content was poor.[122] Thus, because of its force as law, citizens were subjected to it even if the content of the law was terrible or the lawgiver was evil. As Maine phrased it: 'There is nothing to prevent its legislating in the wantonness of caprice.'[123] In his view, this was one of the great dangers of equating law with statute. In addition, he addressed the issue of the contingency of statute law. Drawing on Roman law, Maine argued that statute law was not a panacea. The Romans, for example, only used statute law to resolve 'a great civil commotion'.[124] The point here was undoubtedly a critique of the volume of statutory change visible in Victorian England. Statute law, as a form of law, had to be used in a targeted manner rather than indiscriminately.

5. CONCLUSIONS

This chapter demonstrates that 'ancient law' was a term conceptually crafted and purposefully employed by Maine in his book. Its significance can only be understood in the context of evaluating the work's objective as a critique of natural law scholarship. This becomes particularly apparent when examining Maine's criticisms of specific authors within this intellectual tradition, such as Rousseau.

[120] Ibid. 111.

[121] Ibid. 41–2; Smellie, 'Sir Henry Maine', 72–3; Mantena, *Alibis of Empire*, 107–13, shows that in Maine's later work, he favoured codification for India. His comments on the different forms and content of the code in Roman law and his statements concerning the perils of the continued use of customary law beyond its utility should be viewed in this context.

[122] Maine, *Ancient Law*, 29.

[123] Ibid. 29.

[124] Ibid. 42.

However, the book went beyond a critique of natural law scholarship; it also presented a sophisticated criticism of Bentham's perspectives on agents of legal change and their connection to natural law scholarship.

Maine's discourse on the instrumentalities of legal change was directed at engaging directly with Bentham's views on the nature of law. Consequently, legal fictions were scrutinised to demonstrate their contextual utility. The discussion of Praetorian equity served a broader purpose, aiming first to underscore the significance of the Roman jurists as a body of scholars and their intellectual impact on legal development. The underlying message was clear: law transcends mere legislative will. The second objective was to advocate for the importance of philosophy in legal development.

At the same time, Maine was careful to point out that the concept of natural law carried different layers of meaning, some practical and others philosophical. He viewed it as unwise to focus solely on the most recent layer, epitomised by natural law scholarship post the French Revolution of 1789, as representing the entire concept. This critique enabled him to offer a critical analysis of Bentham's work. Maine asserted that post-1789 conceptions of natural law heavily influenced Bentham's works, and due to his widespread influence, he had imported these issues into English law. This formed the crux of his critique within these chapters.

Chapter 4

The Family and the State

> The exclusive, absolute, and perpetual dominion of the father over his children is peculiar to the Roman jurisprudence, and seems to be coeval with the foundation of the city.[1]

1. INTRODUCTION

Chapter five of *Ancient Law* is the closest thing to a methodology chapter in Maine's book. It is a chapter of two halves. In the first half, Maine describes his motivations for writing the book. He begins by linking his decision to investigate ancient law directly to what he perceived to be shortcomings in the exposition of various legal-philosophical works of the eighteenth century and beyond in which the origins of the State were discussed using insights from natural law.[2] The speculative nature of these discussions and their failure to engage with historical realities prompted Maine, by his admission, to write *Ancient Law*. Having laid out his position, he justified his focus on ancient law as a historical source. From here, he branched into a discussion concerning the origins of the State and the role of law in that process. This marks the transition to the second half of the chapter. The focus here is a discussion of the role of the family in developing ancient law. There can be little doubt that Maine's emphasis on the family was, on some level, a critique of the focus on individualism in the Victorian intellectual discourse of his time.[3] As with other topical issues in the book, and in keeping with the Humanist underpinnings of the work, the matter is discussed obliquely using Roman law as his model.

According to Maine's thesis, the family could not be separated hermetically from the development of ancient law. Ancient law and the State more generally developed out of and around the family. This is likely why it was included in chapter five rather than as a separate chapter, to give a sense of interconnectedness. Still, to the contemporary reader, separating these issues (legal development and the State's formation) in our analysis of his work allows for a better understanding of each. In this chapter, Maine's views on the family will be examined within his broader thesis in *Ancient Law*. As with most topics in his book, Maine's treatment focuses on Roman law – his archetypal 'progressive' legal system. Conveniently for

1 Gibbon and Fernández-Armesto, *The History of the Decline and Fall of the Roman Empire. Vol. 5, Justinian and the Roman Law*, 272.
2 Maine, *Ancient Law*, 113–15.
3 See also Kennedy, 'Savigny's Family/Patrimony Distinction and its Place in the Global Genealogy of Classical Legal Thought', 826, and generally.

Maine, Roman legal sources provided extensive evidence of the development of Roman family law across time.[4] In addition, the Roman *familia*, elegantly defined by the third-century jurist Ulpian in D.50.16.195.1 as a legal construct capable of having several meanings, would have been familiar to much of Maine's audience at Cambridge and later at Middle Temple.

This is an important point. To understand the broader context of Maine's discussion in this chapter, it is essential to remember that family law as a branch of English private law underwent significant changes during the time Maine researched *Ancient Law*. These were comprehensive and ranged from matters of jurisdiction over aspects of family law, the ease of divorce, the custody of children and changes to the property regime of married women.[5] When viewed in the round, these developments appeared to be positive, benefitting individual family members and often at the expense of the traditional powers of the Victorian head of the household. Such changes could be viewed as a growing trend towards individualism, as discussed in Victorian intellectual circles. And yet, Maine does not engage with these developments directly in this chapter. Instead, in keeping with the Humanist aims of the work, Roman law is used as an example, and the audience is left to draw parallels with the contemporaneous developments in English law. In terms of rhetorical technique, the entire chapter reads, at times, like an elaborate use of *praeteritio* – focusing on developments in Roman family law while also making points about contemporaneous English law obliquely.

Before analysing the specifics of Maine's treatment of the family, it is essential to identify the main idea he wished to convey with this discussion.[6] In his view, his archetypal 'progressive' legal system, Roman law, while rooted initially in the family, slowly demonstrated a shift from 'status to contract'.[7] Phrased differently, the development of 'ancient law' is the story of the gradual diminution of the significance of the family and its domestic jurisdiction as the base unit of ancient law in favour of the individual and the simultaneous growth of law. It is important to stress that, in Maine's eyes, this was not a linear or unidirectional trajectory. If anything, his treatment of paternal authority and the later resurgence of marital power over the wife in European legal history suggests a cyclical view of legal change. This was no doubt the critical message of this chapter. Change is inevitable and necessary, but one cannot always assume that it will be for the better.

According to one of Maine's broader insights, societal developments tended to outpace legal change. The changes visible in Roman family law, combined with

4 Capogrossi Colognesi, *La costruzione del diritto privato romano*, 24–8, for a survey.

5 Cornish et al., *Law and Society in England, 1750-1950*, 341–4; Council of Legal Education, *A Century of Law Reform*, 20–2; Howarth, 'Gender, Domesticity, and Sexual Politics', 181–2.

6 Taylor, *Constructing the Family*, 3–24, Taylor's work shows that the nineteenth century was a period of change and development for English family law.

7 Pollock and Maine, *Introduction and Notes*, 34–6, advocated a narrow reading of this statement, especially if projected onto legal developments of the nineteenth and early twentieth centuries. This misrepresents Maine's aims with *Ancient Law*. It was not written to provide a predictive theory for contemporary legal change.

insights from Roman social history, could thus be used to draw inferences about this process. At the same time, however, Roman law was far from an ideal source, and Maine was aware of this.[8] Thus, at the start of chapter one, he noted that the state of philological analyses of Sanskrit and his limited knowledge of this language did not permit him to examine the laws of another Indo-European society in detail when he was writing *Ancient Law*. As will become apparent in this chapter, although his primary source was Rome, the comparative references fulfilled a vital function in his narrative. They were added to elaborate on and support certain general statements about Roman law – often to reconstruct the developmental trajectories of specific phenomena.

Maine's decision to focus on the family in Roman law as his primary example had both advantages and disadvantages. The main advantage was the extent of the source material and its chronological spread over a considerable period. This made it helpful in constructing arguments about the gradual change to this legal order. The main disadvantage, however, was that it did not provide comprehensive evidence for his more general claims, especially for those focusing on the more distant past. It is, therefore, necessary for the modern reader to separate the claims that could be substantiated by Roman legal sources from those that could not. Maine's book focused on 'progressive' legal systems united by their common Indo-European heritage. More specifically, the bulk of his narrative concerned a discussion of legal change in one of those systems in the period when its 'progressive' nature had already become apparent. In his view, this point had been reached once the law had been reduced to writing, as in the Twelve Tables. It is easy to see the conceptual problem this created for Maine here. At this point, the Roman State had already existed for two centuries, according to conventional dating concerning the founding of the city of Rome. It had dispensed with its monarchy and begun experimenting with a Republican constitution, even if, as sources like Livy reveal, social strife between different population sectors remained a problem. Thus, Roman law, his archetypal 'progressive' legal system, provided little concrete evidence regarding the family and its role in forming the Roman State at its inception.

Before discussing the specifics, it is essential to reiterate that the book's aim was not to provide a stadial account of the growth of ancient law in abstract terms from its absolute origins onwards. Thus, the fact that Roman law was less helpful in providing information about the distant past was not fatal. Still, specific comments about this past were necessary for Maine's argument in light of its prevalence as a trope in natural law scholarship. Thus, he had to rely on different sources to discuss the role of the family in the formation of the State.

2. THE FAMILY AND THE STATE

Despite the attention that Maine's discussion of State formation has received in subsequent scholarship, it must be emphasised that it was not a large part of this

[8] Maine, *Ancient Law*, 123.

book, nor was it central to his broader thesis. Maine's narrative begins in earnest only once the law had been reduced to writing – a point at which the State (at least in the Roman experience) already exists. The limited discussion of State formation was purposive and served a twofold function. First, it fed into his broader rationale for writing the book. *Ancient Law* was written to critique the speculative nature of eighteenth century and later natural law scholarship on State formation.[9] Maine used historical insights to critique their methods and lack of historical knowledge. The brevity of his treatment of the issue suggests that he did not think it was a topic about which much could be said. Second, and more abstractly, he could use his account of State formation and the role of the family in it to provide insights into the nature and direction of legal change. More specifically, it could be used to question some of the core assumptions made in earlier works inspired by natural law.

Before launching into a detailed account of Maine's views, it is essential to reflect on his sources. His account of the history of the family and the origins of the State are based exclusively on sources from Graeco-Roman antiquity.[10] These sources, the significance of which will be explored presently, provided Maine with a ready-made narrative about the State's formation and the family's role in it. When his use of these two narratives is compared, the State formation narrative seems less developed than the family narrative. On closer inspection, however, there is more to the matter than first meets the eye. According to Maine, using sources from Graeco-Roman antiquity, the State consisted of increasing circles of relationships starting from the family to form the *gens* and, ultimately, the State.[11] Thus, there were only isolated families in the period before the formation of the State. Since the family was initially founded upon the principle of blood relationships (or purported blood relationships through adoption[12]), expanding circles of relation were created and fostered through a legal fiction to form the State. Thus, the State was a sort of larger family, held together by a legal fiction.[13]

Maine was explicit about his reliance on Graeco-Roman antiquity for this insight. In *Politics*, Aristotle discusses the idea of the family as the basic unit of the State, formed through ever-increasing circles of connection.[14] This was no doubt the source of Maine's idea here. Interestingly, this is where his observations about the State and its formation broadly end. Using the notion of a legal fiction as the metaphorical glue that holds the State together permitted him to skirt around the unresolvable issue, much discussed in natural law circles, as to whether the

[9] Psomiades, *Primitive Marriage*, 91; Widerquist, *Prehistoric Myths in Modern Political Philosophy*, 24–64; Somos, *American States of Nature*, 24–38; Kennedy, *Reforming the Law of Nature*, 107–32.

[10] Kuper, 'The Rise and Fall of Maine's Patriarchal Society', generally; Siedentop, *Inventing the Individual*, 7–18.

[11] Maine, *Ancient Law*, 128–9.

[12] Ibid. 130.

[13] An idea also found in Burke, *An Appeal*, 126. Notably, the terms 'fiction' and 'corporation' also appear in this discussion.

[14] Jarvis, 'The Family as the Foundation of Political Rule in Western Philosophy', for a survey. See also Austin, *Province*, 215–16.

State's formation rested on the people's consent or some other element. In the remainder of the book, possibly except for the final chapter on criminal law, Maine does not appear to have been too interested in the growth of State institutions or their role in legal change. At first sight, this seems a curious oversight. In reality, however, this lack of attention is purposive. Like many supporters of Historical Jurisprudence, he did not support the 'command theory' of law espoused by scholars such as Jeremy Bentham and John Austin. In Maine's view, there was more to the nature of law and its growth than merely the command of the lawgiver. This stance allowed Maine to pay less attention to State institutions and their role in legal change. In addition, the absence of any substantive discussion on the development of the State points to another core feature of *Ancient Law*. The book was not written as a stadial account, from its very origins, of the growth of the State, its institutions and its laws in the premodern world. It was a comprehensive critique of this very idea. Maine assigned a specific meaning to the term 'progress', primarily as a critique of the Victorian understanding of the concept as 'continuous change for the better'.

By contrast, his statements on the origins of law from the family are more fully developed. Before setting these out in detail, it is essential to reflect on their purpose within Maine's book. Since the aim of *Ancient Law* was not to provide a linear, stadial account of the development of law, his statements concerning the origins of law served a different purpose. At the point at which Maine's narrative begins in earnest, the (Roman) State is already in existence, and the law has been reduced to writing. This change from unwritten to written law was seminal to his 'progressive' legal systems theory. Once this fact is appreciated, Maine's statements about the origins of law take on a new significance. Although not discussed in detail, a distinction seems to be made between the family and its organisation before and after the State's formation. In the former scenario, the head of the family is described as a 'patriarchal chieftain', and his rule over the family is defined as 'despotism', not law.[15] The spectre of Aristotle looms large in these words. It is interesting to note Maine's choice of example here. He did not use real-world examples of isolated families seemingly existing without a State. Though many such examples would undoubtedly have been known to him, he relied on an instance from Homer's *Odyssey* in which the *Cyclopes* are described as a people arranged in insular families without a State.[16] In Maine's scheme, 'law' is yet to exist in such a scenario. The despotic commands of the chieftain are sufficient to govern the family, but they are not 'law'. Once the State has been formed from an amalgamation of families into ever larger groups, a gradual emergence of 'law' can be traced.

The role of this narrative point in the book's more significant thesis must be considered. His exposition aimed to provide a historically grounded account of

[15] Maine, *Ancient Law*, 125; Davenport, 'Liberalism's Perverse Pleasures', generally. See also Thomas, *Legal Artifices*, 144–209.

[16] Grote, *A History of Greece*, II, 102, is likely the source of this reference.

the emergence of 'law' to the point where it was reduced to writing for the first time. His evidence for this development was drawn from Greek and Roman history. Thus, in describing the forms of the State before the point at which law is reduced to writing, the narrative of the king, whose authority is gradually curtailed by the rise of an aristocracy, seems to have been inspired by the Roman historian Livy's account of the early history of Rome. It was also extensively discussed by Niebuhr, Maine's likely source here. At the same time, his account of the emergence of 'law', from the despotic commands of the father to the rise of customary law, is drawn from the work of George Grote (1794–1871), *A History of Greece*, published in several volumes from 1846 onwards.[17] It is impossible to determine why Maine chose Grote's work as the source of his ideas in this respect. In all likelihood, his choice is linked to the prominence of Grote's work in the classics curriculum at Cambridge and his use of 'source criticism', also favoured by Niebuhr, as a methodology. Grote's use of comparative material no doubt also appealed to our author.[18] Furthermore, he was famous in Victorian literary circles and influential in Victorian politics.[19] From this work, Maine constructed his account of the gradual emergence of 'law'.[20]

In the earliest phase, the ruler derives the authority for their rulings, *themistes*, from a 'divine agent', *themis*.[21] Since these rulings deal with specific rather than general matters, they cannot be classified as 'law' as such. In addition, Maine pointed out that *themis* in this context did not refer to a deity as such but rather to a more general sense of a 'divine presence' permeating life. This is a curious statement and merits comment. One wonders why Maine did not rely merely on the account of the creation of the Ten Commandments in the Old Testament as his example here. He was certainly not averse to using the Old Testament as a source, as his discussion of the early history of property shows. In all likelihood, the Mosaic laws did not provide a suitable example to Maine here, owing to his views on the gradual separation of law, religion and morality.[22] The written nature of the Ten Commandments may have also been an obstacle. His examples thus had to be drawn from elsewhere. The use of comparative references is noteworthy here. Maine employs two comparisons to make different points. The first is a critical comment regarding the Code of Manu, an early Hindu law code whose nature

[17] Dēmētriou, *Brill's Companion to George Grote and the Classical Tradition*, 1–15.

[18] Liddel, 'The Comparative Approach in Grote's History of Greece', for a survey.

[19] Kinzer, 'George Grote, The Philosophic Radical and Politician'; Gibbins, *John Grote*, for a survey.

[20] Grote, *A History of Greece*, II, 111–12, seems to be the source of this entire discussion. For the complexity of the meaning of the term *nomos* in Greek sources, see Zartaloudis, *The Birth of Nomos*, xiii–xli. For criticisms of Maine's interpretation of the Greek evidence, see Oldham, *Analysis*, 1–2; Pollock and Maine, *Introduction and Notes*, 2–4.

[21] The story of King Numa consulting the nymph Egeria, recounted in Book 1 of Livy, would not be out of place in this context.

[22] Gibbins, 'George Grote and Natural Religion', 103, 109 shows that both Grote and Bentham held hostile views on the role of religion in law. Their view, combined with the tenor of Gibbon's less-than-favourable opinions on the impact of Christianity on Roman law, likely influenced Maine's views.

and purpose were widely misunderstood by Victorian authors.[23] The misunderstanding was caused by Victorian scepticism as to the authorship of this code and, thus, its antiquity. Since this code seemed to have been dictated, in Maine's view, by a deity rather than reflecting a general sense of a 'divine presence', it appeared to have been a later work and would thus be an unsuitable example. The second is a positive reference to both Roman and Hindu law through which he underscores the importance of the 'divine presence' concerning the prominence of the *sacra*, sacrifices to the household gods, in the early Roman law of inheritance, as well as the importance of similar sacrifices in the Hindu law of inheritance. He will later return to this point more fully in the chapter on inheritance.

In the following phase, Maine focused on the rise of an aristocracy as a successor to the king's original authority. Two interesting points concerning legal change are made here. The first is that the king's ad hoc *themistes* are gradually replaced by a body of consistent rulings that cover not only specific circumstances but also provide more generalised rulings. This, to Maine, is the origin of customary law in the sense of unwritten law. Second, unlike the king, the aristocracy did not justify the 'authority' of their growing body of customary law by way of reference to a 'divine agent'. Instead, it was based on their self-fashioning as a small group who could act as keepers of legal knowledge. This, then, was the state of the law at the point before it was reduced to writing.

Given Maine's brief treatment of the topic, it is difficult to determine whether he intended to engage with contemporaneous European legal debate on customary law between Savigny and his opponents. The answer is likely no. Maine's exposition of customary law here is not that of Savigny[24] or Bentham.[25] Instead, given that Grote was his primary source here, it seems to follow the Aristotelian distinction between *ethos* and *nomos*, the latter being linked to general rules of a rational nature.[26] That being the case, explaining its significance in this book becomes essential. Maine's underlying point is that customary law, in the manner in which he identified it, was not 'primitive', nor did it belong to the very earliest history of State formation. The entire discussion on the origins of law, taken from Grote, demonstrated that many developments had to take place before 'true' customary law arose. Instead, it only appeared later in the development of law. Furthermore, customary law was not a phase in the stadial growth of law. The Romans continued to use customary law long after resorting to written law. This made comparative investigations of customary law in Hindu law possible.[27] It is likely within the context of his comments about Hindu law that this account should be read.

[23] Manu, *The Law Code of Manu, a New Translation Based on the Critical Edition by Patrick Olivelle*, xxxviii–xxxix, for an account of the Victorian misunderstanding concerning the nature of this code. For a more expansive discussion, see Maine, *Dissertations on Early Law and Custom*, 9–11.

[24] Kletzer, 'Custom and Positivity', for a survey.

[25] Murphy, 'A Commentary on the *Comment*', 59, for a survey.

[26] Murphy, 'Habit and Convention at the Foundation of Custom', 6–11, for a survey.

[27] Jain, 'Custom as a Source of Law in India', for a survey.

3. THE ROMAN FAMILY

The Roman family was considered an ancient institution even by Graeco-Roman authors.[28] In the Roman experience, for example, it was linked to Romulus, the mythical founder of Rome. The power of the head of the household was explicitly mentioned in the Twelve Tables.[29] Gibbon, one of Maine's primary sources, spent several paragraphs exploring the origins of the Roman family and the extent of the head of the household's authority over its members. Similarly, in book one of Mommsen's *Geschichte*, published around the time that Maine was researching his book, the same themes are discussed, especially concerning the role of the family in the formation of the State. Thus, it was a topical issue for anyone familiar with Roman history. To understand Maine's use of the Roman family in *Ancient Law*, we must turn to its 'definition' provided by the third-century jurist Ulpian:

> D. 50, 16, 195, 1 Ulp. 46 ad ed.
> 'Familiae' appellatio qualiter accipiatur, videamus. et quidem varie accepta est: nam et in res et in personas deducitur. in res, ut puta in lege duodecim tabularum his verbis 'adgnatus proximus familiam habeto'. ad personas autem refertur familiae significatio ita, cum de patrono et liberto loquitur lex: 'ex ea familia', inquit, 'in eam familiam': et hic de singularibus personis legem loqui constat.
>
> Let us see how the term 'family' should be understood. It can have different meanings since it applies to both objects and persons. As an example of its meaning applicable to objects, take the words of the Twelve Tables: 'Let the nearest agnate have the family'. As an example of its meaning applicable to persons, take the words of the law applicable to patron and client: 'From that family,' it says, 'into that family'. Here, it is clear that the law speaks about individual persons. [Own translation]

Although from a much later period than the one discussed here by Maine, this celebrated definition highlights the central role of the family in Roman private law and its various interpretations by the Roman jurists of the third century. As a legal construct, it included 'persons' and 'things' – an important statement for our purposes. The Roman family was a broader concept than the modern nuclear family and played a much more significant role in law throughout the long history of the Roman legal system. It was, in essence, an intergenerational group of people bonded together by blood relationships and presided over by the eldest male relative, the head of the family or household (*paterfamilias*). The legal nature of his control over the family and its assets was termed 'power' (*potestas*), a word also with multiple meanings, as the third-century jurist Paul explained:

[28] Huebner and Nathan, *Mediterranean Families in Antiquity*, provides a recent survey of the complexities surrounding the family concept in Graeco-Roman antiquity.

[29] Gibbon and Fernández-Armesto, *The History of the Decline and Fall of the Roman Empire. Vol. 5, Justinian and the Roman Law*, 272.

D. 50, 16, 215, Paul. l. s. ad l. Fuf. Canin.
'Potestatis' verbo plura significantur: in persona magistratuum imperium: in persona liberorum patria potestas: in persona servi dominium. . . . .

The term 'power' can mean many things. When it refers to the person of magistrates, it signifies *imperium*. When it relates to the person of children, it signifies paternal authority; when it relates to the person of the slave, it means ownership. [Own translation]

The first sentence of this text shows this concept's antiquity and its application to 'persons' and 'things' forming part of the Roman family. This configuration of the family and the power at its base formed the focus of Maine's investigation in the second half of chapter five. As he phrased it: 'It [the family] will be found to have stamped itself on all the great departments of jurisprudence, and may be detected, I think, as the true source of many of their most important and most durable characteristics.'[30]

Thus, the narrative of *Ancient Law* was an account of the gradual growth of law and the State from the decline of the domestic jurisdiction of the family. A survey of the topics covered by Maine in this half of chapter five shows that they broadly align with what contemporary textbook writers classify as aspects of Roman family law.[31] Thus, he begins by examining the power of the head of the household and the importance of agnatic relationships. Then, he focuses on the 'persons' and 'things' forming part of the Roman family. Since, according to Maine's central thesis in *Ancient Law*, the family was the originator of the State and its laws, every chapter in the book demonstrates the development of an aspect of (mainly private) law as the family's role diminishes. In addition, the 'instrumentalities' identified by Maine acted as the agents of change and illustrated how the law develops in response to social change.

4. PATERNAL AUTHORITY

Explaining how Maine harnessed this information to substantiate his narrative is essential. The extent of the head of the household's power over family members in Roman law is well documented.[32] As Gibbon phrased it:

> In the forum, the senate, or the camp, the adult son of a Roman citizen enjoyed the public and private rights of a person: in his father's house he was a mere thing; confounded by the laws with the movables, the cattle, and the slaves, whom the capricious master might alienate or destroy without being responsible to any earthly tribunal.[33]

[30] Maine, *Ancient Law*, 134.

[31] Nelson, *An Analysis*, 78–116, for a summary of this chapter. See also Oldham, *Analysis*, 15–22.

[32] Mackenzie, *Studies in Roman Law*, 125–6, for a near contemporaneous account. Amunátegui Perelló, *Origen de los poderes del paterfamilias*, 43–178, for a recent account. See Bentham, Dumont and Hildreth, *Theory of Legislation*, 252–4.

[33] Gibbon and Fernández-Armesto, *The History of the Decline and Fall of the Roman Empire. Vol. 5, Justinian and the Roman Law*, 272.

The final line of this quotation is telling. 'Law' existed outside the home, not inside it. Such a statement complemented Maine's earlier observations taken from Grote's work. Paternal authority was, in principle, both comprehensive and perpetual. It was only terminated by the death of the head of the household or by the child's emancipation from the family. Roman legal sources show that, during the early Empire, the lifelong power of the head of the household became an inconvenience, especially concerning the inability of sons to own property independently.[34] Imperial interventions were made progressively to the existing law to improve the situation.[35] These changes were central to his argument here. According to Maine, the paternal authority visible in classical Roman law was an echo of a much older idea. It was a diluted manifestation of an earlier scenario in which the 'patriarchal chieftain' had held extensive power over his family and its assets in the earliest history of State formation.[36] It predated 'law'. Since Roman law provided evidence, albeit later and incomplete, of how these powers were curtailed over time, it could be used to make a broader point about legal change. At the same time, however, it provided little information about the earliest history mentioned above. To that end, Maine had to rely on Greek literature, specifically the interactions between Odysseus and his father, Laertes, in Homer's *Odyssey*, to postulate that the patriarchal chieftain's power must have been more expansive in earlier periods and likely linked to the patriarch's physical strength in the earliest history of State formation.[37]

This evidence, together with the later curtailment of parental power also visible in Greek law, allowed Maine to link it to the information provided by Roman law as indicative of an Indo-European legal phenomenon. He does not appear to have been too concerned about the statement in the Institutes of Gaius (Inst. Gai. 1, 55), which described the power the head of the household exerted over his children as '*proprium civium Romanorum est*', or that his other example, the *Galatae* people, had dealt with the matter of parental control over children differently. In Maine's view, the fact that Gaius had found an example of a similar type of power, albeit shared by both parents rather than residing in the head of the household, demonstrated that the idea was older and more widespread. Indeed, he surmised that if Gaius had looked beyond the borders of the Roman Empire, he would have seen versions of it everywhere. It should also be recalled why it was important for Maine to reinforce this point. By this stage in the book, he had already made his claim that the earliest manifestation of the family was patriarchal. The Roman law on this issue thus became evidence supporting his earlier claim.

In the remainder of his treatment of paternal authority, Maine attempted to account for its fate in Roman law.[38] He focused on the nature of paternal authority

[34] Maine, *Ancient Law*, 136–40; Amunátegui Perelló, *Origen de los poderes del paterfamilias*, 341–74.

[35] Gibbon and Fernández-Armesto, *The History of the Decline and Fall of the Roman Empire. Vol. 5, Justinian and the Roman Law*, 273–4, Mackenzie, *Studies in Roman Law*, 126–8.

[36] Zimmerman, *Family and Civilization*, 26–7, for a comment on the undifferentiated power of the head of the household in this history of family law.

[37] Maine, *Ancient Law*, 136.

[38] Ibid. 140–4.

and its impact on members of the Roman family, namely children, wives and enslaved people, who were subjected to such power. The motivations for this were twofold. First, Maine saw the family as the: 'nidus out of which the entire law of persons . . . germinated.'[39] If paternal authority was the binding force that kept the family together, then an investigation into it could be helpful in the context of his broader aims with the book. Second, given Maine's broader thesis concerning the diminution of the family's domestic jurisdiction, the fate of paternal authority could be used to draw inferences about legal change. Through his discussion, he advocated for a holistic assessment of paternal authority. Given its roots in an undifferentiated 'power', its later manifestations in classical Roman law as it applied to children, wives and enslaved people could only be understood fully through a holistic perspective.

According to Maine, the paternal authority visible in classical Roman law, although an echo of the undifferentiated 'power' of the 'chieftain' was much more curtailed in scope. It did not apply to public law, in the case of sons in power, for example, and operated mainly in the sphere of private law. This, again, supported his view concerning the origins of the State in the family. As the State developed, the need for domestic jurisdiction diminished. Two aspects of his treatment of this topic are noteworthy. The first concerns the interaction between paternal authority's personal and proprietary elements.[40] Maine observed that while Roman law was quick to develop a mechanism whereby the personal aspects of such authority could be terminated artificially – through emancipation – the mechanisms designed to curtail the proprietary elements of paternal authority were slow to develop by comparison. It should be recalled that from early on in the history of Roman law, the *mancipatio* procedure could be used to remove paternal authority from the son.[41] In a later chapter, Maine returned to this topic to speculate on how broader societal pressures may have aided or hindered emancipation. As will become apparent, he used his discussion of emancipation to caution against the assumption that its purpose remained unchanged over time.

The reasons for curtailing the proprietary aspects of paternal authority over sons particularly interested Maine. Here, he broadly mounted an argument of the type he would later identify explicitly with legal change. Since legal change tends to lag behind social change, the triggers for the Imperial interventions regarding the curtailment of the proprietary aspects of paternal authority had to be sought at an earlier point, namely the absence of sons while on military service and the inconvenience caused concerning property ownership. At the same time, however, he noticed something peculiar. Roman law possessed '[a] remarkable tendency to innovate on ancient usage only just so far as the exigency of the commonwealth may require'.[42] Thus, even though the proprietary aspects of paternal authority had become cumbersome, this did not warrant discarding the entire

39 Ibid. 152.

40 Gibbon and Fernández-Armesto, *The History of the Decline and Fall of the Roman Empire. Vol. 5, Justinian and the Roman Law*, 274.

41 Maine, *Ancient Law*, 140.

42 Ibid. 137.

concept. Instead, through analogy and based on the pre-existing law relating to the *peculium* of the enslaved person, the idea of the 'military *peculium*' was developed to govern the proprietary capacity of sons in power.[43] The second noteworthy aspect of his treatment is his insight concerning the expansion of paternal authority across the Empire. Maine correctly observed that paternal authority could never be 'a durable' institution due to its restrictive nature. Notwithstanding this, he found it peculiar that this notion would be adopted by newly created Roman citizens across the Empire. Here, he advocated that greater attention had to be paid to the effect of the *Constitutio Antoniniana* of 212 CE, which seems to have extended Roman citizenship to all free inhabitants of the Empire. This last point is important and relates to Maine's arguments concerning legal change.[44] Paternal authority was not a 'durable' concept. And yet it acquired a new lease of life in an entirely different context when it became an integral part of Roman citizenship extended to all free inhabitants of the Roman Empire.

5. KINSHIP

The remainder of chapter five is devoted to the changing legal position of women and enslaved people within the Roman family.[45] The treatment of these two groups followed the same pattern and was designed to make broadly the same points concerning legal change. Throughout Maine's discussion of the various aspects of Roman family law, he reiterated that paternal authority was a multifaceted concept that should be viewed holistically to be understood. This also holds true for his treatment of the legal position of women within the Roman family. A brief discussion of kinship precedes the treatment of women's legal position. Due to their connection in Roman law, Maine viewed kinship as functionally equivalent to paternal authority. He explored the nature of Roman kinship through the lens of agnatic and cognatic relationships.[46] The Roman family functioned on agnatic relationships, namely the relation through the male line to the head of the household. Anyone in the family unrelated through the male line was described as standing in a cognate relationship. To Maine, this relationship was indicative of an archaic notion endemic to the family: '[a]s long as the family was an *imperium in imperio* . . . the limitation of relationship to agnates was a necessary security against a conflict of laws in the domestic forum.'[47]

By severing the power of her birth family and incorporating her into her husband's family, there could be no uncertainty as to where the control over her person and property lay. This statement permitted him to branch out into a discussion

[43] Gibbon and Fernández-Armesto, *The History of the Decline and Fall of the Roman Empire. Vol. 5, Justinian and the Roman Law*, 274. Maine, *Ancient Law*, 140.

[44] Maine, *Ancient Law*, 144–5.

[45] Ibid. 147–52.

[46] Ibid. 147–8. For a survey of Maine's position, see Evans, *Theories and Criticisms*, 64–8. For a near contemporaneous discussion, see Mackenzie, *Studies in Roman Law*, 128–30.

[47] Maine, *Ancient Law*, 150. See Bentham, Dumont and Hildreth, *Theory of Legislation*, 255–78.

of the legal position of women within the Roman family.[48] Since women could not create an agnatic relationship at law in respect of their children, they could not be the head of a household under Roman law.[49] As Maine would later show concerning the changes occurring in the law of inheritance, the exclusion of women from the agnatic relationship would, in time, become inconvenient, too. Thus, the Praetors stepped in to adjust the existing law by giving legal prominence to cognatic relationships in inheritance.

The expansion of the rules on inheritance was one of two examples Maine deployed to demonstrate the changing legal position of women in the Roman family. The other example was the fate of guardianship of women.[50] To the student of Roman law, this example would have been familiar.[51] The fate of guardianship of women followed a similar line of development to that visible regarding the *peculium* of sons in power. Whereas the guardianship of women seemed to have been particularly strict in early Roman law, a gradual relaxation is evident over time, to the point where, according to our sources, it became little more than a formality in the Imperial period. In his Institutes, Gaius expresses it as follows:

> Inst.Gai. 1, 190
> Feminas vero perfectae aetatis in tutela esse fere nulla pretiosa ratio suasisse videtur. nam quae vulgo creditur, quia levitate animi plerumque decipiuntur et aequum erat eas tutorum auctoritate regi, magis speciosa videtur quam vera: mulieres enim quae perfectae aetatis sunt, ipsae sibi negotia tractant, et in quibusdam causis dicis gratia tutor interponit auctoritatem suam; saepe etiam invitus auctor fieri a praetore cogitur.
>
> There appears to be no good reason why women should be subject to guardianship once they have reached a certain age. The popular view, namely that they are easily deceived on account of their *levitas animi* and that it is, therefore, fair that they should be subjected to the power of their guardian, is more deceptive than true. Once they have reached a certain age, women manage their affairs independently, and, in some cases, the guardian will impose his authority. Often, the Praetor can force an unwilling person to act as a guardian. [Own translation]

To account for this line of development, Maine linked it to the paternal authority of the head of the household. Thus, in his view, the original motivation for the imposition of female guardianship in early Roman law had to be located there. Wives who married *cum manu* into the Roman family became legally part of their

[48] Psomiades, *Primitive Marriage*, 99–104, for an account of how Maine's comments here may be read against the backdrop of changes to the law of divorce in Victorian England.

[49] Gibbon and Fernández-Armesto, *The History of the Decline and Fall of the Roman Empire. Vol. 5, Justinian and the Roman Law*, 275, state that: 'a fiction of law, neither rational nor elegant, bestowed on the mother of a family (her proper appellation) the strange characters of sister to her own children and of daughter to her husband or master, who was invested with the plenitude of paternal power.' The use of the term 'fiction' is significant.

[50] Maine, *Ancient Law*, 152–4. See Bentham, Dumont and Hildreth, *Theory of Legislation*, 248–52.

[51] Mackenzie, *Studies in Roman Law*, 136–9, for a near contemporaneous account.

husband's family.[52] They were classified as cognates rather than agnates to that family. They were legally dependent and subject to the paternal authority of the head of the household. It was essential to reinforce this paternal authority, given the centrality of the Roman family and agnatic relationships. Thus, in his view, the guardianship of women was 'a peculiar contrivance of archaic jurisprudence' whereby the wife remained linked to her husband's family even after his demise.[53] Maine went as far as to call this an artificial extension of paternal authority.

The next question he had to address was the gradual demise of guardianship over women visible in Roman law. With the growth of marriage *sine manu* from the later Republic onwards, paternal authority was diluted substantially to the point that, under the marriage *sine manu*, the wife no longer fell under the paternal authority of the head of the household into which she had married. As Maine phrased it, this form of marriage was little more than a 'temporary deposit' of the wife into her husband's family.[54] With the change in the marriage regime also came a shift in the law on the perpetual guardianship of women. Gaius provides a summary of this position in the text quoted above. This text gains new significance in Maine's treatment of the issue. In this text, Gaius mentions one 'common' (*vulgo*) justification for the existence of the perpetual guardianship of women. He dismisses it as 'specious' and recounts that the institution had little significance in his day. Maine used this statement as the starting point for his argument. Why did Roman law change at this point? Apart from a more general trend towards the decline of the importance of the family and paternal authority, a new idea took hold in the case of the perpetual guardianship of women. This unique idea, which Maine linked to the Roman concept of natural law, treated men and women equally regarding their capacity to hold and manage their property. Thus, in his view, what is evident in the Gaius text is an attempt by the jurist to engage critically with an older idea linked to paternal authority and the family.[55]

His argument continued further. To anyone familiar with the subsequent history of family law in Europe and elsewhere, it would have been apparent that married women had again become subject to a form of power within the family.[56] However, this time, it was marital rather than paternal power. In the remainder of his treatment of this topic, Maine attempted to account for this development. It is essential to appreciate the purpose of this segue in the argument. One of the overarching themes in *Ancient Law* is that 'progress' in law is not linear nor unidirectional. This was the main point here. Whereas in classical Roman law, the guardianship of women concerning their property transactions had all but disappeared, the subsequent history of legal development in Europe and elsewhere had

52 Amunátegui Perelló, *Origen de los poderes del paterfamilias*, 178–339; Rey, *Manus*, 59–63.
53 Maine, *Ancient Law*, 153.
54 Ibid. 155.
55 Ibid. 154.
56 Ibid. 154–9.

witnessed a regression of their position on this point of law.[57] Maine attributed this development to a combination of factors, namely the interweaving of Roman law and Germanic customary law in the early medieval period, as well as the impact of Christianity.[58] His broader point was clear. Legal change did not follow a straight path from worse to better. Instead, it was a cycle of forward and backward shifts driven by the interplay of older and newer ideas.

This notion of movement is also visible in Maine's discussion of other forms of guardianship in the context of the Roman family. Orphaned sons were placed under guardianship until the end of their fourteenth year.[59] This early termination of guardianship seemed to Maine to stand in stark contrast to the perpetual guardianship of women under Roman law. Viewed in the broader context of the Roman family, however, these two seemingly contradictory shifts could be explained by reflecting on their common origins in paternal authority.[60] Upon reaching this age, orphaned males could become heads of households. This is why guardianship was terminated at this age. Since women could never become heads of households, the matter was handled differently in Roman law. As Maine pointed out, however, the termination of guardianship for orphaned males at a relatively young age did not leave them legally unassisted. Thus, through statutory intervention, the *Lex Laetoria* (or *Plaetoria*), a Roman statute of the mid-Republic, males over fourteen were given adult assistance in commercial transactions until they reached the age of majority in Roman law.

Before moving on from Maine's discussion of the guardianship of women and orphaned males, his use of comparative sources should be highlighted. Since the Roman legal evidence was extensive, he did not need to use comparative material to any great extent. Where it does appear, it is brief, as seen when he observes that he had been 'informed' of an aspect of Hindu law which proved the existence of agnation.[61] Additionally, his references to legal orders of later periods where, for example, a husband's power over a wife had been reinstated, such as the Salian Franks or English law before the nineteenth century, were used solely to make a point about the cyclical nature of legal change. Taken as a whole, his treatment of the position of women in the Roman family and the gradual demise of guardianship is primarily based on Roman law.

6. SLAVERY

Maine's treatment of the Roman family concluded with a discussion of ancient slavery, a highly contentious topic in light of events unfolding in the British Empire

[57] Maine, *The Early History of the Property of Married Women, as Collected from Roman and Hindoo Law; a Lecture, Delivered . . . 1873 . . .*, returned to this discussion in greater detail with a comparison between Roman and Hindu law.

[58] Maine, *Ancient Law*, 157–8.

[59] Gibbon and Fernández-Armesto, *The History of the Decline and Fall of the Roman Empire. Vol. 5, Justinian and the Roman Law*, 280–1.

[60] Maine, *Ancient Law*, 160–2.

[61] Ibid. 262.

and North America during the mid-nineteenth century.[62] He made several significant points about the Roman family and legal change here. His thoughts on this matter are complex and linked to his broader critique of the linear progression of law from worse to better. Additionally, Maine raised questions about the relationship between law and morality and whether one can infer insights regarding the latter from the former.

His starting point, most likely supported by the definition of the Roman family provided at the beginning of this chapter, was that enslaved people formed part of the family in the earliest history of ancient law. Given that the patriarchal chieftain's power over his family members was not yet differentiated, an enslaved person would have been subjected to the same undifferentiated power as the other family members. In time, not only because of the nature but also the prevalence of slavery in ancient law, attempts were made to justify this practice intellectually. Maine's two preferred legal orders from antiquity, Greece and Rome, provided ample evidence. Thus, in *Politics*, Aristotle[63] included an extensive 'justification' for slavery, while in Roman legal sources, speculative etymology was used to make a similar point:

> D. 1, 5, 4, 1 Flor. 9 inst.
> Servitus est constitutio iuris gentium, qua quis dominio alieno contra naturam subicitur.
>
> Slavery is an institution of the *ius gentium* whereby someone is subject to the ownership of another contrary to nature. [Own translation]
>
> D. 50, 16, 239, 1 Pomp. l. s. enchirid.
> 'Servorum' appellatio ex eo fluxit, quod imperatores nostri captivos vendere ac per hoc servare nec occidere solent.
>
> The term 'slaves' originates from the practice whereby our emperors sell captives, thus 'saving' them from being killed. [Own translation]
>
> I. 1, 3, 3
> Servi autem ex eo appellati sunt, quod imperatores captivos vendere iubent ac per hoc servare nec occidere solent. qui etiam mancipia dicti sunt, quod ab hostibus manu capiuntur.
>
> 'Slaves' are called thus because emperors order captives to be sold, thereby preventing them from being killed. They are also called *mancipia* since they are captured by hand (*manus*) from the enemy. [Own translation]

62 Ibid. 162–3; Rosen, 'Jeremy Bentham on Slavery and the Slave Trade'; Carter, 'The Abolition of Slavery in the United States'; Finkelman, 'Slavery in the United States', for a survey.

63 Ahmad, 'Aristotle's Natural Theory of the Origin of the State', 3; Smith, 'Aristotle's Theory of Natural Slavery', 110; Deslauriers et al., 'Natural Slavery'; Honoré, 'The Nature of Slavery'; Helmholz, 'The Law of Slavery and the European *Ius Commune*', for a survey.

Maine was sceptical of the intellectual implications of these statements. He viewed them as creating an 'imaginary principle', introduced by both the Greek and Roman authors, to justify the existence and extent of slavery in their legal systems.[64] This was only part of the problem with justifications of this kind. As he phrased it: 'what they do is they soothe the conscience of the master and probably also lead to the debasement of the slave.'[65] This was the essence of his criticism and provided a digression into Maine's second point about ancient slavery. Given the controversies surrounding slavery in the British Empire and North America when Maine was researching *Ancient Law*, it stands to reason that these aspects also filtered into his narrative. More specifically, he was concerned about the use of these Graeco-Roman 'justifications' by supporters of slavery in North America to advocate the continued existence of the practice. Contemporaneous examples of this may be seen in the works of Thomas Cobb, published in 1858, in which an argument was made explicitly that slavery in North America was 'patriarchal' and that the enslaved person was, therefore, in a 'better' position than the free labourer because of it.[66] Maine was emphatic that the connection between the enslaved person and the family in ancient law could not be used to justify slavery in nineteenth-century North America. More specifically, its use as an 'admission of moral defensibility' of slavery in nineteenth-century America had to be explicitly called out.[67] This statement connects to a more significant theme in *Ancient Law*: morality is contingent. Just because enslaved people were legally considered part of a family in the earliest stages of Roman law did not mean that any conclusions could be drawn about their treatment.

Maine's final comments on slavery are brief but tie into a central theme of the book overall. The observant reader of the Roman legal texts providing 'justification' for slavery will have noted the appearance of the term *ius gentium*. In Maine's view, although this did not 'justify' the institution of slavery, it did impact how the Roman jurists viewed slavery and the legal status of the enslaved person, namely as existing legally in the liminal space between the law of persons and property. This point of view had to be contrasted to the position of English common law, in which duality was not recognised, and enslaved people were viewed as property.[68] The statement allowed Maine to draw a more generalised conclusion. Even though legal systems of the nineteenth century in which slavery was still prevalent rarely contained vestiges of slavery in ancient law, their approach to slavery was nonetheless different. Thus, Maine observed that the treatment of enslaved people tended to differ in those legal systems based on written (Roman) law from those based on unwritten law. This would later become known as the much-debated Tannenbaum thesis regarding the distinction between slave systems based on written law and

64 Maine, *Ancient Law*, 162–3. See Bentham, Dumont and Hildreth, *Theory of Legislation*, 238–47.

65 Maine, *Ancient Law*, 162–3.

66 Cobb, *An Inquiry into the Law of Negro Slavery in the United States of America*, ccxvii–ccxviii.

67 Maine, *Ancient Law*, 163–4.

68 Ibid. 166.

unwritten law.[69] It is crucial to appreciate that Maine's point here was solely about difference, and no doubt also tied into his statement concerning the value of written over unwritten law.[70]

7. THE PATRIARCHY CONTROVERSY

Maine's comments about patriarchy and the controversy that followed the publication of *Ancient Law* are well documented.[71] It centred around several of his statements concerning the role of patriarchy in the earliest history of the development of the State and the law.[72] Before exploring this controversy's details, identifying its role in Maine's narrative is vital. The bulk of *Ancient Law* is devoted to the family's decline and the individual's rise, as reflected in Roman law. Since the Roman family was a particular type of family grounded in paternal authority, a way had to be found to 'prove' the antiquity and ubiquity of this type of family across the systems he chose to focus on. After providing several examples, Maine's conclusion was summarised through a rather emphatic statement: 'the primeval condition of the human race is . . . the Patriarchal theory.'[73] It is not difficult to see why this statement became a lightning rod for criticism.[74] It reads very broadly, and probably deliberately so. There is, however, more to this statement than first meets the eye. As mentioned above, Maine was less interested in the origins of the State than the law. His comments about State formation are sparse and distinguish between two epochs: before and after the State's formation. Given his labelling of the head of the household during the first epoch as a 'patriarchal chieftain' who governed the family 'despotically', this is likely the context in which the statement above should be read. To construct his proof, Maine resorted to two types of evidence. The first and oldest were biblical descriptions of the families of the 'Hebrew patriarchs' in the Old Testament. Of these, none is perhaps more telling than his observation that '[t]he families of Jacob and Esau separate and form two nations'.[75]

One aspect of this use of a biblical narrative that deserves specific comment is the reason for its deployment. He used biblical references throughout *Ancient*

69 Watson, *Slave Law in the Americas*, xiii.

70 Cairns, 'Slavery without a Code Noir', for a survey of this debate.

71 Kuper, 'Ancestors', 274–6; Capogrossi Colognesi, *Modelli di stato e di famiglia nella storiografia dell'800*, 247–78; Evans-Pritchard, *A History of Anthropological Thought; Edited by André Singer; with an Introduction by Ernest Gellner*, 82–90; Kuper, 'The Rise and Fall of Maine's Patriarchal Society', 104–5. For a more general discussion of patriarchy in Victorian society, see Howarth, 'Gender, Domesticity, and Sexual Politics', 189–90. See also Pollock and Maine, *Introduction and Notes*, 27–34; Nelson, *An Analysis*, 92–5.

72 Smellie, 'Sir Henry Maine', 79. For criticism of Maine's extrapolation of the patriarchal theory to Hindu law, see Derrett, *Sir Henry Maine and Law in India, 1858-1958*, 51–2. Kuper, 'The Rise and Fall of Maine's Patriarchal Society', 105–10.

73 Maine, *Ancient Law*, 122. See also Smellie, 'Sir Henry Maine', 68.

74 Pollock and Maine, *Introduction and Notes*, 27–8.

75 Maine, *Ancient Law*, 124.

Law to make particular points, usually in the context of his critique of post-revolutionary French philosophy. In his discussion of the recent history of natural law, Maine pointed out that those scholars writing in the aftermath of the French Revolution of 1789 tended to dismiss biblical sources due to their association with the Church and the power structures of the *Ancien Régime*. The aversion to using historical information from biblical sources to Maine indicated a broader malaise affecting natural law scholarship: its lack of grounding in concrete evidence. This is no doubt why he insisted on using biblical sources here. To Maine, in this respect, the bible provided historical proof.

The second type of evidence was comparative and demonstrates one of the underlying problems of Maine's method. In his view, there was ample evidence from Roman law, Hindu law and the laws of the 'Sclavonians' to support his assertion about the ubiquity of the patriarchal theory. He did not see the need to bolster this statement with any references, but there are indications that he was concerned about the potential scope of his claim.[76] He noted that the comparative examples he could trace were all limited to the Indo-European family of nations, suggesting that the patriarchal theory might not apply to nations that did not form part of this group. This misgiving does not appear to have concerned our author too much. Undeterred, he made the case for the Patriarchal theory based on biblical evidence. There is an interesting digression in Maine's argument here. He refers, in passing, to a debate between John Locke and Robert Filmer concerning the divine right of kings. Although, as Maine himself observed, it was a 'not very profitable' debate, it is worth pointing out that Filmer's argument relied to a great extent on the assumption that the divine right of kings was derived from Adam's dominion of the earth and that a king, as a descendant of Adam, ruled over his subjects like a father over his family.[77] Although this is merely a passing reference, it demonstrates that Maine used the biblical evidence tactically.

Twenty-two years later, towards the end of his life, Maine returned to the Patriarchy theory in his *Dissertations on Early Law and Custom*. In one chapter, entitled 'Theories of Primitive Society', he defended his position in *Ancient Law* against the attacks subsequently levelled against it by various authors, including John Ferguson McLennan[78] (1827–1881) and Lewis Henry Morgan (1818–1881). Those criticisms boiled down to one essential issue. Critics of Maine's theory argued that one could come to different conclusions by examining the same source material. Thus, they were unconvinced that the family, presided over by a Patriarchal chieftain, was the earliest unit of society. In this context, various alternatives were proposed. These included the 'horde' as the origin of society

[76] Ibid. 123.

[77] Becker, 'A Preliminary Comparison of the Political Thought of Locke and Filmer'; Parker, 'A Critical Analysis of Filmer's and Locke's Use of Genesis in the Development of Their Political Philosophies'; Harris, 'Treatises of Government and Treatises of Anarchy'; Harris, 'Of the Origin of Government', for a survey.

[78] Evans-Pritchard, *A History of Anthropological Thought; Edited by André Singer; with an Introduction by Ernest Gellner*, 61–8.

and the role of matriarchy as a stage in the growth of society.[79] The defence of his earlier position demonstrates several interesting points. First, it is clear from his statements that the two camps in this debate were speaking at cross purposes. Those who supported the 'horde' as the origins of society, or matriarchy as a phase in its development, adopted a stadial approach. On the other hand, Maine was at pains to stress that this was not what he had meant.

> It was not part of my object to determine the absolute origin of human society. I have written very few pages which have any bearing on the subject, and I must confess a certain distaste for inquiries which, when I have attempted to push them far, have always landed me in mudbanks and fog.[80]

Maine's position here is emphatic. He never intended to claim that the family was the absolute origin of all societies. Rather, his claim in *Ancient Law* was that it was an early, historically grounded phenomenon, described by Greek philosophers through observation and corroborated by earlier biblical evidence.[81] It also seemed prevalent among the Indo-European legal orders, especially in Roman law. This was the totality of his claim. It cannot go unnoticed, too, that in the quotation above, Maine criticised the methods of those wishing to investigate the origins of society. He would later return to this criticism when discussing Darwin's work.

In addition to defending the Patriarchal theory, Maine made several insightful comments regarding the aim of his work in this later rebuttal. First, he noted plainly that *Ancient Law* had been inspired by Niebuhr's discovery of the Gaius palimpsest. This discovery permitted Maine to appreciate that law is made up of different layers of ideas, much like the geological layers of the earth. This geological image resonated throughout *Ancient Law*. In addition, an appreciation of the layering of ideas permitted Maine to harness material from Roman law. Thus, he argued that paternal authority in Roman law echoed a much earlier idea. What Gaius described in his work was a version of this earlier idea. His second and perhaps most profound insight concerned the attempts by scholars, especially those influenced by anthropological methods, to identify a stock 'primitive society' through observation. In Maine's description of the distant past, in which isolated families dominated, he used the *Cyclopes* as an example. His later comments in *Dissertations on Early Law and Custom* explain this choice: '[n]o community, when first seen by the historian, can be certainly said to occupy its original seat.'[82]

The significance of this statement is clear. Maine did not believe it was possible to identify the very starting point of any State, not only those in the past

[79] Pollock and Maine, *Introduction and Notes*, 27–8, for a summary. See also Kuper, 'Ancestors', 279–85; Göttner-Abendroth, *Matriarchal Societies*, 1–42, for a survey of the historiography of the matriarchy controversy.

[80] Maine, *Dissertations on Early Law and Custom*, 192.

[81] Ibid. 193–4, 196–7.

[82] Ibid. 212.

but also those in the present. It is impossible to return to any society's very beginning. For this reason, any stadial account of the development of society, such as those preferred by MacLennan and Morgan, was doomed to fail.[83] There is more to Maine's use of *Cyclopes* as his example, though.[84] The reader may ask why he relied on a mythical example from Graeco-Roman antiquity rather than a 'living' contemporaneous example. European literature from the early modern period onwards did not lack examples from explorers' accounts. Herein lies the issue. Maine did not believe in stadial accounts of 'civilisation'. Thus, classifying contemporaneous people as falling at the 'primitive' end of the spectrum of 'progress' never features in *Ancient Law*.[85] It also explains why 'progressive', as a term, should not be considered classificatory. Maine demonstrated this point most clearly as follows:

> It appears to me that, while the Patriarchal theory and the counter-theory of which I have been speaking each explain reasonably well a certain number of ancient social phenomena, both are open to considerable objection as universal theories of the genesis of society.[86]

With the benefit of hindsight offered by the twenty-two years since the publication of *Ancient Law*, Maine took the opportunity to explain how his efforts there related to those of Charles Darwin. This insightful passage shows that their seemingly similar endeavours were quite different.[87] In *Ancient Law*, Maine had pondered why families dominated in the earliest history of State formation. He had left the matter open and speculated that information from other branches of science would be needed to answer this question satisfactorily. This is where Darwin proved helpful. According to Maine, Darwin's account in his *The Descent of Man* supported his notion of the family as the earliest unit of society. Not satisfied with this level of support, he also used it to criticise the alternative options raised by McLennan and Morgan.[88]

Towards the end of this chapter, Maine distilled the importance of accepting the family as the earliest unit of society into two specific points. These points reverberate throughout *Ancient Law* and are therefore worth noting. First, the family is a structure based on power, possibly physical power in its earliest form.[89] This insight feeds into several features of the family, including agnation and the legal position of women. If, as Maine surmised, the family is the base unit of the State, then an understanding of the power at its core could also shed light on

83 Ibid. 201.
84 Ibid. 198.
85 Bock, 'Comparison of Histories', 246–9; Geroulanos, *The Invention of Prehistory*, 63–72.
86 Maine, *Dissertations on Early Law and Custom*, 203–4.
87 Maine, 206–7; Kuper, 'Civilization, Culture, and Race', 418; Capogrossi Colognesi, *Dalla storia di Roma alle origini della società civile*, 203–32; Capogrossi Colognesi, *Modelli di stato e di famiglia nella storiografia dell'800*, 99–140.
88 Maine, *Dissertations on Early Law and Custom*, 206–13.
89 Ibid. 215–17.

conceptions of power, such as sovereignty, at more elevated levels of the State. Second, given the ubiquity of the family as a base unit in the legal orders he chose to investigate in *Ancient Law*, it should be evident that the organic changes experienced by the family (as well as the law) could be a fruitful area of study.[90] His investigation in *Ancient Law* demonstrated that legal change did not follow a stadial or 'progressive' path. It happened, as Maine put it, in 'infinite variations'.

8. CONCLUSIONS

The family and its role in the development of the law was the crux of Maine's work. It stands to reason, therefore, that it would be examined in some detail. As this chapter has shown, while Roman law provided much evidence supporting Maine's broader thesis, it was limited by the lack of evidence for the more distant past. It had to be augmented with comparative material to make such claims. Maine's choices in this regard reflect his focus in the book. As is evident from his treatment of the earliest phases of law using the information from Grote, he was not particularly interested in trying to construct the earliest history of law. It would seem that he was aware of the intellectual dangers inherent in such an endeavour. As such, he limited his analysis to the period in which he had the most evidence in Roman law. This analysis contains a wealth of insights. At its core, Maine demonstrated a cycle of legal change. At the same time, he was careful to point out that this cycle should not be seen as a linear line of 'progress' in Victorian terms. Instead, as subsequent European family law developments showed, legal change oscillated between positions. To understand the motivations for these, one had to focus on the instrumentalities of legal change.

[90] Ibid. 219–21.

Chapter 5

Freedom of Testation and the Family

> The personal title of the first proprietor must be determined by his death; but the possession, without any appearance of change, is peaceably continued in his children, the associates of his toil, and partners of his wealth.[1]

1. INTRODUCTION

Succession was essential to Maine's overall thesis concerning ancient law since, as a branch of law, it governed the intergenerational transmission of assets. Notably, it is the first area of law discussed by Maine after his account of the legal significance of the family. It served an essential function in this context since it underpinned his claim about its 'corporate' nature. Given its prominence, it merited extensive treatment across two chapters. When the content of these two chapters (six and seven) is compared, it is evident that they were written to support a broader set of themes operative throughout the book. To what extent Maine expected his audience to draw parallels with contemporaneous changes to the English law of succession is challenging to ascertain, given that the Wills Act of 1837, which introduced various changes to the English law of succession, had already been embedded as law when Maine was researching the book. Still, the general trend in the English law of succession during the nineteenth century was one of legal change benefitting wives and children, often at the expense of the Victorian head of the household. Parallels could be drawn easily.[2] In rhetorical terms, this resembles a *praeteritio* – an allusion to a topic without mentioning it directly.

Both chapters focus on Roman law, although the final part of chapter seven also considers the origins of primogeniture in subsequent epochs of legal development. This is not an artificial digression but flows naturally from a discussion about disinheritance in Roman law in the first part of the chapter. To appreciate Maine's broader arguments in these two chapters, it must be reiterated that each chapter of *Ancient Law* was placed in a specific order to construct a narrative arc within the book. The chapters on succession represent the start of this arc, which concludes with the chapter on delict and crime at the end of the book. The purpose of the narrative arc was to demonstrate how, in Roman law, his chosen

[1] Gibbon and Fernández-Armesto, *The History of the Decline and Fall of the Roman Empire. Vol. 5, Justinian and the Roman Law*, 283.

[2] Cornish et al., *Law and Society in England, 1750–1950*, 350–1; Lovelass, *The Law's Disposal of a Person's Estate Who Dies without Will or Testament*, 127–62.

example of a 'progressive' system, the State and law developed out of and around the family. As the State develops and the individual is afforded more rights, the legal significance of the family diminishes accordingly. In addition, Maine aimed to show how the law developed through specific instrumentalities and in response to social change. The arc was not meant to represent a linear line of unidirectional 'progress'. *Ancient Law*, in its entirety, is a critique of this very idea. Instead, the arc represented a cycle of legal change.

Each chapter in *Ancient Law* consists of one or two large claims, supported by comparative evidence, alongside several minor claims, often merely mentioned in passing. Maine's primary claim in chapter six is that superficial comparisons between past and present areas of law, even if these appear substantively related doctrinally to contemporary scholars, are intellectually vacuous and should be avoided.[3] The central claim of chapter seven is connected to this prior claim in chapter six. Even if aspects of law in the past and the present are shown to be intellectually related, one cannot assume that their contours or functions have been or will remain identical or broadly similar without investigating their respective historical contexts. It is to these two significant claims, together with their various minor claims, that we now turn.

2. SUPERFICIAL SIMILARITIES

Maine chose succession as the focus of these two chapters primarily because it was a topic likely to capture the attention of his audience, who were familiar with nineteenth-century English law. The testament in nineteenth-century English law had civilian roots through the influence of medieval canon law.[4] Thus, it could be used as an example to demonstrate the value of Historical Jurisprudence as a method and to caution against the dangers of superficial comparisons between past and present law. Maine's critique focused on two issues: the role of the testament in the law of succession more generally and the historicity of its form and content as reflected in nineteenth-century English law.[5] In true Humanist style, he does not state these aims explicitly, but the implication is clear. In classical Roman law and beyond, the testament played a significant role.[6] The Roman jurists discussed it in detail, especially the making of the testament and the form in which its provisions had to be worded. It would be easy to deduce from the available Roman legal texts that the testament was the most crucial aspect of the Roman law of succession at all times in its history. As Maine argues in this chapter, it cannot be assumed that the testament, and thus also testate succession, was at the core of the law of succession at all times in the past. In addition, those features of the testament so familiar to his audience based on their knowledge of nineteenth-century English law, – namely, a) that the provisions of the

3 Maine, *Ancient Law*, 189; Bentham, Dumont and Hildreth, *Theory of Legislation*, 211–22.
4 Ibid. 171–3.
5 Ibid. 174.
6 Rüfner, 'Testamentary Formalities in Roman Law', for a survey of the Roman law.

testament were secret, b) that the testament was revocable until the death of the testator and c) that its provisions only took effect upon their death – were by no means immanent. Such a superficial comparison, Maine argued, was intellectually unfounded, especially since the features on which this comparison was based could not be said to have existed in all periods in the history of the testament in Roman law. He phrased it as follows:

> Testaments very slowly and gradually gathered round them the qualities I have mentioned; and they did this from causes and under pressure of events which may be called causal, or which at any rate have no interest for us at the present, except so far as they have affected the history of law.[7]

This quotation, which also reflects Maine's approach to causation and legal change (a matter discussed elsewhere), cuts to the heart of the issue. Superficial comparisons between past and present law create illusions of similarity, undermining legal history's dynamic and contingent nature. This critique was likely aimed also at contemporaneous textbooks on Roman law in the Pandectist tradition, which placed significant emphasis on the testament.[8]

Having established this central claim, Maine advocated for the adoption of a broader perspective. Focusing on the Roman testament and its features at a single point in its historical development was intellectually questionable since testaments developed these features over time. Historical context was important. Testaments were only a tiny part of a much larger topic. More fundamentally, the origins of the testator's right to dictate the intergenerational transfer of assets had to be examined. This was the early notion at the heart of the law of succession. This exciting aspect of Maine's narrative demonstrates his engagement with Roman law and the broader civilian tradition. Whether the testator's right was grounded in natural law was a much-discussed topic in European legal scholarship of the early modern period and beyond. It is raised in, for example, Gibbon and Blackstone, where references to the views of civilian jurists such as Pufendorf and Barbeyrac may be found.[9] It cannot be determined definitively which of these two works inspired Maine here. Given that he took extensive inspiration from Gibbon on many points, it is the likely source.

Gibbon observed that '[t]he principle of hereditary succession is universal; but the order has been variously established by convenience or caprice'.[10] This quotation demonstrates the issue's complexity, namely whether the law of succession

[7] Maine, *Ancient Law*, 174.

[8] Mackeldey and Dropsie, *Handbook of the Roman Law . . . Translated and Edited by M.A. Dropsie from the Fourteenth German Edition*, 489–90, provides a good example.

[9] Gibbon and Fernández-Armesto, *The History of the Decline and Fall of the Roman Empire. Vol. 5, Justinian and the Roman Law*, 283–7; Blackstone, *Commentaries*, II.32 (330–51).

[10] Gibbon and Fernández-Armesto, *The History of the Decline and Fall of the Roman Empire. Vol. 5, Justinian and the Roman Law*, 283. See also Taylor, *Elements of the Civil Law*, 519–20, a popular eighteenth-century textbook on Roman law where the matter is discussed in detail with extensive references to sources.

was a creation of State or natural law. This controversy lay at the heart of these two chapters.[11] Maine used this debate to critique earlier natural law scholarship. He pointed out two intellectual flaws in the natural law position with his usual sharp focus. These flaws related to the two meanings afforded to the term 'natural law' in these discussions, namely that it denoted either a universal or a primordial practice. First, if 'natural law' meant a 'universal' practice in this context, subsequent statutory interventions, such as those in the Napoleonic Code enacted at the start of the nineteenth century, undermined this interpretation.[12] The Napoleonic Code was widely proclaimed as a code inspired by natural law. Since the law of succession was subjected to extensive and specific regulation within this code, the succession principle could not be described as 'universal' in this sense. Second, the claim that the intergenerational transfer of assets using a testament was primordial could not be sustained either since, as Maine showed in this chapter, it was not permitted in all periods of history. This latter point was a core element of Maine's broader thesis throughout this chapter and deserves detailed scrutiny.

To Maine, a narrow focus on the law of succession, specifically testate succession, was the wrong starting point. Instead, as he argued, the focus should be on universal succession – a broader concept.[13] This would have been familiar to many in his audience who knew Roman law since it is featured prominently there. In the Institutes of Gaius, the following statement occurs:

> Inst.Gai. 2, 97
> Hactenus tantisper admonuisse sufficit, quemadmodum singulae res nobis adquirantur: nam legatorum ius, quo et ipso singulas res adquirimus, opportunius alio loco referemus. videamus itaque nunc, quibus modis per universitatem res nobis adquirantur.
>
> How individual objects are acquired in ownership has been dealt with sufficiently. The right of legacies, through which we obtain ownership of particular objects, will be discussed elsewhere. Let us now turn to the different ways in which we acquire ownership of property collectively. [Own translation]

This is a transition passage in the Institutes where Gaius segues from his treatment of the law of property into a discussion of the law of succession. He begins this section by discussing the larger concept of succession *per universitatem*, before addressing intestate and testate succession in detail. Universal succession in Roman law referred to the notion that one person could acquire the totality of another's rights and duties, of which inheritance was one example (and adoption another). This idea was necessary for Maine's broader thesis in *Ancient Law*. Since, in classical Roman law, the link between universal succession and the person of the acquirer (the heir) was well developed, it permitted him to make two further

[11] Maine, *Ancient Law*, 175–6.
[12] Savigny and Hayward, *Of the Vocation of Our Age for Legislation and Jurisprudence, Translated from the German . . . by A. Hayward*, 70–99, for a critical account of the merits and demerits of this code.
[13] Maine, *Ancient Law*, 179–86. See also Austin, *Province*, xlii–xliv.

claims. First, universal succession through inheritance permitted the acquirer to assume the legal personality of the deceased.[14] As he phrased it, the acquirer was 'instantly clothed with his entire legal person'.[15] Second, the acquirer does not need to be a single person but could be several individuals designated 'co-heirs'. These two claims allowed Maine to build an argument based on the history of the Roman law of succession that supported his broader thesis about the importance of the 'corporate' family in ancient law.[16]

3. THE IMPORTANCE OF HISTORICAL CONTEXT

The two standard textbooks on Roman law from antiquity, the Institutes of Gaius and of Justinian, discuss testate and intestate succession extensively. Gaius devotes a few paragraphs to the historical origins of the Roman testament, but there is little historical context on this matter provided in the Institutes of Justinian. Thus, Niebuhr's discovery of Gaius' palimpsest provided much-needed historical context to Maine. It will be recalled that Maine opposed the treatment of the Roman testament in its developed form as either a universal or primordial feature of the law of succession. To counteract this poor use of history visible in natural law scholarship, he advocated for a greater awareness of the earliest history of the Roman position.

Maine's central premise in *Ancient Law* is that the family rather than the individual predominated in ancient law.[17] At its core, the family, united through actual or purported blood relationships (established through adoption), had a corporate nature – it continued to exist irrespective of the demise of individual family members. Maine's inspiration for this idea was likely Plato's discussion of this matter in *The Laws*.[18] The family's assets were held in common, and an individual was elected to care for them (the *paterfamilias* in the Roman context). In this act of transferring control of the family's assets from one representative to the next upon death, Maine found the origins of the law of succession. He phrased it as follows:

> It seems, in truth, that the prolongation of a man's legal existence in his heir, or in a group of co-heirs, is neither more nor less than a characteristic of the family transferred by a fiction to the individual. Succession in corporations is necessarily universal, and the family was a corporation. Corporations never die.[19]

[14] Maine, *Ancient Law*, 184–6.

[15] Ibid. 181.

[16] Ibid. 188–90.

[17] Savigny, *System of the Modern Roman Law, Translated from the German . . . by W. Holloway. Vol. I*, 317, for a similar view. For contemporary criticisms of this view, see Cornell, *The Beginnings of Rome*, 284–6.

[18] Taylor, *Elements of the Civil Law*, 522–3. Comte, *Positive Philosophy*, II.132 also treats the family as the base unit of society.

[19] Maine, *Ancient Law*, 186.

The term 'fiction' here is telling and feeds into Maine's more extensive point regarding the instrumentalities of legal change. As will be recalled, legal fictions were one mechanism of legal change designed to give the appearance of continuity of an existing situation while masking a change. This supported Maine's point regarding the corporate family. The family continued to exist even though its headship may have changed.

Having laid the groundwork, Maine proceeded to discuss intestate succession. His motivation for doing so was twofold. First, he viewed intestate succession as the older of the two notions. Even though he does not discuss the individual legal rules as they existed at specific points in the history of Roman law in detail, he found sufficient evidence to substantiate his view that the overarching purpose of these rules was to facilitate the continued existence of the corporate family and its assets upon the death of its chosen caretaker (the *paterfamilias* in the Roman context).[20] The second motivation for doing so concerns a specific aspect of the early Roman succession law. In the Roman law of the Republic, the heir was also liable for maintaining the *sacra* of the family. This term referred to religious rites that had to be performed to honour the ancestors and were legally associated with the inheritance. The Roman law on this issue, mainly known from disparate comments by Cicero, was undoubtedly known to Maine as a classicist. He mentions Cicero by name, although he does not provide a pinpoint reference. As those familiar with the classics would have known, Cicero discussed the *sacra* extensively in *De Legibus*.[21] When viewed in its entirety, the development of the Roman law on the *sacra* demonstrated a particular issue beneficial to Maine's broader narrative. The origins of the heir's obligations to maintain the *sacra* are unclear, but it is generally viewed as being of considerable antiquity. While the obligation to maintain the *sacra* was unproblematic when the heir had inherited the bulk of the estate, it became financially burdensome when much of the estate had been divested through legacies.[22] By the second half of the Republic, this obligation was becoming onerous. Legal reforms were introduced to assign the responsibility for maintaining the *sacra* to the person who had inherited the largest share of the estate. It seems to have fallen into desuetude after that.

Appreciating the *sacra*'s role in Maine's broader thesis is essential.[23] At the start of *Ancient Law*, Maine posited that 'progressive' legal systems tended to begin to separate law from religion early, usually once the law had been reduced to writing. This was a continuous process. To our author, the eventual fate of the *sacra* in the Roman law of succession from the mid-to-late Republic provided evidence. It had served its purpose and had become an inconvenience. Maine's use of the *sacra* as an example also had a broader function. It helped to substantiate one of his comparative observations concerning the relationship between law and

[20] Ibid. 191.

[21] Harries, 'The Law in Cicero's Writings', 114; Macrae, '"The Laws of the Rites and the Priests"'; Beltrão, '*Sacra Privata Perpetua Manento*. A Reading of Cicero's *De Legibus*', generally.

[22] Ortolan, *Explication historique des Instituts de l'empereur Justinien*, 318–19 (note 4).

[23] Ibid. 34–7, for a discussion of the connection between the *sacra* and the *gens*.

religion. To explain this point, he referred here to Hindu law. To our author, Hindu law was a 'progressive' legal system according to his definition. When compared to his chosen system, Roman law, Hindu law's position concerning religious rites as an aspect of the law of inheritance could be used to draw various parallels.[24] In this instance, its failure to achieve a separation between law and religion, as in Roman law, had problematic consequences:

> Among the Hindoos, the religious element in law has acquired a complete predominance. Family sacrifices have become the keystone of all the Law of Persons and much of the Law of Things. They have even received a monstrous extension, for it is a plausible opinion that the self-immolation of the widow at her husband's funeral, a practice commemorated in the traditions of several Indo-European races, was an addition grafted on the primitive *sacra*, under the influence of the impression, which always accompanies the idea of sacrifice, that human blood is the most precious of all oblations.[25]

It cannot be determined from this quotation where Maine obtained his information regarding *Sati* (widow immolation). It is mentioned in Elphinstone's book on the history of India, a work he used to make various points about Hindu law.[26] By the time Maine was researching *Ancient Law*, there were already several English-language works on Hindu law in which the matter had been discussed. It was also an issue that provoked public opinion in Britain in the first part of the nineteenth century.[27] Although the British colonial government had already banned this practice in some regions by the time Maine was researching *Ancient Law*, it persisted in others.[28] It would have been a relevant matter familiar to many in his audience. Appreciating the specific point of criticism our author raises here is essential. He is not critical of the *sacra* as a practice or the content of Hindu law. His point is that failing to separate law from religion has long-term negative consequences. These are twofold. First, it permitted the rise of a religious elite that dominated the interpretation of the law. Second, this situation resulted in the creation and adoption of religious practices, such as *Sati*, by analogy. Again, it is a point about historical contingency. The *sacra* had a place in the history of Roman law, but it was not maintained artificially once it had become a burdensome formality.

Maine's segue into Hindu law here permitted him to return to the central thrust of this chapter, namely the role of the testament in the law of succession.[29] Having made the case that intestate succession was likely older than testate

24 Maine, *Ancient Law*, 197.

25 Ibid. 192–3. When discussing the *sacra* in Hindu law, Maine quotes a passage he attributes to the 'Hindoo Doctor'. It is unclear who he is referring to. See Macnaghten, *Considerations*, 135, where the same passage is discussed verbatim in the context of the Code of Manu.

26 Elphinstone, *The History of India*, 357–8.

27 Grimshawe, *An Earnest Appeal to British Humanity in Behalf of Hindoo Widows*, generally.

28 Strange, *Elements of Hindu Law*, I.238.

29 Derrett, *Sir Henry Maine and Law in India, 1858–1958*, 52–3, for criticisms of Maine's extrapolation of the discussion of testaments to Hindu law.

succession on account of its role in the transfer of assets of the corporate family, he now had to account for the rise of the testament and its eventual dominance. To understand Maine's point here, contemporary readers should take account of the historiography of the study of Roman law in the early modern period.[30] There, the importance of testate succession had been emphasised over intestate succession because of its association with the individual's will. An excellent example of this position is the Dutch jurist Hugo Grotius's (1583–1645) *De Iure Belli ac Pacis*, where he describes intestate succession as: 'having its natural origin in the conjecture of the will of the last possessor'.[31] The implication is clear. Testate succession was the default, expressing the testator's will, whereas intestate succession was an intellectual extension through 'conjecture'. This position led to a debate, prominent in the scholarship of the early modern period and beyond, concerning the philosophical roots of testate as well as intestate succession and their connection to natural law, as can be seen in the work of, for example, Johann Gottlieb Heineccius (1681–1741), one of the most celebrated German jurists of the early eighteenth century.[32] Maine alluded to this debate as an example of the poor use of history. As he phrased it: 'we must be careful not to attribute to it [the testament] in its earliest shape the functions which have attended it in more recent times.'[33]

This appeal for greater awareness of the testament's historical origins allowed him to state his case. If, as Maine had argued, the original purpose of succession was to allow for the intergenerational transfer of assets of the corporate family through the rules of intestate succession, then the origins of the testament and its increased use must be linked to this in some way. Furthermore, this change had to be explained in terms of 'causal' factors.

How Maine constructed this link is interesting as it reflects his method. Two legal systems (Roman and Hindu law) provided the information he needed for his narrative. At the same time, several others (Athenian law, the law of Bengal and the 'vulgar' Roman law of the Germanic tribes) were used to support his claims within the Indo-European family of legal systems.[34] In keeping with his approach to 'early jural conceptions', these comparators could be used to speculate more generally about the earlier and later manifestations of the testament and of testate succession in general. As for the two primary examples, it is crucial to appreciate Maine's method. Both Hindu law and Roman law had a role to play here. When the insights from these two legal systems were combined, they provided Maine with evidence that the original function of the testament in his archetypal system, Roman law, was quite different from its role in modern times. Not only was its role different, but the testament itself had to be viewed as part of a series of strategies,

30 Maine, *Ancient Law*, 195.

31 Grotius, *Grotius on the Rights of War and Peace*, 112.

32 Heineccius, *A Methodical System of Universal Law*, 220–2.

33 Maine, *Ancient Law*, 194.

34 Ibid. 196–7. Heineccius, *A Methodical System of Universal Law*, 221, also refers to ancient Greece and Tacitus's description of the Germans.

the oldest of which was adoption, deployed to ensure the continuation of the family and its assets. According to Maine, Hindu law provided more expansive evidence of the earlier position than Roman law.

The prevailing opinion among English jurists of the nineteenth century was that Hindu law did not have the institution of a testament:

> It is admitted that the idea of a will is wholly unknown to Hindu law, and that the native languages do not even possess a word to express the idea. In early times, when the family property was vested in the family corporation, and when the members had nothing more than a right of usufruct, the idea that any individual could exercise a power of disposal to commence after his own death, would have been a contradiction in terms.[35]

The absence of a testament in Hindu law was helpful to Maine's narrative since it supported his notion of the corporate family whose assets were transferred intergenerationally. It could thus be used to conjecture what the position may have been in archaic Roman law. The comparison was not exact, however. Unlike Roman law, not all members of this intergenerational corporate family in Hindu law had an equal stake in the property. While the male and female family members formed part of the corporate family in Hindu law, the male members were described as coparceners.[36] This status was acquired at birth (or through adoption), and they were the only ones in the family who could insist on a division of assets. Female members did not have this capacity.

The testament was an alternative strategy designed to preserve the family and its assets, for which Roman law provided the evidence. It was, however, necessary, Maine stressed, that the testament and its form in classical Roman law should not be taken to be the same as its original form or function. To that end, the remainder of chapter six focused on the historical development of the Roman testament. As mentioned at the start of this chapter, natural law scholars had focused on three elements of the Roman testament as though they were immanent. These are a) the secrecy of its provisions, b) its revocability until the death of the testator and c) that its provisions only took effect upon the death of the testator. Maine set about disproving the immanence of these elements using Roman law.

Our primary source of information concerning the history of the testament in Roman law is the Institutes of Gaius.[37] This again underscores the importance of the Verona palimpsest for Maine's endeavour. In several paragraphs, Gaius provides a concise history of the original testament, which was essentially a verbal declaration either spoken in front of the curiate assembly or during preparation

[35] Mayne, *A Treatise on the Hindu Law and Usage*, 322. See also Strange, *Elements of Hindu Law*, I.253, where the view is attributed to Sir William Jones (1746–1794), a notable Victorian jurist and expert on the history of India. For context, see Vesey-FitzGerald, 'Sir William Jones, the Jurist', generally. See also Pollock and Maine, *Introduction and Notes*, 37–40.

[36] Strange, *Elements of Hindu Law*, I, 260; Mayne, *A Treatise on the Hindu Law and Usage*, 332.

[37] Inst.Gai.2.100–3.

for battle. This supported Maine's first point, namely that the provisions of the Roman testament were not initially secret. These two testament forms were later augmented by a third form, the testament, using the *mancipatio* and involving the bronze and the scales. Again, this testament was spoken in the presence of witnesses. It survived longer, while the former two testament forms eventually fell into disuse. Maine does not discuss the verbal testament pronounced in front of the assembly in detail. However, some elements supported his claim about the early purpose of testaments and their publicity, and required mention. According to the Roman law of intestate succession, the ultimate benefactor of a person's estate was the *gens*, an accumulation of families of common descent. Since the *gentes* were represented in the curiate assembly, before which the verbal testament had to be declared, it lent support to Maine's position that the rise of the testament had to be connected to a scenario where the legal rules on intestate succession had somehow become inconvenient.[38]

The remainder of chapter six discussed the testament using the *mancipatio*. Maine's decision to focus on this type of testament was purposive. In his view, this was the form of the testament that had the most significant impact on the subsequent development of Roman succession law. In addition, the presence of the *mancipatio* permitted him to make more significant claims supporting his hypothesis.[39] Most of our information is based on a passage from Gaius' Institutes:

> Inst.Gai. 2, 103
> Sed illa quidem duo genera testamentorum in desuetudinem abierunt; hoc vero solum, quod per aes et libram fit, in usu retentum est. sane nunc aliter ordinatur quam olim solebat. namque olim familiae emptor, id est qui a testatore familiam accipiebat mancipio, heredis locum optinebat, et ob id ei mandabat testator, quid cuique post mortem suam dari vellet; nunc vero alius heres testamento instituitur, a quo etiam legata relinquantur, alius dicis gratia propter veteris iuris imitationem familiae emptor adhibetur.
>
> Indeed, those two kinds of testaments have fallen into disuse, and only the one using the bronze and the scales remained in use. It, too, operates differently than before. Initially, the 'purchaser of the family', the person who acquired the family from the testator through a sale, became the heir, and the testator charged him with distributing the estate according to his wishes. These days, one person is appointed the heir by the testament and must distribute the legacies according to it. In contrast, another person is described as the 'purchaser of the family' in imitation of the earlier law. [Own translation]

This text reveals various aspects of the original situation involving this type of testament and subsequent developments. It also introduces the reader to the figure of the purchaser of the family (*familiae emptor*) and his role in this form of testament. There can be no doubt that Gaius's discussion in this text influenced

[38] Maine, *Ancient Law*, 199–201.
[39] Ibid. 203–5.

Maine's views on this issue. He focused on three issues. The first concerned the likely target audience of this type of testament. During the mid-nineteenth century, this testament was called the 'plebeian testament'. This can be seen, for example, in Ortolan's account[40] and Niebuhr's work.[41] Since plebeians did not have a *gens*, these scholars argued, they could not have used the curiate assembly to validate their testaments. This was either because they would not have been admitted to it, or because, even if they were admitted, the reception would have been hostile. It was from this scenario that the testament using the *mancipatio* developed. Maine supported this position as he consistently referred to this form of testament as the 'plebeian testament'. The second point of focus was the term 'purchaser of the family'. To Maine, this provided more evidence that the original aim of succession as a branch of law was the continuation of the corporate family and its assets. The final point of focus was a technical one. At the start of chapter six, Maine cautioned against assuming that the elements of the testament in modern times existed at all points in the past. Specifically, he warned against assuming that provisions of testaments were always secret. Given the public nature of the *mancipatio* procedure, this, to Maine, demonstrated the exact opposite.

This then brings us to the other two features of the Roman testament on which scholars of natural law focused, namely the revocability of its provisions until the death of the testator and the fact that its provisions did not take effect until that point.[42] As the concise history presented in the Gaius text quoted above shows, the role of the 'purchaser of the family', initially central to the operation of the *mancipatio* testament, eventually became ceremonial. While they were still appointed in name only, as Gaius tells us, the true heir was named in the testament and was instructed to distribute the legacies. This rather terse statement by Gaius belies a somewhat complex process of legal change. Since the *mancipatio* transferred legal rights immediately and irrevocably, and as it was unlikely that a testator would wait until they were near death to transfer the estate to the 'purchaser of the family', it stood to reason that this form of testament was neither revocable nor did its provisions take effect only upon the death of the testator. This is how Maine interpreted the text, as it served his broader thesis. Although his interpretation was not far from the mark, subsequent scholarship pointed out that the testator was not entirely at the mercy of the 'purchaser of the family' after the *mancipatio*.[43] One final aspect of the text quoted above deserves mention. Gaius uses an interesting phrase to describe the ceremonial role of the 'purchaser of the family', namely *propter veteris iuris imitationem*. Maine's discussion of this

40 Ortolan, Nasmith and Prichard, *The History of Roman Law, from the Text of Ortolan's 'Histoire de La Législation Romaine et Généralisation Du Droit' (Edition of 1870). Translated . . . and Supplemented by a Chronometrical Chart of Roman History by I.T. Prichard and D. Nasmith*, 82.

41 Niebuhr, *Niebuhr's History of Rome, Epitomised from the Larger Work, and Adapted to the Use of Schools and Colleges by Travers Twiss; with Chronological Tables and an Appendix.*, 123.

42 Maine, *Ancient Law*, 206.

43 Muirhead, *Historical Introduction to the Private Law of Rome, by James Muirhead; Revised and Edited by Henry Goudy*, 154–5.

issue suggests that he was aware of the significance of this phrase. He argued that the change in the law must have occurred through Praetorian innovation based on 'equity', thus linking the matter back to his discussion on mechanisms of legal change.[44]

The last part of chapter six is devoted to a brief survey of the transition from the verbal testament using the *mancipatio* to a written document sealed by witnesses in classical Roman law, as well as the rise of the Justinianic will.[45] His treatment of these two forms of the Roman testament is brief. It makes one obvious point, namely that it is intellectually vacuous to focus on the form and content of the Roman testament at a certain point in its history without considering its development. The final section of Maine's treatment briefly mentions Savigny and his comments on the continued usage of Roman law on testaments in the Middle Ages. It seems to reference Savigny's work on the history of Roman law in that period.[46]

4. FREEDOM OF TESTATION

Maine's primary claim in chapter six regarding the function of succession as a branch of law is carried over into chapter seven. There, it takes the form of an extensive discussion regarding freedom of testation in Roman law and the related issue of primogeniture.[47] Gibbon noted that the 'insolent prerogative of primogeniture' did not exist in Roman succession law.[48] His discussion likely inspired Maine's inclusion of the subject here. Despite its absence from Roman law, however, it still profoundly impacted the development of civil law in subsequent epochs.[49] It is this development which Maine set out to trace in the final part of chapter seven.

Before examining his treatment of the matter in detail, the more significant motivations behind Maine's arguments must be outlined. This section is about freedom of testation and, more specifically, the restrictions imposed by law on the testator's ability to disinherit family members without cause. The broad thrust of the development of the Roman law of testamentary succession, when viewed as a whole, is that it became progressively more difficult legally to disinherit spouses and children without cause. Both in the Roman law of the Republic and the early Empire, legal measures (such as the 'claim of the unduteous will', or reserve portions for children in the estate) were introduced, often under the guise of Praetorian 'equity', to improve the testamentary entitlements of these categories of

[44] Maine, *Ancient Law*, 209–10.

[45] Ibid. 210–14.

[46] Savigny, *The History of the Roman Law during the Middle Ages, Translated from the Original German of Carl von Savigny by E. Cathcart. Vol. I.*, 91.

[47] Maine, *Ancient Law*, 215–16.

[48] Gibbon and Fernández-Armesto, *The History of the Decline and Fall of the Roman Empire. Vol. 5, Justinian and the Roman Law*, 284.

[49] Mayne, *A Treatise on the Hindu Law and Usage*, 322–3, for a survey.

persons. This is the proper focus of Maine's arguments here.[50] One can go further, however. Once this trend towards restricting the testator's right to disinherit spouses and children without cause in Roman law had been identified, he could use it to critique the tendency to project conclusions drawn from this development onto the law of succession in earlier periods of Roman history. This was the primary purpose of chapter seven. Maine was interested in the motivation for these restrictions and what they revealed about the development of the law of succession more generally. To explain his position on this issue, it is best to start with a quotation by Gibbon, the likely source of this discussion:

> A domestic monarch, who reigned over the lives and fortunes of his children, might distribute their respective shares according to the degrees of their merit or his affection; his arbitrary displeasure chastised an unworthy son by the loss of his inheritance, and the mortifying preference of a stranger.[51]

When Gibbon uses the term 'domestic monarch,' he refers to the earliest history of society when the State had barely begun to exist and was still little more than a group of families, each presided over by a figure with almost unlimited domestic jurisdiction. As this quotation shows, it is easy to interpret this statement regarding the extent of the right to disinherit as also representative of the legal position in early Roman law.

Maine objected to the tenor of this statement.[52] In his view, there was no evidence to support the contention that mean-spirited heads of households in early Roman law had abused their unlimited power to disinherit children, thus necessitating a change in the law. Building upon his argument in chapter six, he argued that the early law on inheritance after the enactment of the Twelve Tables needed to be contextualised historically. When viewed in this way, based on his earlier argument, it becomes clear why the legal sources of this period do not mention disinheritance. Maine had previously argued that intestacy was the norm in early Roman law and that the rules governing it were explicitly created to facilitate the intergenerational transfer of the corporate family's assets to a new administrator. Where these rules failed, for whatever reason, a testament was permitted to rectify the problem. The function of the testament, then, was not, as in modern times, to divest assets away from the family through disinheritance. It had the opposite purpose: ensuring a fairer distribution of the family's assets than what would have been provided for under the existing law. To interpret the silence of the sources as evidence of a 'boundless license of disherison', as Maine called it, was to misunderstand legal history.[53] The absence of evidence is not evidence of absence.

50 Montesquieu et al., *Spirit*, Part 6, Book 27 also discusses the matter in detail.

51 Gibbon and Fernández-Armesto, *The History of the Decline and Fall of the Roman Empire. Vol. 5, Justinian and the Roman Law*, 286.

52 Maine, *Ancient Law*, 216–17.

53 Ibid. 216.

This being the case, it remains to be investigated whether any aspect of the existing rules of intestate succession may have precipitated a shift towards using the testament. To that end, Maine focused on the two branches of the law of succession as depicted in Justinianic law, namely the original civil-law rules of intestate succession and the Praetorian changes which were introduced subsequently. The original civil-law rules on this matter preferred the agnatic line of succession and did not consider emancipated children or widows in its inheritance allocation.[54] It was these exclusions that praetors sought to correct. Given the limited information, Maine also cautioned against creating a narrative of widespread abuse of the freedom to disinherit. There is no evidence for this, and it does not align with the broader purpose of inheritance law. If anything, it was a further deduction based on an incorrect premise.

The restrictions imposed on the testator's ability to disinherit were examples of corrective Praetorian 'equity' and served two functions in Maine's argument. First, it permitted him to offer some insights into the nature of legal change. Maine had argued earlier in the book that social change often outpaces legal change. This is also the tenor of his comments here. At some point, Maine proposed, the rules on intestate succession fell out of step with 'popular sentiment'.[55] This led to a conflict. As he phrased it:

> Every dominant sentiment of the primitive Romans was entwined with the relations of the family. But what was the family? The law defined it one way – natural affection another. In the conflict between the two, the feeling we would analyse grew up, taking the form of an enthusiasm for the institution by which the dictates of affection were permitted to determine the fortunes of its objects.[56]

Phrased differently, change was needed to ensure that the legal understanding of the family and its role in inheritance aligned more closely with societal views of the family. As Maine had pointed out in his discussion on the instruments of legal change, it was in the interests of every society to ensure that the gap between law and society remained as narrow as possible.

The second function that the reference to Praetorian 'equity' served in the context of Maine's discussion was to critique a well-known phrase, namely that the Romans had a 'horror of intestacy'.[57] This phrase is commonly interpreted to indicate the Roman preference for testate succession over intestate succession. In Maine's view, and given his argument about legal change through Praetorian 'equity', this phrase acquires additional meaning in the context of the larger purpose of the law of succession as a vehicle for the intergenerational transfer of assets within the corporate family. This is one of Maine's most impressive insights. It cannot be presumed that the Praetorian innovations occurred in a structured

[54] Ibid. 221, 223.
[55] Ibid. 218, 220.
[56] Ibid. 222–3.
[57] Ibid. 218.

manner. The source material only reveals the outcome of a process of trial and error that must have been occasionally somewhat messy. This is most likely where this 'horror' originated. Despite the changes brought about through Praetorian innovation, the original sentiment persisted: '[e]verybody conversant with the philosophy of opinion is aware that a sentiment by no means dies out, of necessity, with the passing away of the circumstances which produced it.'[58]

Thus, even though the initial exclusion of emancipated children and widows may have been rectified through Praetorian innovation, the notion that it was better to have a testament than to let the rules of intestate succession govern the matter persisted in Roman cultural memory. In his view, this explained the rise of the testament as the preferred form of inheritance in Roman law.

5. PRIMOGENITURE

Chapter seven's final part focused on the rise of primogeniture in later European legal thought. As mentioned at the start of chapter six, this institution had a profound impact on English law and continued to be debated until the publication of the book. Since this topic could be tied into his discussion about freedom of testation, it provided a suitable conclusion to chapter seven.[59] It was yet another example of a limitation of the freedom of testation imposed by law. Given its impact on English law, it would also have been a familiar topic to Maine's audience. As will presently become clear, there was more to Maine's discussion of primogeniture than meets the eye. To appreciate this, one must look more closely at a statement at the start of chapter six where he mentions 'a line of progress' between the testament in its nineteenth-century form and its origins in Roman law. This phrase is essential since, as previously argued, Maine wrote *Ancient Law* primarily to critique the notion of a linear unidirectional progression of law from primitive to sophisticated prevalent in the Victorian intellectual discourse. Once this larger aim is understood, it becomes clear that the discussion of primogeniture was designed to critique 'progress' in the sense of continuous improvement. Maine did not see primogeniture as improving the Roman legal position regarding succession. If anything, he saw it is a regression. Once this is appreciated, it becomes clear that to Maine, legal change was cyclical – oscillating between periods of equality and inequality in the distribution of the inheritance assets by law.

Maine was emphatic about its origins. In his view, primogeniture, unknown to Roman law, was a product of feudalism and promoted inequality in the distribution of assets, mainly immovable property, through inheritance.[60] As with many aspects of Maine's book, the discussion here seems to have been influenced by a statement in Gibbon's *Decline and Fall* where primogeniture is referred to as an 'insolent prerogative' which did not feature in Roman law. Similarly, Montesquieu's *De L'Esprit*

58 Ibid. 223.
59 Ibid. 227–43.
60 Ibid. 225–6.

contains a detailed discussion of the history of feudalism.[61] Jamoussi has shown that discussions concerning primogeniture and its relationship to natural law were a stock feature of intellectual debates in European legal literature of the seventeenth and eighteenth centuries.[62] These discussions also influenced Bentham's criticism of the matter, especially concerning its impact on immovable property in English law. This was the intellectual backdrop to the discussion in *Ancient Law*. The gist of Maine's discussion centres around the inequality primogeniture produces. After surveying Roman law, supported by examples from Hindu law and early Germanic law to confirm whether this phenomenon occurred elsewhere, he concluded that the notion of primogeniture was not a feature of a 'progressive' legal system according to his definition. Instead, his examples led him to deduce that the distribution of assets through the law of inheritance tended to be more equal in such systems.[63] This being the case, he was interested in the potential origins of primogeniture and its prevalence in subsequent periods of European legal history. His discussion of the purported origins of primogeniture makes two more prominent points. Both speak to the underlying tenor of the discussion, namely, the equality of distribution of assets through inheritance. Maine's first point is that primogeniture is linked to feudalism, and its origins must be sought in the practice of benefices awarded by chieftains to soldiers during the early medieval period, particularly under the Carolingians later on. Having set out his views on this matter, he questions why it became so popular. Maine had an answer, albeit a rather uncomfortable one: '[t]he answer, I think, is that European society decidedly retrograded during the dissolution of the Carlovingian empire.'[64]

This statement is interesting for several reasons. First, it directly supported Maine's critique of linear progress. Second, it connected the rise of feudalism with a weakening of the State. Benefices, which Maine argued were the origin of primogeniture, were not originally hereditary but became so through custom in the aftermath of Charlemagne's death and the division of the Frankish Empire among his heirs. This tied into his critique of linear progress.

The second reason why the statement above is interesting is that it permitted Maine to build an argument regarding the reasons for the spread of primogeniture in European legal thought across subsequent epochs. His views on this are best summarised as follows:

> Nothing in law springs entirely from a sense of convenience. There are always certain ideas existing antecedently on which the sense of convenience works, and of which it can do no more than form some new combination.[65]

[61] Evans-Pritchard, *A History of Anthropological Thought; Edited by André Singer; with an Introduction by Ernest Gellner.*, 5; Siedentop, *Inventing the Individual*, 165–77; Maine, *Dissertations on Early Law and Custom*, 291–328. See Montesquieu et al., *Spirit*, Part 6, Books 30–1.

[62] Jamoussi, *Primogeniture and Entail in England*, 69–134; Cecil, *Primogeniture*, 26–53.

[63] Maine, *Ancient Law*, 227–33.

[64] Ibid. 235.

[65] Ibid. 233.

It is important to unpack this statement in the context of Maine's discussion on primogeniture. Primogeniture provided counter-evidence to the notion of linear progress. As a product of feudalism, it was a regression of the Roman legal principles of succession. To appreciate why primogeniture became so popular in subsequent epochs of European legal development, one must look beyond the weakening of the State and consider the benefits it afforded both to lords and vassals in the context of feudalism. In addition, as Maine noticed, the interpretation of feudal customs by secular and religious courts founded upon principles of the European *ius commune* must have also permitted an intermingling of the Roman legal concept of ownership and primogeniture.[66]

6. CONCLUSIONS

Maine's discussion of the Roman law of succession initially seems overwhelming to the casual reader. It covers a wide range of topics and is often approached by the author superficially yet with enthusiasm. However, once the historical context of these two chapters is mapped out to the reader, it becomes clear that it is a clever piece of rhetorical prose designed to address the shortcomings of legal scholarship on the law of succession in the natural law tradition.

The two chapters devoted to succession critique the supposed connection between succession and natural law, specifically focusing on testate and intestate succession. Additionally, it suggests parallels with developments in contemporaneous English law. Maine's critical insight in these chapters is that fixating on past law at a given moment in time solely because it resembles present law is intellectually vacuous. Instead, one should recognise that past law consists of layers of different ideas that, while seemingly similar to present law, might be very different in scope and function. This is the central message of these chapters.

The other core message relates to the concept of 'progress'. Maine did not subscribe to the Victorian interpretation of this term, as he was wary of its underlying intellectual assumptions. Instead, he advocated viewing legal change as a cycle in which different legal ideas rose and fell. Understanding the mechanisms of legal change was crucial to his work.

[66] Ibid. 238.

Chapter 6

The Origins of Property, its Acquisition and Protection

> The savage who hollows a tree, inserts a sharp stone into a wooden handle, or applies a string to an elastic branch, becomes in a state of nature the just proprietor of the canoe, the bow, or the hatchet.[1]

1. INTRODUCTION

The narrative of *Ancient Law* operates on two levels. On one level, the book was written to critique earlier natural law scholars' poor use of history. In terms of the development of the law of property in European legal thought, the roots of this discourse could be traced back to the eighteenth century and had, more recently, been reinvigorated by the French Revolution of 1789 and its impact on landownership.[2] On another level, *Ancient Law* was written in the context of, and perhaps even in response to, the more significant geo-political events surrounding the British colonial presence in India, where issues of landownership also came to dominate.[3] Nowhere do these two narrative levels present themselves more clearly than in the chapter on property.[4] To Maine, these two narratives found common ground in the work of Niebuhr, who, in his discussion of the history of landownership in Republican Rome, used comparative evidence from India to reinforce his arguments.[5] Maine's chapter on property explains how this concept developed in Roman law, his archetypal 'progressive' legal system.[6] It recounts a trajectory, also seen in the chapter on succession, whereby property rights held by

1 Gibbon and Fernández-Armesto, *The History of the Decline and Fall of the Roman Empire. Vol. 5, Justinian and the Roman Law*, 281–2.

2 Capogrossi Colognesi, *Dalla storia di Roma alle origini della società civile*, 15–18; Tuori, *Lawyers and Savages*, 48–52; Lerminier, *Introduction générale à l'histoire du droit*, 174–86.

3 Dewey, 'The Influence of Sir Henry Maine on Agrarian Policy in India', generally; Stokes, *The English Utilitarians and India*, 81–139; Bayly, 'Maine and Change in Nineteenth-Century India', generally.

4 Kuper, 'Ancestors', 276–7; Tuori, *Lawyers and Savages*, 68–74.

5 Niebuhr, *Niebuhr's History of Rome, epitomised from the Larger Work, and Adapted to the Use of Schools and Colleges by Travers Twiss; with Chronological Tables and an Appendix*, 192; Capogrossi Colognesi, *Dalla storia di Roma alle origini della società civile*, 23–6. See also Capogrossi Colognesi, *Dalla storia di Roma alle origini della società civile*, 31–4, for an account of the impact of Savigny's views on this matter relating to Niebuhr.

6 For a provocative account of the origins of property, rooted in anthropology, see Widerquist and McCall, *The Prehistory of Private Property*, 127–61. For the philosophical angle, especially in German philosophical thought of the nineteenth century, see James, *Property and its Forms in Classical German Philosophy*, generally.

individuals are established in the context of the decline of the common property regime of the family. While the family never completely disappears, its impact on the law progressively diminishes. At various points in the narrative, where Roman law could not be used to support his claims, he augmented his account using examples from other 'progressive' legal systems, both historical and contemporaneous. The reasons for the inability of Roman law to assist at specific points in this regard were either because the information was lacking or because the Roman position had been distorted, in his opinion, by subsequent natural law scholarship. These additional examples were deployed primarily to reinforce his broader thesis concerning the historical contingency of certain 'early jural conceptions' and their development trajectories in the legal systems he chose to discuss.[7]

Instead of providing a complete survey of the development of this branch of Roman law focusing on specific rules or doctrines of law, Maine chose to examine three issues: the role of first-taking, or occupancy as he called it, in establishing property rights; the role of joint ownership in the development of property law; and, finally, the different ways in which limitations imposed on the alienation of property were overcome. These issues are interconnected and were chosen deliberately. Gibbon's account of Roman law in chapter 44 of his *Decline and Fall* likely provided the basis for Maine's narrative here. Not only did Gibbon start his account of property with occupancy, but he also discussed the issues subsequently treated by Maine broadly in the same order. While Gibbon's treatment provided a convenient order to discuss these issues, there was more to this choice of topics than merely emulating Gibbon. Given the natural law context of Gibbon's narrative, it also provided a set of topics which could be used to enter into a dialogue with earlier scholarship.[8] As will become apparent in this chapter, these topics, consequently, also provided a convenient set of issues that Maine could use to engage with contentious matters of his day, including sovereignty and Empire.

As previous chapters have shown, *Ancient Law* was written as a critique of both natural law and German historicist scholarship. Maine's criticism of natural law scholarship was directed primarily at their poor use of history. By challenging what he saw as the superficial use of history prevalent in such scholarship, Maine made a case for the historical contingency of property law.[9] This, in turn, permitted him to critique claims to the supposed universality of certain aspects of property law in natural law scholarship. This was only part of Maine's aim with this chapter, however. He also used it as an opportunity to comment on what he perceived to be the intellectual failings of German Historical Jurisprudence. In Maine's opinion, as Grossi has shown, the drawback of their methodology was that, despite their manifest erudition, they had failed to engage fully with contemporaneous issues.[10] By contrast, he believed that 'ancient law', as an intellectual construct, could be

[7] Evans, *Theories and Criticisms of Sir Henry Maine*, 32–42, for a summary of Maine's theory on property, taking his subsequent works into account. See also Nelson, *An Analysis*, 146–78, as well as Pollock and Maine, *Introduction and Notes*, 45–9, and Oldham, *Analysis*, 22–4.

[8] Crow, 'A Melvillean Moment', 28.

[9] Mantena, *Alibis of Empire*, 122.

[10] Grossi, 'An Alternative to Private Property', 28–9.

used to engage with actual historical examples and broader societal issues of his day. Thus, for example, he used his discussion of the early history of property to deliver a critique of the British in India.[11]

This chapter will examine Maine's three points of focus in his account of the early history of property. Using his text, combined with the comments of later scholars who wrote summaries of it, an attempt will be made, in keeping with the broader thesis of *Ancient Law*, to reconstruct the historical and intellectual contexts in which the book was written and how its audience would have understood it. This will be done to illuminate Maine's aims with this work.

2. OCCUPANCY

Maine's account of occupancy is somewhat sparse on references, but there is little doubt that it was rooted in Roman law. As Gibbon observed at the start of his discussion of property, occupancy, as the 'original right of property', had been 'established by the philosophy of the civilians'.[12] This statement is telling. Roman law and the legal and philosophical tradition of Graeco-Roman antiquity provided the starting point for European legal and political thought on many issues, including this one.[13] Maine would have been familiar with this intellectual tradition as a classics scholar, as well as with the key texts and controversies in this debate.[14] To that end, although he does not cite any Roman law text on this point, it seems prudent to quote the *locus classicus* from Roman law on the issue of occupancy:

> D. 41, 2, 1, 1 Paul. 54 ad ed.
> Dominiumque rerum ex naturali possessione coepisse Nerva filius ait eiusque rei vestigium remanere in his, quae terra mari caeloque capiuntur: nam haec protinus eorum fiunt, qui primi possessionem eorum adprehenderint. item bello capta et insula in mari enata et gemmae lapilli margaritae in litoribus inventae eius fiunt, qui primus eorum possessionem nanctus est.
>
> And according to Nerva the Younger, ownership (*dominium*) arose out of natural possession, and glimpses of this are still visible in, for example, property captured on earth, in the sea, and in the air since it immediately becomes the taker's through first possession. Similarly, property captured in war, islands arising in the sea, and gems and pearls found on the beaches become the property of those who first take possession. [Own translation]

[11] Fitzmaurice, *Sovereignty, Property and Empire, 1500–2000*, 215, points out that Empire was one reason for the continued importance of occupancy as a topic in nineteenth-century legal scholarship. See Sturman, *The Government of Social Life in Colonial India*, 35–69, for the significance of history in the debates concerning property rights in colonial India.

[12] Gibbon and Fernández-Armesto, *The History of the Decline and Fall of the Roman Empire. Vol. 5, Justinian and the Roman Law*, 281.

[13] Fitzmaurice, *Sovereignty, Property and Empire, 1500–2000*, 33, shows that in medieval learned law, it was generally accepted that *occupatio* originated in natural law and provided a justification for the origins of property.

[14] Garnsey, *Thinking about Property*, 111–21.

In this well-known Digest text, the Roman jurist Paul, quoting an earlier jurist, Nerva the Younger, put forward a theory on the historical origins of the legal concept of ownership (*dominium*) in Roman law. According to Paul, ownership arose from 'natural possession' (*ex naturali possessione*). This could be deduced from the fact that whatever was captured on land, at sea or in the air became the property of the captor due to their initial possession of these items. Several examples were added to illustrate the central point in the latter part of this text. These included taking possession of war booty, islands in the sea, and gems and pearls found on beaches.[15]

At first sight, this text is an example of intellectual speculation often visible in Roman legal texts. It cannot be determined what sources (if any) Paul or Nerva the Younger had at their disposal to substantiate the claim of the historical relationship between ownership and possession, nor can it be said whether the Roman jurists universally held this claim. One suspects not. What is more important, though, is that Paul, one of the intellectually more significant Roman jurists, lent his support to this theory, citing Nerva the Younger with approval. On the strength of Paul's approval of this theory and its eventual inclusion in Justinian's Digest, a link was drawn between the historical development of ownership and possession in Roman law. That link lay in the principle of occupancy (*occupatio*), namely that unowned property (whether because it had not been owned before or because it had become ownerless through, for example, intentional abandonment) could be acquired through first-taking. It is worth noting here that in the Roman legal tradition, represented by Paul (and Nerva the Younger), as well as earlier in the works of Cicero, there was no attempt, as Garnsey has noted '[t]o justify the advent of *occupatio*'.[16] This would become one of the central points of discussion in subsequent natural law scholarship on the issue.

Although Maine never directly cites this Roman law text, it was central to his account. The starting point of his critique of occupancy can be linked to the phrase 'natural possession' in the first sentence of the Roman legal text quoted above. Maine argued that earlier scholars of natural law, as the quotation from Gibbon shows, had latched on to this notion, thus interpreting this mode of acquiring property ownership as 'natural' and aligned with natural law.[17] The consequence of this association was far-reaching. The occupancy principle was expanded progressively to the point that it became an a priori rule of natural law from which other conclusions were drawn. As he phrased it: '[t]heory has made them its favourite food, and has enabled them to exercise the most serious influence on practice.'[18]

[15] Fitzmaurice, *Sovereignty, Property and Empire, 1500–2000*, 35–6, while the examples from the Digest are confined to movable property, statements from the works of Cicero have also been used to argue that according to Roman legal thought, the principle of occupancy also included immovable property.

[16] Garnsey, *Thinking about Property*, 121.

[17] Maine, *Ancient Law*, 244–6. Somos and Peters, *The State of Nature*, 2–3, ('Introduction') for an account of the complexity of the term 'state of nature'.

[18] Maine, *Ancient Law*, 245.

Maine's criticism here is twofold. Not only had the issue become heavily discussed theoretically, but it also had a 'most serious' influence on legal practice. Having wrenched the principle of occupancy from its historical context, earlier natural law scholars began to use it for two different, yet related, purposes. First, it became the justification in international law for the acquisition of ownership of property captured in war (based on the example in the latter part of the Roman law text), and second, it provided a theory concerning the origins of property. As Fitzmaurice observed, occupancy had become 'one of the most common explanations in Western political thought for the origin of property and, for that matter, the beginning of political society'.[19] Maine was aware of these associations and chose to make them the focus of his critique.

2.1 *Occupatio* and Spoils of War

In the Roman legal text cited above, the reader is told, in the list of examples enumerated: '*item bello capta . . . qui primus eorum possessionem nanctus est.*' This roughly translates as: 'he who first acquires possession of goods captured in war, (also acquires ownership of them through occupancy).'

As Maine pointed out, for all the apparent clarity of this statement, its elevation to an a priori rule in natural law scholarship was problematic.[20] Thus, according to one view, the reason for the acquisition was rooted in the fact that when a State was conquered in war, it ceased to exist, and all property reverted to a state of nature as *res nullius*, ostensibly since private property did not exist in a state of nature. However, this view was not universally shared. An opposing view, which connected the existence of private property to the law of nature, maintained that it was merely according to 'a fiction of jurisprudence' that the property of those defeated in war was treated as *res nullius*.[21]

Although Maine's summary of these positions is brief, it alludes to a vast debate in European legal scholarship from the medieval period onwards, in which various attempts had been made to rationalise the existence of the occupancy principle. In his summary of this debate, Maine makes two points. First, in the historical development of the principle of occupancy in European legal and political scholarship, it had become linked not only to the acquisition of rights in property but to the very notion of sovereignty and, thus, the creation of the State.[22]

[19] Fitzmaurice, *Sovereignty, Property and Empire, 1500–2000*, 1. For a similar quotation, see Maine, *Ancient Law*, 246.

[20] Maine, *Ancient Law*, 246.

[21] Fitzmaurice, *Sovereignty, Property and Empire, 1500–2000*, 33, 36–9, for a survey of the differing positions in medieval learned law concerning this point. See also Benvenisti, 'The Origins of the Concept of Belligerent Occupation', 624–35, and Benvenisti, *The International Law of Occupation*, generally. For a recent survey, see Fitzmaurice, 'Discovery, Conquest, and Occupation of Territory', 841–8; Straumann and Kingsbury, 'The State of Nature and Commercial Sociability in Early Modern International Legal Thought', generally.

[22] Lee, 'Private Law Models for Public Law Concepts', for a survey.

This had, in turn, given rise to the two opposing points of view on whether rights could exist outside the State's confines. As Fitzmaurice noted:

> It is possible . . . to identify a particular nineteenth-century preoccupation with the occupation of sovereignty in legal discourse – an attempt to develop a legal framework for commercial empires. The idea of occupation was used by nineteenth-century jurists to extend the progressive theory of history through the development of a hierarchical understanding of sovereignty.[23]

As will become apparent in this chapter, this 'preoccupation', as Fitzmaurice called it, also informed Maine's discussion of the early history of property law.

The second important point was that the Roman law texts on which these natural law discussions were based did not deal in sufficient detail with the legal consequences flowing from it, namely the relationship between conquest in war and the continued existence of private property. Phrased differently, by reducing the idea that spoils of war became the property of the first taker through occupancy to an a priori rule of natural law, scholars of natural law failed to engage with the historical contingency underlying this rule.[24] In Maine's view, the shortcomings of this approach could be seen clearly when the notion of occupancy was viewed in its historical context. To that end, he provided an account of the occupancy principle in Roman law.

The gist of his account is the following. If the Roman law on this issue were traced back through the *ius naturale* to the *ius gentium*, from which it most likely originated as a common practice observed by many nations, its underlying rationale becomes apparent.[25] Thus, the Roman law rule could only be adequately understood in the context of the actual Roman practice adopted regarding the property of those conquered in war. In the Roman context, according to Maine, the rule about the acquisition of ownership of the property of vanquished enemies through occupancy had applied originally only to movable property since the acquisition of immovable property was dealt with differently.

Maine does not provide any reference here, but it is a crucial point in his narrative and deserves greater scrutiny. Two aspects are noteworthy. First, it must not be forgotten that Maine was constructing an argument here and thus organised his evidence accordingly. The fact that in Roman law, the acquisition of ownership of spoils of war was restricted to movable property neatly suited his more significant claims concerning the origins of property in Roman law and its connection to the family in its earliest phases. It was, therefore, worth highlighting specifically. Second, Maine also claimed here that external evidence (in other words, evidence not found in Roman legal sources) substantiated this interpretation.[26] This statement is interesting. Being a trained classicist, Maine would

[23] Fitzmaurice, *Sovereignty, Property and Empire, 1500–2000*, 6.

[24] Maine, *Ancient Law*, 248.

[25] Ibid. 247; Mantena, *Alibis of Empire*, 124.

[26] Churchill, '*Ex qua Quod Vellent Facerent*', for a survey of the position in Roman law.

have been well acquainted with the works of the Roman historian Livy or his Greek predecessor Polybius on the history of the early Roman Republic. These works frequently discuss how the Roman State dealt with immovable property acquired through conquest in war. Still, their focus was not on legal technicalities and left much unsaid about the practicalities surrounding the occupancy of immovable property of a defeated State. By signposting the historical context in which the scope and limitations of the Roman law rule should be understood, his underlying point was that a greater sensitivity towards the complexity of the historical context of Roman law was needed. Whether Maine obtained this historical information first-hand from the primary sources or in a digested form from Niebuhr's *Geschichte*, a work he relied on when writing *Ancient Law*, cannot be determined. Either way, these accounts revealed a much more complex historical scenario and, more importantly, legal regime than those presented in the works of the earlier natural law scholars.

The works of Polybius and Livy provided evidence that the acquisition of ownership of immovable property was dealt with differently from that of movable property in Roman law. This, in turn, also provided Maine with intellectual ammunition against the works of earlier natural law scholars in which the principle of occupancy had been treated in an ahistorical manner. It cannot be denied, however, that Maine did not need to champion 'external evidence' to find support for such a position. He could have also found evidence for it in Roman law. This can be seen, for example, in the following Roman legal text:

> D. 49, 15, 20, 1 Pomp. 36 ad Sab.
> Verum est expulsis hostibus ex agris quos ceperint dominia eorum ad priores dominos redire nec aut publicari aut praedae loco cedere: publicatur enim ille ager qui ex hostibus captus sit.
>
> Lands captured by enemies should indeed be returned to their former owners once they have been expelled. These lands should not be declared public land nor considered spoils of war. But land captured from the enemy is declared public land. [Own translation]

In the latter part of this text, Pomponius, a Roman jurist of the second century CE, noted that land captured from the enemy became State property and was not considered spoils of war.

The careful reader may wonder why Maine chose to emphasise this point. It was certainly not unknown information, even to natural law scholars in the early modern period. For example, in his *De Iure Belli ac Pacis*, the Dutch jurist Hugo Grotius (1583–1645) clearly distinguished between the legal rules on spoils of war applicable to movable property and immovable property such as enemy land.[27] The most plausible answer is that, to Maine, the rule/or rules on acquiring ownership of war spoils through occupancy only made sense in context. Or as he

[27] Grotius, *Grotius on the Rights of War and Peace*, 340. For a survey of the later history up to the nineteenth century, see Phillimore, 'Booty of War', generally.

phrased it: 'The idea would occur spontaneously to persons practising the ancient forms of warfare, when victory dissolved the organisation of the conquering army and dismissed the soldiers to indiscriminate plunder.'[28] The more it became abstracted in discussions of natural law scholars, the less persuasive it became as a general rule of law. What seemed, at first sight, to be an unambiguous statement which could be used to create an a priori rule of natural law was, in fact, historically contingent. There may also be another element to this issue. In Ferdinand Mackeldey's *Lehrbuch*, one of the most famous European textbooks on Roman law of the nineteenth century, the acquisition of property through defeat in war is also portrayed as an unambiguous legal rule with limited reference to the distinction drawn in Roman law between movable and immovable property.[29] Statements such as these may also have been the focus of Maine's critique.

Maine's final point about using occupancy as a justification for acquiring ownership of spoils of war also had a colonial context. Ever since the popularisation of occupancy in the context of European expansion by scholars such as Grotius, jurists who wrote in the natural law tradition had grappled with questions which the a priori principle of natural law could not resolve. As mentioned, the Roman source material did not focus on the issue of 'legitimacy', as Garnsey called it, of acquisition of ownership through occupancy. Similarly, Maine identified two additional issues which had become the object of discussion in the history of European legal thought. These issues concerned the extent of the territory acquired in this manner and the actions needed to establish and maintain possession of it. To understand Maine's point here, it should be seen against the backdrop of the development of the principle of occupancy in European legal scholarship of the early modern period. As Fitzmaurice noted:

> Between the seventeenth and eighteenth centuries, the idea of occupation was increasingly used – for example, by John Locke and Adam Smith – to explain the historical progress of human societies from a hypothetical state of nature to an agricultural state. These philosophers and historians would argue that it was through the occupation of land and goods that humans were able to preserve themselves and, in so doing, create civil societies. . . . Moreover, early modern authors stressed that occupation could not simply be a taking of something 'with the hands', as it had been for medieval authors. Rather, they argued that occupation was only achieved by use or, in Locke's terms, improvement.[30]

It was this debate – namely whether occupancy alone (or an additional element such as labour as Locke argued) – that Maine alluded to here.[31] It provided further evidence that occupancy in its abstracted form developed by natural law scholars was not fit for purpose.

[28] Maine, *Ancient Law*, 247.

[29] Mackeldey and Dropsie, *Handbook of the Roman Law . . . Translated and Edited by M.A. Dropsie from the Fourteenth German Edition*, 216–17.

[30] Fitzmaurice, *Sovereignty, Property and Empire, 1500-2000*, 3.

[31] Ibid. 98–101. See also Garnsey, *Thinking about Property*, 136–76; Nelson, *An Analysis*, 87–9.

Of the two issues at hand (the extent of the land acquired in this manner and the establishment of occupancy), Maine did not discuss the second in detail. The reason for this is easy to fathom. Since he did not believe in applying this rule to a colonial context, there was no point in elaborating upon it. In rhetorical terms, this resembles a *praeteritio* – commenting on something by not commenting on it. As for the first issue, Maine limited his observations to two aspects of it, namely, first, that the claims to territory based upon this vague notion of occupancy alone had never been entirely accepted intellectually by those nations involved in colonial expansion such as the Dutch, the English and the Portuguese.[32] This provided additional ammunition against the idea of occupancy as an element of (universal) natural law. Furthermore, never missing an opportunity to take a swipe at his *bête noir*, Jeremy Bentham, Maine argued that even *he* could not justify the application of this principle in such an abstract manner but instead preferred to focus on the authority of the Papal Bull, *Inter Caetera*, decreed by Pope Alexander VI in 1493 whereby the Spanish monarchs were granted ownership of all lands discovered west of an imaginary vertical line drawn west of the Azores, thus including most of the Americas.

Maine often criticised Bentham in *Ancient Law*, not always fairly, so it must be determined whether what he said amounted to 'grotesque . . . praises' of this Papal Bull.[33] The most likely source from which Maine drew this statement was an 1840 English translation by Hildreth of the French text of Etienne Dumont's edition of Bentham's *Theory of Legislation*. The statement is certainly not without complications, chief among them being that it does not appear in the first French edition of 1802 and is seemingly only inserted in the second edition of 1820.[34] In this work, Bentham's comment on the matter occurs in a footnote where he states:

> Lines of demarcation will be necessary; but it will not answer to wait till the event has arrived, and the value of the land is known, for then all will entertain hopes, which some only can realize. The event must be anticipated, and expectation not yet formed will then be docile in the hands of the legislator.[35]

Whether this can be said to be 'grotesque . . . praises' is open to interpretation. It certainly does not seem to be the case. Instead, it may be observed that Bentham's view on the matter is typical of his worldview. The fact that the Papal Bull had created a legal rule, and a rule backed by the legislator's authority more specifically, would have been attractive to Bentham. Nevertheless, it succeeded in reinforcing Maine's point, namely that even Bentham could not bring himself to support the natural law rule on occupancy, wrenched from its historical context, but instead preferred a rule backed by the lawgiver.

32 Maine, *Ancient Law*, 249.

33 Ibid. 249.

34 I am grateful to Professor Philip Schofield and Dr Chris Riley of the UCL Bentham Project for bringing this reference to my attention.

35 Bentham, Dumont and Hildreth, *Theory of Legislation*, 194 in the note.

2.2 *Occupatio* and the Origin of Property

In D. 41, 2, 1, 1 Paul. 54 ad ed., the jurist Paul, citing Nerva the Younger, proposed that the Roman legal concept of ownership was derived from 'natural possession'. This link between possession, especially if acquired through *occupatio*, and the idea of ownership was the focus of the second leg of Maine's critique. In his view, the notion of a link between ownership and 'natural possession' had been adopted in contemporaneous jurisprudence with 'eager curiosity' but without reflecting fully on the intellectual implications of this statement. Maine targeted the views of two authors, William Blackstone and Friedrich C. von Savigny, to make this point. There is every reason to suspect that the choice of these two authors was purposive. Blackstone represented the English legal tradition, while Savigny, an influential figure in German Historical Jurisprudence, represented its European counterpart. Maine chose to quote a passage from Blackstone's *Commentaries*, Book 2, Chapter 1, as the basis of his critique:[36]

> In the beginning of the world, we are informed by holy writ, the all-bountiful creator gave to man 'dominion over all the earth; and over the fish of the sea, and over the fowl of the air, and over every living thing that moves upon the earth.' This is the only true and solid foundation of man's dominion over external things, whatever airy metaphysical notions may have been started by fanciful writers upon this subject. . . . And, while the earth continued bare of inhabitants, it is reasonable to suppose, that all was in common among them, and that every one [sic] took from the public stock to his own use such things as his immediate necessities required. . . . Thus the ground was in common, and no part of it was the permanent property of any man in particular: yet whoever was in the occupation of any determinate spot of it, for rest, for shade, or the like, acquired for the time a sort of ownership, from which it would have been unjust, and contrary to the law of nature, to have driven him by force; but the instant that he quitted the use or occupation of it, another might seize it without injustice. . . . But when mankind increased in number, craft, and ambition, it became necessary to entertain conceptions of more permanent dominion; and to appropriate to individuals not the immediate use only, but the very substance of the thing to be used.[37]

There is much to unpack in this statement. As a starting point, it is essential to remember that Blackstone's statement should be viewed within the broader context of an intellectual discourse concerning occupancy stretching back to the late medieval period.[38] With his usual sharp focus, Maine pinpointed the very core of the problem with this theory:

> Their object in so stating their theory was to reconcile the doctrine that in the state of Nature *res nullius* became property through occupancy, with the inference which they drew from Scriptural history that the Patriarchs did not at first permanently appropriate the soil which had been grazed over by their flocks and herds.[39]

36 Maine, *Ancient Law*, 251–2; Mantena, *Alibis of Empire*, 125–6.
37 Blackstone, *Commentaries*, 1–2.
38 Grossi, 'An Alternative to Private Property', 38.
39 Maine, *Ancient Law*, 253.

To phrase it differently, the occupancy principle was too vague to account for how nomadic peoples' intermittent use of immovable property was transformed into a legal entitlement as strong as ownership.[40] As noted above, this observation ties in with discussions in the legal literature of the seventeenth and eighteenth centuries about whether occupancy alone or occupancy combined with another element was required to acquire land ownership.

Still, Maine's criticism was not limited to the vagueness of the principle. Grossi noted that Maine also objected to the contemporaneous ideologies latently woven into these accounts.[41] The circumstances in which people found themselves in the past differed significantly from those in the present, a recurrent theme in much of Maine's work. Once this was appreciated, the modern observer also had to accept that 'the same sentiments and prejudices' likely did not exist in the past.[42]

Having critiqued Blackstone's position as essentially ahistorical, Maine set his sights on Savigny, who could not be accused of the same folly.[43] As he pointed out, while the positions of Blackstone and Savigny on the subject were similar, Savigny's observations were limited to Roman law and thus did not claim to be universal. Nevertheless, Savigny's position was not without its problems. To assess this position, it is necessary to set it out in greater detail. Savigny's position was that: 'all property is founded on adverse possession ripened by prescription.'[44] Although Maine does not provide a pinpoint reference, Savigny's position on this was well known, having been proposed already in his *Das Recht des Besitzes: eine civilistische Abhandlung*, published in 1803 and articulated further in his *System*, published in several volumes between 1840 and 1849.[45] Already in Maine's lifetime, it was acknowledged that Niebuhr's account of the Roman Republican controversies surrounding the Agrarian laws and the acquisition of possession of public lands by the Patricians in his *Geschichte*, first published in 1811–1812, was an essential point of reference for many legal scholars in this debate.[46] To Maine, Savigny's

[40] Fitzmaurice, *Sovereignty, Property and Empire, 1500–2000*, 117–18. See also Pollock and Maine, *Introduction and Notes*, 48, specifically on the Blackstone quotation. For a discussion of the link between the state of nature and discussions of 'barbarism', see Eberl, *Naturzustand Und Barbarei*, 171–361.

[41] Grossi, 'An Alternative to Private Property', 38–9.

[42] Maine, *Ancient Law*, 254.

[43] Ibid. 254–5.

[44] Ibid. 254.

[45] Savigny, *Von Savigny's Treatise on Possession, or, The Jus Possessionis of the Civil Law, Translated from the German by Sir Erskine Perry . . .*, 9. See also Nelson, *An Analysis*, 168.

[46] Niebuhr, *Niebuhr's History of Rome, Epitomised from the Larger Work, and Adapted to the Use of Schools and Colleges by Travers Twiss; with Chronological Tables and an Appendix*, 191–7. For a recent account of this episode, see Capogrossi Colognesi, *Law and Power in the Making of the Roman Commonwealth*, 182–6; Capogrossi Colognesi, *Dalla storia di Roma alle origini della società civile*, 19–22. Capogrossi Colognesi, *Dalla storia di Roma alle origini della società civile*, 45–65, has shown that Niebuhr's interest in the history of landownership was partly driven by the then newly discovered technical manuals of the Roman agronomists and their use of Roman law. For a critical assessment, see Cornell, *The Beginnings of Rome*, 327–9; Capogrossi Colognesi, *La costruzione del diritto privato romano*, 103–12.

position demonstrated the critical problem with the narrative of occupancy. As he phrased it:

> [H]owever closely we approach in tracing them [ideas of property] to the infancy of law, we can get no farther than a conception of ownership involving the three elements in the canon – possession, adverseness of possession . . . and prescription. . . .[47]

Thus, much like his criticism of Blackstone, Maine's criticism of Savigny related to matters of historical contingency.[48] Although the latter's treatment of the subject was more clearly rooted in a historical episode from the Roman Republic concerning the possession of public lands, it still did not provide enough detail to explain the transition from possession to ownership. Or, as Gibbon expressed it: 'the steps are silent, the shades are almost imperceptible.'[49] Maine did credit Savigny's account with an important insight which, in his view, was the real crux of the issue, namely the passage of time. '[W]hy was [it] that lapse of time created a sentiment of respect for his possession . . . .' he asked.[50] In rhetorical terms, this is an excellent example of *erotema* – the dramatic use of a rhetorical question that cuts to the heart of the issue, planted in the audience's minds as an intellectual seed waiting to germinate. In his view, this was the core issue that needed to be examined, though he ruled it outwith the scope of his present work. While this may seem somewhat elusive, as indeed it is, Maine's position here is not without merit. To investigate the significance of the passing of time on the creation of a legal principle would have merited a completely different approach, and any attempts to force it into his discussion here would have necessitated a considerable digression. Instead, in keeping with his rhetoric here, he left it to his audience to form their own view.

In summary, Maine's criticism of occupancy, both as a justification for the acquisition of property captured in war and for the origins of property, was that the lack of acknowledgement of the historical contingency of the Roman law had given rise to more problems than solutions. However, it was not only the vagueness of the concept to which he objected. Maine was also uncomfortable with the ideology imported by the occupancy principle. As he pointed out towards the end of his discussion on this topic, the principle itself presupposed a sophisticated (i.e. modern) understanding of property in terms of which, by default, everything should have an owner.[51] In addition, since the Roman legal concept of ownership, as interpreted by legal scholars since the late medieval period, had come to be interpreted in a highly individualistic manner in subsequent epochs of European legal thought, the default being the single *dominus*, this individualism implicit

47 Maine, *Ancient Law*, 255.

48 Mantena, *Alibis of Empire*, 126.

49 Gibbon and Fernández-Armesto, *The History of the Decline and Fall of the Roman Empire. Vol. 5, Justinian and the Roman Law*, 282.

50 Maine, *Ancient Law*, 255–6.

51 Ibid. 257.

within the idea of occupancy was at odds with Maine's broader thesis, namely that early law prioritised the group's interests over that of the individual.[52]

3. COMMON PROPERTY

Having stated his position that, in ancient law, the family held more legal significance than the individual, Maine set out the main thrust of this chapter.[53] In his view, ancient law did not distinguish between the law of property and that of persons as neatly as in developed Roman law but treated them in an undifferentiated manner.[54] Given that the developed Roman law of property, as interpreted by natural law scholars in the subsequent epochs of European legal history, was resolutely individualist, Maine suggested that it would not serve as a helpful exemplar.[55] He thus had to find a way to link the group to the notion of property. This was achieved by arguing that common property related to the family was a 'rudimentary jural conception' characteristic of legal systems connected through the Indo-European language family. Since Roman law could offer only limited assistance in making this case, as shown in his critique of Savigny, Maine had to look further afield, specifically to contemporaneous legal cultures where common property linked to the family remained a stock feature. His aim with these examples was not to make any point about temporality or 'progress' but to demonstrate the resilience and plasticity of this 'rudimentary jural conception'.

The definitive example, in his view, was the village community found in India.[56] Such an example was not without problems, however. First, there was the issue of Maine's knowledge of the subject. Since *Ancient Law* was written and published before his departure to India, he could not have relied on empirical research to substantiate his claims. Instead, as the text shows, he relied on the information in 'archives' in the North of India and works by English scholars on Muslim and (mainly) Hindu law, such as Mountstuart Elphinstone, for this information.[57] This information pointed to subtle differences in the composition and organisation of

[52] Compare Crone, *Pre-Industrial Societies: Anatomy of the Pre-Modern World*, 115–41, for an account of the individual's place within society in the pre-modern world. Crone's account is not rooted in specific historical examples, thus making it difficult to critique. For a recent account of the creation of this individualist sense of ownership based on Roman law from the eighteenth century onwards, see Di Robilant, *The Making of Modern Property*, 98–130. Kantor, Lambert and Skoda, *Legalism*, 55–74, provides a good survey of the complexities of the situation in Roman law.

[53] Mantena, *Alibis of Empire*, 127–8; Collini, *Liberalism and Sociology*, 27.

[54] Maine, *Ancient Law*, 259.

[55] Ibid. 259–60.

[56] Ibid. 260–2. Pollock and Maine, *Introduction and Notes*, 49–51. McDonagh, 'Towards a Genealogy of the Village in the Nineteenth-Century British Colonial World', 149–54, for an account of the colonial significance and influence of Henry Maine's treatment of the village community. For criticisms of Maine's theory and the limitations of his knowledge concerning the village community in India, see Diamond, *Primitive Law*, 275–6. See also Capogrossi Colognesi, *Modelli di stato e di famiglia nella storiografia dell'800*, 154–64.

[57] Elphinstone, *The History of India*, 120–5; Maine, *Ancient Law*, 262–3; Derrett, *Sir Henry Maine and Law in India, 1858–1958*, 53.

groups owning communal property within village communities between the North and the South of India. The differences are related not only to the nature of the rights assigned to members of the group concerning the common property but also to the connection between members of the group, whether through familial bonds or, more loosely, through purported familial bonds.[58] To counteract any potential criticism based on this diversity, Maine focused on the commonalities, namely that the village community, in its basic form, was an intergenerational group, usually descended from a single family, that owned a body of common property held by and managed by someone appointed by the group for that purpose. The group also devised structures to secure the management and protection of the common property.

Maine carefully addressed the different manifestations of the village community across various legal systems, suggesting that he was aware that the analogy could prove contentious. In rhetorical terms, this is an example of *prolepsis* – countering any anticipated criticism by offering various justifications in advance. To counteract any such criticism further, he argued for plasticity in the concept itself, notably using one of his 'instruments of legal change', namely the legal fiction:

> No institution of the primitive world is likely to have been preserved to our day, unless it has acquired an elasticity foreign to its original nature through some vivifying legal fiction. The village community then is not necessarily an assemblage of blood-relations, but it is either such an assemblage or a body of co-proprietors formed on the model of an association of kinsmen. The type with which it should be compared is evidently not the Roman family, but the Roman gens or house.[59]

The use of the term 'vivifying legal fiction' in this quotation is telling. While Maine would also refer to other legal systems in this chapter, his discussion of Hindu law is the most comprehensive and thus requires more significant investigation. First, in his view, using Hindu law as a comparator was legitimate because he believed in the theory of the connection of specific 'progressive' legal systems through the Indo-European language family.[60] This is not an unimportant point. Hindu law was 'ancient law' for his discussion on this issue. Given the distortion of the Roman law of ownership through natural law and, consequently, the marginalisation of joint ownership in Roman law, it could not be used as the default example here.[61] Instead, Hindu law provided the example that Maine's narrative needed.

Two aspects of his use of Hindu law as his example in this instance are worth noting. The first was an issue of temporality, one of the core themes running through *Ancient Law*. By highlighting the existence of the village community's common property regime in nineteenth-century Hindu law, Maine was delivering a critique of the notion of the linear 'progress' of legal systems from 'primitive' to

[58] Maine, *Ancient Law*, 262–3; Mantena, *Alibis of Empire*, 129–31.

[59] Maine, *Ancient Law*, 264.

[60] Mantena, *Alibis of Empire*, 132.

[61] Grossi, 'An Alternative to Private Property', 40.

'sophisticated', the former based on common property and the latter defined by its individualised notion of ownership. This is not incidental. Much of the European intellectual debate of the preceding two centuries had supported a view of history based on 'progress', especially in their discussions on the history of property law. These works and the notion of 'progress' contained in them were the focus of Maine's critique. As Maine argued, the persistence of the village community and its common property regime in Hindu law was fatal to such a view. As he phrased it: '[b]ut in India this order of ideas is reversed, and it may be said that separate proprietorship is always on its way to becoming proprietorship in common.'[62]

This observation is telling. The village community and its common property regime were not static 'primitive' remnants. Rather, they were dynamic forces in Hindu law, continuing to shape it in the present. Here, as Maine observed in *Village Communities*, the distinction between past and present fell away. This is one of the clearest examples of Maine's support for a cyclical view of legal change.

The second issue relates to the interpretative lens through which those trained in one legal tradition viewed another system. Maine's comments here were squarely aimed at the politics of his day, and he offered a twofold critique of the British colonial administration in India.[63] The first leg of his criticism related to the attempts by colonial administrators to separate real rights from personal rights when dealing with the property regime found in village communities. In his view, this amounted to 'some of the most formidable miscarriages of Anglo-Indian administration'.[64] A recurring theme throughout this chapter, and one in the early history of contract, is that the distinction between contract and property as conceptual categories was more blurred in 'ancient law'. Any attempt to impose a rigid civilian distinction on a system where such a distinction was not as clearly defined was doomed to failure. The second leg of his criticism was directed at how the colonial administration misunderstood the resilience of the village community in the context of the legal system. At various points throughout Maine's discussion of the village community, not only in Hindu law but also in Russian law and further afield, he stressed its resilience in the face of high-level changes imposed on the legal system. To those who chose to ignore the importance of the village community for Indian law, Maine's warning was clear: '[T]he most beneficent systems of government in India have always been those which have recognised it as the basis of administration.'[65]

Having established the importance and resilience of the village community and its common property regime in Hindu law, Maine marshalled several examples from other legal systems to reinforce the idea that it was a widespread phenomenon. These included examples from Russian law and the law applicable to lands on the disputed border between Turkey and the Austrian Empire. For Russia, he

62 Maine, *Ancient Law*, 261.

63 Mantena, *Alibis of Empire*, 138–45.

64 Maine, *Ancient Law*, 260.

65 Ibid. 261.

relied on two books recently published on the Russian Empire, Haxthausen[66] and Tęgoborski,[67] respectively. He does not reveal his sources of information for 'Serbia, Croatia, and the Austrian Sclavonia' or his brief comment about the Scottish Highlands.[68] While the details of these comparisons are not without interest, Maine's use of them is the more critical point. He used these comparisons to make two points central to his argument. First, the village community, no matter how it was constituted, with its common property regime, was a resilient phenomenon: 'The greatest interest of these phenomena . . . arises from the light they throw on the development of distinct proprietary rights inside the groups by which property seems to have been originally held.'[69] Maine's second point was that internal variations in how individuals were assigned common property within the different manifestations of the village community across various systems should not be seen as stages in the development of individual ownership from common property. This point again speaks to his critique of 'progress'. He was, however, prepared to formulate a general rule, namely that: '[P]rivate property, in the shape in which we know it, was chiefly formed by the gradual disentanglement of the separate rights of individuals from the blended rights of a community.'[70]

Maine rounded off his discussion of this topic with a return to his comment concerning the interconnectedness of the law of persons and of property in the 'infancy of law'. Once this is accepted, the development of the law of persons, from family to individual, must also be mirrored in the development from shared to individual property.[71] As is his wont, he concluded the discussion with two rhetorical questions – another clear example of *erotema*. These questions cut to the very heart of the issue; namely, why members of the village community began to respect the rights of individuals to parts of the common property and why certain members of the village community separated from the community at large.[72] Maine wanted his audience to continue contemplating these two central issues even after the lecture had finished.

Before moving away from the notion of common property, it is worth pointing out that Maine did not engage, in his chapter, with a scholarly controversy precipitated by the publication of Mommsen's *Geschichte* in 1854–1856. According to Mommsen's theory, substantiated by references from Cicero, Dionysius of Halicarnassus and Plutarch, at or shortly after the foundation of the Roman State, there must have been a period where the Roman State owned all land before it was gradually distributed out to groups.[73] There is no way to determine whether Maine, writing *Ancient Law* at the same time, was aware of Mommsen's theory.

66 Haxthausen, *The Russian Empire*.

67 Tęgoborski, *Commentaries on the Productive Forces of Russia*.

68 Maine, *Ancient Law*, 267–8.

69 Ibid. 268.

70 Ibid. 269–70.

71 Grossi, 'An Alternative to Private Property', 41.

72 Maine, *Ancient Law*, 270.

73 Momigliano, 'From Mommsen to Max Weber', for a general overview of the issue.

Even if he was, though, there is every reason to suspect that he would not have engaged with it to any great extent. The reasons for this are twofold. First, Maine focused on common property owned by the family group. When his narrative about early (Roman) law starts, the group already holds property in common. Thus, it would not have been necessary to explore how this came to be. This would have brought his audience back to the realm of speculation – a fundamental objection raised by Maine throughout this chapter. Second, even if we assume that Maine was aware of Mommsen's theory, he may not have agreed with it. As Fustel de Coulange would later point out, this theory was not supported by the primary sources on which it was purportedly based.[74]

4. THE ALIENATION OF PROPERTY

Having postulated that ownership, as it came to exist in Roman law of the classical period, emerged from a gradual separation of individual property from common property, Maine now turned his attention to the processes that were likely involved. Given the persistence of common property as a 'rudimentary jural conception', Maine's base assumption was that this line of development could not have been easy, thus necessitating various workarounds by the legal order. These workarounds and the associated instrumentalities of legal change are discussed in detail in the remainder of his chapter.

The first of these is the issue of classification.[75] Here, his critique focuses on how natural law scholars have interpreted Roman property classifications. In his view, their interpretation of Roman legal material gave rise to a priori assumptions that cannot be justified. There is, however, more to this section than merely a critique of the interpretation of Roman legal classifications. As will become apparent, Maine's critique was also aimed at two additional matters, namely the ideologies latent within the Roman legal classifications on the one hand and the role played by agents of legal change, such as courts, in developing and maintaining classifications when the need arose. As such, this section of Maine's work was also devoted to analysing legal change.

The first Roman-law classification addressed by Maine is the distinction between *res mancipi* and *res nec mancipi*.[76] This property classification, traditionally considered to have been introduced in the earliest stages of Roman law, separated (mainly) agricultural property into two categories. Ownership of property of the first category could only be transferred using a complex act known as *mancipatio*. In contrast, the transfer of property ownership in the second category did not

[74] Ashley, Ashley and Fustel de Coulanges, *The Origin of Property in Land*, 100–6.

[75] Maine, *Ancient Law*, 272–3.

[76] Maine, 272–3. See also Pollock and Maine, *Introduction and Notes*, 51–3. Compare Ortolan, Nasmith and Prichard, *The History of Roman Law, from the Text of Ortolan's 'Histoire de La Législation Romaine et Généralisation Du Droit' (Edition of 1870). Translated . . . and Supplemented by a Chronometrical Chart of Roman History by I.T. Prichard and D. Nasmith*, 136–7. See also on the supposed agricultural origins of this distinction, 134–5.

require such formality. The rediscovery of Gaius's Institutes, where this act is discussed in detail, would have strengthened Maine's case.

Maine used this classification to further his argument, made in the first part of this chapter, regarding common property. Once the property of an individual had been separated from that of the group, it had to be clearly distinguished, not only from the group's property but also from that of other individual owners.[77] Evidence of this, for Maine, could be seen in the complexity of the act known as *mancipatio*, and the fact that its requirements had to be strictly observed. In fact, according to Maine, it could be argued that the label, *res mancipi*, did not initially apply to this category. Instead, property of this kind was merely called 'property,' the only assets recognised as such.

This foray into the significance of *res mancipi* permitted Maine, in turn, to present an argument about legal change. The argument has two parts. The first concerns the ideology underlying the distinction between *res mancipi* and *res nec mancipi*. As he pointed out, this distinction is not value-neutral (i.e. 'natural'), like the classification between movable and immovable property adopted later in Roman law, but instead it elevates one category to greater importance.[78] In time, however, the significance of this category and the cumbersome mode of conveyance declined. The reasons for this decline form the second part of the argument. As is well known from the history of Roman law, the Roman jurists of later epochs chose not to expand the category of *res mancipi* to include newly encountered objects. Instead, the category remained closed, thus leading to a proliferation of objects classified as *res nec mancipi*, ownership of which could be transferred eventually with much less formality using the conveyance known as delivery (*traditio*). Although he does not go into detail, Maine proposed that this expansion of the category of *res nec mancipi* and its conveyance through *traditio* must have occurred through the operation of legal fictions and equity. To Maine, the fact that the category was resolutely closed was significant. It demonstrated the 'stubbornness of classification' in early law and indicated another point: that such early classifications were not founded on general intellectual categories.[79]

This discussion of the historically contingent nature of the classification of *res mancipi* and its associated mode of conveyance, *mancipatio*, allowed Maine to critique the natural law view regarding delivery as a mode of conveyance. The crux of the matter is the following text:

> Inst.Gai. 2, 65
> Ergo ex his, quae diximus, apparet quaedam naturali iure alienari, qualia sunt ea, quae traditione alienantur, quaedam civili: nam mancipationis et in iure cessionis et usucapionis ius proprium est civium Romanorum.

[77] Maine, *Ancient Law*, 271–2.
[78] Ibid. 272.
[79] Ibid. 275.

> Thus, from what we have said above, some things are alienated according to natural law, such as property alienated via delivery. In contrast, other things are alienated according to civil law. *Mancipatio*, *cessio in iure*, and *usucapio* are confined to Roman citizens. [Own translation]

Again, Maine does not cite this text, but it is the basis of his discussion and is worth quoting. Based on Gaius's classification of *traditio* as a mode of conveyance according to natural law (*iure naturali*), later repeated in Justinian's Institutes, scholars of natural law in the early modern period and beyond proposed that delivery must therefore predate *mancipatio*. Maine postulated that this was the exact opposite of the historical reality, given the significance of *mancipatio* in developing individual property.[80] However, this was not the end of his treatment of the distinction between *res mancipi* and *res nec mancipi*. Having set out the historical contingency, and thus the peculiarity, of this distinction, he also pointed out that the line of development witnessed in the Roman law here is not necessarily 'typical'.[81] To show how the matter was dealt with differently, namely by classifying property according to the source, he used examples from nineteenth-century India and early Germanic law.

At this point, Maine's argument becomes somewhat dissipated. Structurally, it resembles *aposiopesis*, but instead of leaving the sentence unfinished, as is more common for this type of rhetorical device, the argument itself is left incomplete. Having earlier argued that the distinction between movable and immovable property, later adopted in Roman law, was a value-neutral one, he returned to this point to comment that, due to the utility of this classification, it had proven resilient in civilian systems of the nineteenth century and even in English law where it was still having an impact on academic discussions on the distinction between movable and immovable property.[82] On the back of his comment that the civilian law of movable and immovable property had influenced many civilian systems and even English law to some extent, Maine listed two further examples of the relaxation of strict formalism in Roman law. These two examples, *usucapio* and *cessio in iure*, had a twofold significance in Maine's argument.[83] On the one hand, it permitted Maine to comment on what he perceived to be the remarkable ability of Roman law to develop new ideas, thus also delivering a critique of the slowness with which similar notions were recognised in English law. On the other hand, especially concerning *cessio in iure*, it permitted Maine to introduce courts as an agent of legal change in the remainder of his chapter.

In the rest of the chapter, Maine addresses two topics. The first of these, in keeping with his focus on classifications, is the distinction between ownership and possession.[84] He strongly emphasised the role of courts in maintaining the distinction between the two concepts. In his discussion on courts, Maine engaged

[80] Ibid. 279.
[81] Ibid. 280.
[82] Ibid. 283.
[83] Ibid. 284–90.
[84] Nelson, *An Analysis*, 155–6.

both with continental scholarship and the context of English law. Regarding continental scholarship, Maine touched on Savigny's views regarding the etymology and origins of the concept of possession in Roman law. Maine indicates that Savigny's opinions on the matter were drawn from Niebuhr.[85] Given the chronology of the publication of these two authors, Maine must be referring here to Savigny's *System*, first published between 1840 and 1849 across several volumes. Niebuhr's *Geschichte*, first published in two volumes in 1811–1812, had been translated into English twice by the time Maine researched *Ancient Law*. Thus, whether taken from Niebuhr's English translation or the original German work, Maine was aware that Savigny's account of the development of possession was based on a specific historical episode from the Roman Republic involving the possession of public land and the Agrarian laws. Although he does not cover this episode in detail, his reference again supports his broader thesis about the historical contingency of Roman legal classifications. There was another reason Maine used this episode: namely, to draw attention to an analogous situation in early 1800s English law concerning tenants of church lands.[86] This segue also permitted Maine to comment on the use of possessory interdicts. In broad terms, Maine argued that once a more comprehensive range of persons, not only possessors but also owners, are granted possessory interdicts, it harms the continued existence of the real action traditionally used by owners.

The final part of the chapter is an excursion into the relationship between the Roman conception of ownership and its feudal counterpart.[87] Maine cast doubt on the view that feudal tenure resulted from a post-Roman development, most likely in the aftermath of the collapse of the Western Roman Empire in 476 CE. The aim of this section is twofold. First, it permitted Maine to showcase his historical knowledge and thus also to criticise the assumption above as an example of the poor use of history. Second, he could use this digression to demonstrate one of his legal change agents – equity. His argument was, in essence, that feudal tenure was not a post-Roman development, but rather that an aspect of Roman law likely provided the foundations for feudal tenure, namely *emphyteusis*. In Maine's view, this land tenure was a product of equity. It was gradually adopted within and on the boundaries of the Empire, where Germanic peoples encountered it.

5. CONCLUSIONS

Maine's chapter on the early history of property contains complex arguments requiring careful analysis. The three focus points in this chapter, namely occupancy, common property and restrictions on the alienation of property, were deliberately chosen to support his more significant thesis concerning the importance of acknowledging the historical contingency of property law. As such, the

[85] Maine, *Ancient Law*, 290–1.

[86] Ibid. 295.

[87] Ibid. 298–302; Evans, *Theories and Criticisms of Sir Henry Maine*, 38–42. See also Nelson, *An Analysis*, 156–7.

first focus point, occupancy, may be said to contain a refutation, while the other two focus points serve to construct Maine's alternative.

Maine's critique of occupancy was squarely aimed at its use by natural law scholars. At the heart of his criticism was the ahistorical use of this Roman legal principle to justify two essential claims: acquiring ownership of spoils of war and explaining the origins of property. Regarding the first claim, Maine argued that the historical context of occupancy as a Roman legal principle demonstrated a diversity of practices, undermining the notion that there was a single legal rule on this issue that could be transplanted to an early modern context and beyond. It also argued against the idea that the rule was a manifestation of natural law. The second claim, namely as a justification for the origins of property, was equally problematic. It was too vague to be applied to other contexts and fed into a narrative about 'progress', which Maine found troubling.

The remaining two points of focus in this chapter were devoted to producing an alternative hypothesis concerning the development of property law. To appreciate Maine's point, it is important to stress that his aim was never to describe a trajectory of law from beginning to end. In fact, given his discussion of the Indian evidence, his argument appears to suggest the opposite. For Maine, clues about property development had to be sought in the relationship between the group and the individual, or to phrase it differently, between recognising individual ownership as an offshoot of communal ownership. This process would have been familiar to anyone with knowledge of Roman law. Evidence of this process was evident in property law and in related areas regarding the recognition of the ability of spouses and children in power to own property separately from the *paterfamilias*. How, then, should the Indian evidence be interpreted? Maine's point here is about 'progress'. It was not the inevitable destiny of all 'progressive' legal systems to transform from communal to individual ownership. These two concepts did not represent stages in the progress of a legal system. Rather, they were the consequences of various competing legal forces that operated in cycles. His attempt to explain the interaction between communal and individual ownership in Roman law using the drivers of legal change, such as legal fictions and equity, was explicitly aimed at drawing attention to these interactions. It was also meant as a critique against Roman legal scholars who, by focusing on individual ownership in the works of earlier natural law scholars, had neglected to discuss communal ownership as a continuing force, even in developed Roman law.

Chapter 7

The Individual and the State: Contract, Delict and Crime

> The general duties of mankind are imposed by their public and private relations, but their specific obligations to each other can only be the effect of, 1, a promise; 2, a benefit; or 3, an injury; and when these obligations are ratified by law, the interested party may compel the performance by a judicial action.[1]

1. INTRODUCTION

The quotation from Gibbon's famous chapter on Roman law provides a good starting point for Maine's treatment of contract, delict and crime, as it likely provided the kernel of the idea behind his discussion. In *Ancient Law*, the development of contract law is covered in a single chapter, while delict and crime are addressed together in the subsequent chapter. As the quotation above shows, it is impossible to separate these topics entirely, as they are intellectually connected. Given Gibbon's influence on Maine's work and how his book was used to signpost debates in European legal and political scholarship on natural law, it stands to reason that these topics should be addressed collectively. The crux of the issue that connects these three topics is the legal obligation.[2] In the legal and political discourse of the seventeenth and eighteenth centuries, the legal obligation had come to play a central role in discussions concerning the origins of the State, on the one hand, and the extent of an individual's legal duty not to harm another, on the other hand. Maine alludes to these debates, especially those surrounding the 'social contract' as set out in the works of Hobbes, Locke and, especially, Rousseau in his chapter on contract. More specifically, the focus of his concern was the extent to which natural law scholars of that period had assumed that the formation of the State was based on contract, thus implying that contract played a vital role in the very early stages of the State and the development of its legal system.[3] A similar concern is visible in his discussion of delict and crime, namely,

[1] Gibbon and Fernández-Armesto, *The History of the Decline and Fall of the Roman Empire. Vol. 5, Justinian and the Roman Law*, 287–8.

[2] Hägerström, 'Rights, Obligations and the Binding Force of Contracts in Roman Law and in Natural Law Theory', for a survey of the debate. See also Hart, *Essays on Bentham*, 127–61.

[3] As pointed out by Vinogradoff, *The Teaching of Sir Henry Maine; an Inaugural Lecture Delivered in Corpus Christi College Hall on March 1, 1904*, 4, Maine's scepticism of this idea was an important thread throughout his works. See Cassirer, *The Philosophy of the Enlightenment*, 253–74; Woodard, 'A Wake (or Awakening?) For Historical Jurisprudence', 226–8.

the extent to which members of a society are duty-bound not to harm others or their property. There, Maine also engages with statute law as an 'instrumentality' of legal change. These are the central themes of the two chapters in *Ancient Law*.

2. CONTRACT

Maine's chapter on the early history of contract is a comprehensive critique of its scope in ancient law. The discussion of contract (as well as delict and crime) marks the end of the narrative arc in Maine's book. This form of repetition has a rhetorical quality to it. The essence of the first sentence of chapter one of *Ancient Law* is repeated at the end of the book's cyclical narrative arc in the discussion of legislation – what begins with a code also ends with a code. As with most topics discussed in *Ancient Law*, the crux of Maine's criticism resides in the limited attention paid by earlier natural law scholars to historical realities. A lack of historical understanding of the original scope and subsequent development of contract in ancient law had given rise to ahistorical fallacies perpetuated in works of the early modern period and beyond. His criticism focused on the views proposed by legal scholars who, seeing the extent to which contract underpinned vast swathes of Victorian society, argued that this scenario must have prevailed in the past.[4] More specifically, given the significance of natural law and the state of nature in discussions about the social contract, these scholars assumed that ancient society must have also been founded on contractual relationships, thus assigning an expansive role to contract in ancient law.

An excellent example of this may be found in Gibbon's opening statement on contract, as quoted above. The gist of Gibbon's statement is clear: legal obligations play a significant role in society because of the broad scope of their application (across the law of contract and delict) and because they are the product of 'universal reason and justice' – a shorthand reference to natural law.[5] In addition to Maine's criticism of natural law scholarship, this chapter was almost certainly also a commentary on the state of contract law in nineteenth-century English law in which individualism and the will theory played an important role, as the work of Atiyah and others have shown.[6] Still, these issues are not addressed directly by Maine, thus reinforcing the Humanist purpose of this work.[7]

Maine questioned the view scholars of natural law held that contract played a prominent role in ancient law on two grounds. The first was the misguided belief that everything in the present must have some origin in the past. Or, as he put it: '. . . the mistake of supposing that every wheel and bolt in the modern

[4] Atiyah, *The Rise and Fall of Freedom of Contract*, 324; Tuori, *Lawyers and Savages*, 91–2; Maine, *Ancient Law*, 304, 313–14.

[5] Gibbon and Fernández-Armesto, *The History of the Decline and Fall of the Roman Empire. Vol. 5, Justinian and the Roman Law*, 288.

[6] Atiyah, *The Rise and Fall of Freedom of Contract*, 226–37.

[7] Ibid., 324–58. See also Ibbetson, *A Historical Introduction to the Law of Obligations*, 220–61; Swain, *The Law of Contract 1670–1870*, 274–82.

social machine had its counterpart in more rudimentary societies.'[8] To illustrate this point, he cited an example of this type of reasoning in Montesquieu's *Persian Letters*.[9] This work, published in 1721, was a series of letters written by two fictitious Persian noblemen who had settled in France during the latter part of the eighteenth century. Four of these letters (11–14) discuss the fate of the Troglodytes, a people of the Arabian Peninsula who, as described in letter 11, 'lacked all notion of justice and equity'.[10] As a result of this fundamental flaw, Troglodyte society eventually self-destructed. On realising their error, only two Troglodyte families came to observe justice and equity and consequently flourished.

Montesquieu used the account of the fate of the Troglodytes as a morality tale designed to warn against the dangers of lawlessness. More specifically, in keeping with the view of natural law scholars, the underlying implication was that only a social compact guaranteed the rise of 'justice and equity'. Without it, there could only be chaos, to paraphrase Hobbes's famous statement in *Leviathan*. Maine's criticism of such a narrative extended to the additional inferences drawn from this view. He phrased it as follows:

> If the inference be obtained from it that society could not possibly hold together without attaching the sacredness to promises and agreements which should be on something like a par with the respect that is paid to them by a mature civilisation, it involves an error so grave as to be fatal to all sound understanding of legal history. The fact is that the Troglodytes have flourished and founded powerful states with very small attention to the obligations of contract. The point which before all others has to be apprehended in the constitution of primitive societies is that the individual creates for himself few or no rights, and few or no duties.[11]

The final sentence of this passage is telling. According to Maine, a society can flourish ('progress') without giving contracts a prominent place within its legal system. This was his central point. This more limited role of contract in ancient society tied into Maine's earlier statements concerning the prominence of the family rather than the individual. This focus would have affected the existence and growth of rights and duties connected to the individual. More generally, this statement contains a crystallisation of Maine's primary idea underlying his book: ancient law was not constructed around the individual, but around the family. Since contract, as understood by the Victorians, tended to be an expression of individualism, it stands to reason that this situation could not be universal or primordial. It was historically contingent.

The second issue criticised by Maine related to the role of morality in contract. According to natural law scholars, as ancient society was based on contract, such societies must have had a more refined concept of morality than in the present.

[8] Maine, *Ancient Law*, 310–11, 315.
[9] Ibid. 311; Levy, 'Constitutional History', 260–4.
[10] Davidson, *Montesquieu*, 55–9 (Broadway translations).
[11] Maine, *Ancient Law*, 311.

As an example of this position, Maine used a work by Rousseau, published in 1750, called *Discourse on the Sciences and Arts*.[12] The work, originally written as an entry to an essay competition to debate the question of the impact of arts and science on morals, consisted of a critical account of 'progress' and an argument that scientific progress had not universally benefited civilisation. In his essay, Rousseau pointed to several pre-modern civilisations, including the ancient Persians, who had been negatively affected by progress. He put it this way:

> Contrast these scenes with that of the mores of the small number of peoples who, protected against this contagion of vain knowledge, have by their virtues brought about their own happiness and the model for other nations. Such were the first Persians, a singular nation in which virtue was learned just as science is among us, that subjugated Asia so easily, and that alone has enjoyed the distinction of having the history of its institutions taken for a philosophical novel.[13]

Maine's critique of this statement extended to two issues. First, the implication that ancient societies had somehow possessed a more refined form of morality (the learning of 'virtue' juxtaposed against the learning of 'science') was historically doubtful. He phrased it as follows:

> The veracity and good faith attributed to the ancient Persians are repeatedly pointed out as traits of primitive innocence which have been gradually obliterated by civilisation; and at a later period he found a basis for all his speculation in the doctrine of an original social contract. The social contract or compact is the most systematic form which has ever been assumed by the error we are discussing.[14]

As this quotation shows, Maine objected to the underlying implication of a 'primitive innocence' at the heart of Rousseau's statement. Not only was it a manifestation of the 'golden age' fallacy, but it also implied a close connection between a supposed more elevated form of morality in the past and the foundation of the State through the social contract.[15] It was these implicit assumptions to which Maine objected. Additionally, although discussions surrounding the social contract had declined somewhat by the mid-1800s when *Ancient Law* was written, Maine showed that the legacy of this debate continued to affect contemporary scholarship:

> The favourite occupation of active minds at the present moment, and the one which answers to the speculations of our forefathers on the origin of the social state, is the analysis of society as it exists and moves before our eyes; but, through omitting to call

12 Riley, 'Rousseau, Fénelon, and the Quarrel between the Ancients and the Moderns', 87–8.

13 Rousseau, *Basic Political Writings*, 9–10.

14 Maine, *Ancient Law*, 308–9.

15 Noone, 'Rousseau's Theory of Natural Law as Conditional', 37; Carbonneau, 'The Implicit Teaching of Utopian Speculations: Rousseau's Contribution to The Natural Law Tradition', 140, generally. See also Hart, *Essays on Bentham*, 79–104.

> in the assistance of history, this analysis too often degenerates into an idle exercise of curiosity, and is especially apt to incapacitate the inquirer for comprehending states of society which differ considerably from that to which he is accustomed. The mistake of judging men of other periods by the morality of our own day has its parallel in the mistake of supposing that every wheel and bolt in the modern social machine had its counterpart in more rudimentary societies.[16]

There is much to unpack in this quotation. According to Maine, speculations about the social contract had, by the nineteenth century, transformed into a pre-occupation with continuous improvement, or 'progress', as the Victorians called it. In his view, focusing on societal (and legal) change without considering history was futile. This was his other central point in this chapter. In addition, the strength of the final sentence deserves specific mention. To Maine, morality was a contingent element of society which had to be assessed in context and, in the case of ancient society, using actual history rather than philosophical speculation. Any speculative statements implying that those in ancient cultures had a more refined form of morality, now lost, due to their willingness to enter into a social contract to form a society, should be avoided. At best, it was a version of the 'golden age' fallacy. It was a fundamental mistake to judge earlier societies and their laws through the lens of contemporary morality.

Having made these two broad points, Maine devoted the remainder of the chapter to an account of the growth of the various parts of the Roman law of contracts. As will presently become clear, his account was designed to support the two central claims made above. It was not meant to be a detailed survey of the specifics of each contract as could be found in textbooks of Roman law. Instead, he highlighted specific aspects of these contracts to the extent that they supported his two central claims.

Maine's argument in the chapter on contract rested on the premise that Roman law provided a good account of how ideas change within a legal system over time. According to his definition, it could thus be used as an example of legal change in a 'progressive' legal system. Although he did not regard Roman law as wholly typical, there was enough typicality to permit it to be used as an example, thereby reaffirming his use of Roman law as a model in *Ancient Law*.[17] Towards the end of the chapter, he also made a case for the intellectual importance of the Roman law of contracts for other subjects such as theology, politics and moral philosophy, likely to reinforce his view of the general intellectual importance of studying Roman law.

The broad thrust of Maine's argument is as follows. The development of the Roman law of contracts demonstrates the gradual movement (a cycle) from an insistence on external formalities as indicators of legal validity in archaic Roman law to an almost complete abandonment of formalities in later phases of Roman law,

[16] Maine, *Ancient Law*, 310–11.
[17] Ibid. 339.

replaced by a reliance on the parties' will.[18] Given the prominence of the will theory in Victorian contract law, there can be little doubt that his treatment of the topic in this manner was purposive. His underlying point was that the prominence of the will theory was a contingent phenomenon of Victorian society and its law. It should not be projected onto the past.

Furthermore, given Maine's views on linearity and time, the other likely point was that the will's prominence in Victorian contract theory was part of a cycle destined to change. To Maine, the scope of contract was relatively narrow in archaic Roman law compared to the broader concept of contract characteristic of classical Roman law and beyond. He used several Roman contracts to demonstrate this cycle of development. To the casual observer, his use of Roman law initially appears slight. There are no pinpoint references to Roman law texts, nor does he cite contemporaneous literature to support his assertions. As will become apparent, however, this first look belies a sophisticated understanding of Roman legal sources. It cannot be denied, however, that one work influenced Maine's discussion in terms of content and the arrangement of material here. Gibbon similarly provides an overview of specific Roman contracts; his work seems to have inspired Maine here.

Maine discusses five contracts in Roman law, roughly in the order familiar to scholars of Roman law. These are *nexum*, *stipulatio*, literal contracts, real contracts and consensual contracts. Each fulfilled an essential role in his narrative regarding legal change. *Nexum*, that early form of debt bondage discussed in detail by Livy, provided a convenient starting point for Maine's discussion of the development of contracts in Roman law. Nineteenth-century works such as those of Niebuhr, another clear source of Maine's ideas, show that it was a popular topic of discussion.[19] Although the existence of *nexum* likely predated the enactment of the Twelve Tables, the fact that it was mentioned in writing as a provision of the Twelve Tables meant that its nature and eventual changes through statute could be discussed from that point onwards, rather than having to delve into the uncertainties of the law prior to that time, and fed into Maine's more significant concern with written, rather than unwritten law.[20] Maine used *nexum* to make three central points about the development of the Roman law of contracts.

The first point related to *nexum* as an act *per aes et libram*. Acts of this type involved ritual and required the presence of the parties to the agreement, a scale holder and at least five witnesses who had to be Roman citizens. The parties to the agreement had to express the content carefully, using precise wording, and signify the ritual transfer of money using a piece of uncast bronze tapped against

[18] Watson, *The Evolution of Law*, 3–42, for a survey. For criticisms of the formalism of 'ancient law' in the abstract, as a general rule, see Diamond, *Primitive Law*, 350. See also for general criticism of his chapter on contract, in anthropological terms, Diamond, *Primitive Law*, 391.

[19] Niebuhr, *Niebuhr's History of Rome, Epitomised from the Larger Work, and Adapted to the Use of Schools and Colleges by Travers Twiss; with Chronological Tables and an Appendix*, 146–7.

[20] Cornell, *The Beginnings of Rome*, 280–3, for a survey.

the scales. Maine used the nature of this transaction to reinforce his point about the insistence on external formalities in creating a contract in archaic Roman law.

The second point concerns the absence of specialisation in legal terminology in archaic Roman law.[21] Taking his cue seemingly from the definition of Festus whereby *nexum*, from the verb *nectere*, means 'to tie or to bind', a point which he would later reinforce in his discussion on the rise of the abstract concept of the obligation in law, Maine used the fact that the term *nexum* was used in different senses by different Latin authors (Livy and Cicero, for example) to make a more significant point about formalism in archaic Roman law.[22] In archaic Roman law, a single term could denote various things, and with time, as circumstances demanded, legal terminology tended to become more specialised. Thus, in Maine's view, the debate about whether *nexum* should be seen as a contract or as a conveyance missed the point:

> Now conveyances transfer proprietary rights, contracts create obligations – how then can the two be included under the same name or same general conception? This, like many similar embarrassments, has been occasioned by the error of ascribing to the mental condition of an unformed society a faculty which preeminently belongs to an advanced stage of intellectual development, the faculty of distinguishing in speculation ideas which are blended in practice.[23]

This statement permitted Maine to circumvent the problematic issue, discussed in Roman law textbooks of the time, of the differing definitions of *nexum*. It provided a convenient reason not to address the related issue of the relationship between *nexum* and *mancipatio*.[24]

Finally, and perhaps most controversially, Maine used *nexum* to demonstrate how, in his view, specialisation of legal terminology occurred in Roman law. This is the most compelling example, demonstrating Maine's knowledge of Roman law. The matter revolves around two famous statements concerning the meaning of *nexum* by Varro and Festus respectively.[25] Varro's account provides two definitions of *nexum*. One is attributed to Manilius, who defines *nexum* as every act *per aes et libram*, including *mancipatio* (*in quo sint mancipia*); another is attributed to Mucius, who employs a similar definition but excludes *mancipatio* (*praeterquam mancipio detur*). Festus's account of this issue cites Aelius Gallus, who essentially follows the definition of Manilius and includes *mancipatio*. Much had already been written about this problem when Maine wrote *Ancient Law*. His solution to the

[21] Maine, *Ancient Law*, 340. See also Ibid. 316.

[22] Roby, *Roman Private Law in the Times of Cicero and of the Antonines*, II, 70, 296–310, for a slightly later and comprehensive summary of the issue.

[23] Maine, *Ancient Law*, 315.

[24] Capogrossi Colognesi, *La costruzione del diritto privato romano*, 46–53, on *mancipatio*. See also Tuori, *Lawyers and Savages*, 131–6.

[25] Roby, *Roman Private Law in the Times of Cicero and of the Antonines*, II, 296–310, for a survey of the primary sources.

issue was to attribute the later technical use of *mancipatio*, as a form of conveyance, to the process of specialisation of the vocabulary around *nexum*:

> There seems to have been one solemn ceremonial at first for all solemn transactions, and its name at Rome appears to have been *nexum*. . . . But we have not very far to move onwards before we come to a period at which the notion of a contract has disengaged itself from the notion of a conveyance. A double change has thus taken place. The transaction 'with the copper and the balance,' when intended to have for its office the transfer of property, is known by the new and special name of mancipation. The ancient *nexum* still designates the same ceremony, but only when it is employed for the special purpose of solemnising a contract.[26]

Given that so much surrounding *nexum* remains unresolved, due to the scarcity and opacity of the sources, Maine's account presents a helpful solution to the problem. His view that *nexum* was the oldest contract in Roman law also casts light on his use of sources. It is highly likely that this position, which was not shared universally by Roman law scholars of the early nineteenth century, was derived from the French jurist Ortolan, whose historical commentary on the Institutes of Justinian ran through several editions and was influential during the first part of the nineteenth century.[27] Unlike Savigny, who championed *mutuum* as the earliest form of Roman contract, Ortolan argued that *nexum* must have been the original contract from which other contracts were derived.[28] As Roman law scholars in the generations after Maine would point out, however, the scarce source material failed to make a credible case for this position.[29]

The next phase in developing the idea of contract in Roman law upon which Maine focused was what he referred to as 'the intermediate stage'. At this point, the concept of the obligation as a legal tie that binds the parties to the contract had already been formed, but a formless obligation was not yet sufficient to create a contract under Roman law. The parties still had to fulfil additional requirements, as outlined in the categorisation of the fourfold division of Roman contracts (real, verbal, literal and consensual).

Maine covered, in order, verbal, literal, real and consensual contracts in this chapter. He did not devote space to each contract, especially in the latter three categories, but only picked out specific examples. The order in which the contracts were discussed permitted him to make meaningful observations regarding legal change in this area of law. In Maine's view, verbal contracts, specifically in the form of the verbal question and answer form known as the stipulation, were:

26 Maine, *Ancient Law*, 317–18.

27 Ortolan, Nasmith and Prichard, *The History of Roman Law, from the Text of Ortolan's 'Histoire de La Législation Romaine et Généralisation Du Droit' (Edition of 1870). Translated . . . and Supplemented by a Chronometrical Chart of Roman History by I.T. Prichard and D. Nasmith*, 272–3. Nelson, *An Analysis*, 195–6 notes the similarity between Maine and Ortolan on this point.

28 Hunter, Cross and Gaius, *A Systematic and Historical Exposition of Roman Law in the Order of a Code*, 537, for a summary of Savigny's view.

29 Ibid. 539.

'the eldest known descendant of the primitive *nexum*'.[30] This notion of the connection between *nexum* and stipulation, known as the 'derivative theory' of stipulation, was taken from continental literature, having been mooted by Ortolan at this point, which is the likely source of his idea.[31] To Maine, the formal question-and-answer component of the stipulation demonstrated the 'intermediate state' in which the legal obligation remained bound to some element of formalism. He phrased it as follows: '[t]his question and answer constituted the additional ingredient which, as I have just explained, was demanded by the primitive notion over and above the mere agreement of the persons interested.'[32]

As Roman law scholars in the generation after Maine would point out, no source material supports the idea that stipulation was a *nexum* from which the formalities had been removed.[33] If anything, the evidence of stipulation in archaic Roman law suggested that this contract was of considerable antiquity.

The remainder of Maine's discussion on stipulation concerned the intricacies of the question and answer, and more specifically, the extent to which the verbal nature of the process, at first sight, seemed to provide little protection in law to the promisee.[34] This section is one of the few places where source material is cited directly. Maine used citations from two plays by the Roman playwright Plautus to demonstrate the workings of the stipulation. Not much can be inferred from these citations, however. The two passages were known in Victorian literature and were used here mainly to demonstrate the legal position of the promisee in the stipulation. According to Maine, the fact that the promisee was the one who phrased the question showed that he was, in fact, more protected in law than previously surmised.[35] This permitted Maine to make a more significant claim about the reason for the longevity of stipulation as a form of contract, namely its utility.

Maine's treatment of the literal contract, specifically of debts evidenced by ledger entries, is brief but makes two essential points. By the time *Ancient Law* was written, the discovery of Gaius's Institutes, where the matter is discussed with great clarity, had begun to replace the earlier and less reliable source material for this contract. Nonetheless, despite the clarity of Gaius's account, not all matters were resolved, and the question of how the obligation was created and the legal significance of the different types of entries remained an ongoing concern.[36] Maine seems aware of this controversy and left it open. For his narrative, the more important point was the entry itself. To him, the entry indicated that contract in

30 Maine, *Ancient Law*, 326.

31 Ortolan, *Explication historique des Instituts de l'empereur Justinien*, II, 333; Ortolan, Nasmith and Prichard, *The History of Roman Law, from the Text of Ortolan's 'Histoire de La Législation Romaine et Généralisation Du Droit' (Edition of 1870). Translated . . . and Supplemented by a Chronometrical Chart of Roman History by I.T. Prichard and D. Nasmith*, 273.

32 Maine, *Ancient Law*, 326.

33 Hunter, Cross and Gaius, *A Systematic and Historical Exposition of Roman Law in the Order of a Code*, 539.

34 Maine, *Ancient Law*, 326–7.

35 Ibid. 330.

36 Ortolan, *Explication historique des Instituts de l'empereur Justinien*, II, 335; Maine, *Ancient Law*, 331.

Roman law had now dispensed with all the original formalities, provided the debt was evidenced in writing. For Maine, it was 'another step downwards in the history of contract-law'.[37]

Maine's account of the real contract, specifically the loan of money (*mutuum*), is somewhat brief. In his view, this category of contract demonstrates 'a great advance in ethical conceptions'.[38] His motivation for this statement lies in the fact that this category of contract creates an obligation by the delivery of the object. To him, this indicates that '[f]or the first time . . . moral considerations appear as an ingredient of contract-law, and the real contract differs from its two predecessors in being founded on these . . .'.[39] Later in the chapter, where Maine summarised his argument, he phrased it as follows:

> In the real contract a moral duty is for the first time recognised, and persons who have joined or acquiesced in the partial performance of an engagement are forbidden to repudiate it on account of defects in form.[40]

There is much to unpack in this short overview, not just in the phrase 'partial performance', but most significantly the fact that Maine does not discuss the link between *nexum*, the earliest form of the loan agreement in Roman law, and the subsequent creation of *mutuum*. In addition, he does not raise the issue concerning the fundamental difference between *mutuum* and the other contracts grouped within the category of real contracts, namely that in *mutuum*, ownership of the object is transferred. It would have been helpful had he unpacked the content of the 'ethical conceptions' somewhat more expansively to explain the significance of this phrase more fully. Maine's reference here was likely because the loan of money, the archetypal instance of *mutuum*, was essentially gratuitous. More than anything, this suggested a prior trust relationship between the parties to the contract.

The final group of contracts, the consensual ones discussed by Maine, played an essential part in his narrative.[41] As will be recalled, the fourfold classification of contract, to Maine, represented a later epoch in developing the idea of contract in Roman law. Two aspects of this group of contracts deserved specific attention. The first was the relationship between the obligation at the core of the contract and the consensus required for these contracts to exist. Maine pointed out that the obligation and the requirement of consent were two separate issues.[42] Thus, consent was the formality required by Roman law for this group of contracts to exist, much like the delivery of the object was a requirement in real contracts. The second aspect on which Maine focused was the classification of these contracts as

[37] Maine, *Ancient Law*, 331.
[38] Ibid. 331.
[39] Ibid. 332.
[40] Ibid. 338.
[41] Ibid. 332–4.
[42] Ibid. 333.

originating from the law of nations (*ius gentium*).[43] In his view, this association was likely a later development. In subsequent epochs, when the law of nations and the law of nature had become conflated, it had led to the erroneous assumption that these contracts were 'natural' under the law of nature and thus had to be the most ancient Roman contracts. As Maine argued, these were probably the most recent contracts to develop in Roman law.

Maine's discussion on the history of contract closes with a short account of the final stage of its development, namely when contract had shed all the formalities associated with it in early Roman law. In his view, this stage came about through the work of the Roman Praetor, specifically when it came to giving legal effect to naked pacts. In this way, Maine ties his discussion back to his account of the different ways legal change occurs. Here, specifically, 'equity' – in the sense of Praetorian legal intervention – advances the law of contract:

> The revolution of the ancient law of contract was consummated when the Praetor of some one year announced in his Edict that he would grant equitable actions upon pacts which had never been matured at all into contracts, provided only that the pacts in question had been founded on a consideration (*causa*). Pacts of this sort are always enforced under the advanced Roman jurisprudence. The principle is merely the principle of the consensual contracts carried to its proper consequence . . . .[44]

To the scholar of Roman law, the brevity of Maine's account of the progressive recognition of pacts as binding legal obligations is breathtaking. At the same time, his narrative did not require an in-depth discussion of the substantive law. To Maine, it was enough to show that Roman law had seemingly arrived at a point where all external formalities had been discarded in favour of a formless agreement relying on the parties' will. As subsequent scholarship on the recognition of a general principle of contract in European legal thought has shown, however, this process would take considerable time, and the doctrinal development needed was not straightforward.[45]

3. DELICT AND CRIME

Maine's chapter on delict and crime contains little substantive discussion of individual examples from Roman law.[46] It is, therefore, difficult to determine its exact intellectual inspiration or its choice of focus. Some of his statements echo Gibbon's in broad terms. Still, the substance is different.[47] First, Gibbon provides a more

[43] Ibid. 334–5.

[44] Ibid. 337. Compare Gibbon and Fernández-Armesto, *The History of the Decline and Fall of the Roman Empire. Vol. 5, Justinian and the Roman Law*, 288.

[45] Nanz, *Die Entstehung des allgemeinen Vertragsbegriffs im 16. bis 18. Jahrhundert*, generally.

[46] Evans, *Theories and Criticisms of Sir Henry Maine*, 69–70; Nelson, *An Analysis*, 197–206; Oldham, *Analysis*, 27–31.

[47] Gibbon and Fernández-Armesto, *The History of the Decline and Fall of the Roman Empire. Vol. 5, Justinian and the Roman Law*, 290–303.

detailed survey of these two branches of law and focuses on individual examples drawn from Roman law. Second, there is less of a narrative in Gibbon's account, whereas an explicit narrative drives Maine's work, especially in this chapter. It is also difficult to draw a more general line of influence to the circumstances of Maine's own time. The criminal law reforms of the early nineteenth century had already been embedded as law by the time Maine was researching *Ancient Law*, and even though Bentham's law reform agenda was widely discussed at the time, Maine does not seem to direct criticism specifically at him in this chapter.[48]

The absence of any discussion of specific delicts or crimes in Maine's book cannot be attributed entirely to a lack of information. Besides the titles devoted to the subject in the Digest, delict is extensively discussed in the Institutes of Gaius and of Justinian. As Mackenzie's near-contemporaneous work on Roman law shows, Roman criminal law did not feature prominently in either of these textbooks.[49] Nevertheless, there was no shortage of monographs on aspects of Roman criminal law written in French and German during the first half of the nineteenth century.[50] This suggests that Maine's focus in this chapter is an authorial choice and should be examined in detail.

A comparison of Maine's chapter on delict and crime with the one on contract reveals subtle differences. This is expected since the two chapters had different roles in his broader narrative. The overarching purpose of Maine's chapter on contract was to question its supposed prominence in the early stages of ancient law. This, in turn, allowed him to critique, albeit indirectly, the social contract theory dominant in natural law scholarship of the eighteenth century and beyond. The purpose of the delict and crime chapter was different. Whereas delict in Roman law was not without statutory intervention, they played a much more significant role in developing Roman criminal law. Since legislation was one of the 'instrumentalities' of legal change identified by Maine earlier in the book, this chapter, focusing on Roman criminal law and the body of statute law on which it was based, afforded him space to evaluate statute law and its limits more generally.

Although contract and delict were linked intellectually in classical Roman law as sources of a legal obligation, the two branches of law were very different structurally; the Roman law of contracts in its developed form consisted mainly of four categories of 'named' Roman contracts with individual contracts grouped within these, while the 'named' Roman delicts were all said to be of the same 'genus'.[51] In classical Roman law, these were surrounded by various ad hoc cases that did not fit neatly into these categories but were nonetheless afforded protection in law. By contrast, despite the statutory reforms of Sulla

48 Rustigan, 'A Reinterpretation of Criminal Law Reform in Nineteenth Century England'; McGowen, 'The Image of Justice and Reform of the Criminal Law in Early Nineteenth-Century England', generally. See also Sverdlik, 'Bentham on Temptation and Deterrence', generally.

49 Mackenzie, *Studies in Roman Law*, 329.

50 Laboulaye, *Essai sur les lois criminelles des Romains concernant la responsabilité des magistrats*; Zumpt, *Das Criminalrecht der Römischen Republik*, for example.

51 Inst.Gai.3.182.

and later Augustus, Roman criminal law consisted of a raft of individual crimes established by specific statutes.[52] Irrespective of this difference, Maine's focus in this chapter is not on individual delicts (or crimes). He spends a few paragraphs discussing theft and its associated remedies, but only to make a more significant point about the calculation of penalties in early Roman law. Instead, in this chapter, he focuses on the legal change from the earliest Roman law to the law of the Empire and beyond. This does not mean that classification was unimportant to him. As will become apparent later, classification in Roman criminal law permitted Maine to make an important point about the limitations of legislation as an instrumentality of legal change.

Determining which legal systems Maine chose to illustrate his examples in this case is essential. Throughout the book, Maine uses Roman law as an example of a 'progressive' system. There was undoubtedly no scarcity of source material in Roman law to demonstrate the development of criminal law. Still, the available material did not adequately substantiate his more speculative claims, especially regarding the law in earlier periods. For these, he had to rely on the early medieval Romano-Germanic law codifications (including 'Anglo-Saxon' law) and, to some extent, archaic Greek law.[53] The function of these comparisons, as elsewhere in the book, was limited to supporting these more speculative claims and, in substance, the chapter focuses on Roman law.

The starting point of Maine's chapter is the earliest phases of ancient law. The available evidence, drawn primarily from the Romano-Germanic codifications, permitted Maine to lay down a fundamental premise for this part of the book. In the earliest phases of ancient law, the law of 'wrongs' had a much more expansive place in the legal order than it would later inhabit.[54] This is because other branches of law had not yet developed, primarily due to factors such as the dominance of the family and the underdeveloped notion of contract. Since the same barriers did not apply to the law of 'wrongs', its scope was potentially much broader. Maine argued that the code of Draco and the Romano-Germanic codes contained sufficient evidence to extrapolate a more general premise, also applicable to the period surrounding Twelve Tables, even if the evidence was less strong there, namely: '[T]he more archaic the code, the fuller and more minuter is its penal legislation.'[55] There is little doubt that Maine framed this premise expressly to make a broader allusion, central to his running critique of

52 Ferguson, *The History of the Progress and Termination of the Roman Republic By Adam Ferguson, LL.D. Professor of Moral Philosophy in the University of Edinburgh. In Three Volumes. Illustrated with Maps.*, I, 452–3, for a discussion of these changes.

53 Maine, *Ancient Law*, 367. Kemble, *The Saxons in England*, is the only book directly cited in this chapter to support his claims about 'Anglo-Saxon' law. For archaic Greek law, he returns to the Homeric trial scene discussed in detail earlier in the book in the context of his comparative observations on the 'wager' in the Roman actions-at-law system.

54 Maine, *Ancient Law*, 367.

55 Ibid. 368. Compare Gibbon and Fernández-Armesto, *The History of the Decline and Fall of the Roman Empire. Vol. 5, Justinian and the Roman Law*, 291–2.

natural law discussions about the original state of man and his warlike nature, as famously described by Hobbes in *Leviathan*. Maine preferred a more sophisticated explanation for the phenomenon. While it cannot be ruled out that the presence of violence in ancient society may have been a factor, in his view, the more likely answer for the expansive nature of the law of 'wrongs' was that the other areas of private law had not yet developed.[56] At first sight, this does not appear too convincing, especially given the state of the evidence, but Maine's point is more complex, and in general terms, has an air of plausibility. In the early stages of ancient law, the State had not yet developed to the point where it could prosecute perpetrators of crime on behalf of its citizenry. Thus, citizens had to rely on the concept of 'wrong' in civil law to obtain legal redress.[57] In Maine's view, this accounted for the expansive scope of this area of law in ancient society.

This is the central theme of this chapter, and there can be little doubt that it was explicitly developed to offer a critique of natural law scholarship. One of Maine's recurring criticisms of this type of scholarship is its poor use of history. This criticism forms the foundation of his narrative in this chapter. Once the social contract had been formed, according to natural law scholarship, the State came into existence immediately. Maine objected to the view that the State had sprung from the head of Zeus fully formed. Instead, as he argued in this chapter, and to some extent in his discussion of the early development of law, it would take considerable time and intellectual growth for the State to acquire the ability to prosecute individuals on behalf of its citizenry. This fact could only be appreciated by focusing on actual historical examples.

Using information from archaic Roman law, Maine posited the existence of an undifferentiated concept of 'wrong' in the earliest stages of ancient law.[58] This would separate into more circumscribed categories in later periods. He referred to the earliest concept as 'a wrong', which would later divide into crime (punished by the State), delict (redressed by the victim or their family through civil procedure) and sin (punished by the gods).[59] Although he alludes to it indirectly, he suggests that the separation between 'wrong' and 'sin' happened first.[60] It is worth recalling Maine's earlier statement concerning the manifestation of 'progressiveness' in a legal system. Maine had argued that this was connected to recording the law in writing, as the Romans had done with the Twelve Tables. At the same time, he also posited that 'progressive' legal systems tended to be those that had begun to separate law from other societal forces, such as religion, at an early point. This influenced his comments about the distinction between crime, delict and sin. He posited that a distinction between 'wrong' and 'sin' began to

56 Maine, *Ancient Law*, 369.

57 Diamond, *Primitive Law*, 279–80, 346, for criticisms of this theory as a general feature of 'ancient law' in the abstract.

58 Maine, *Ancient Law*, 370.

59 Ibid. 371.

60 Ibid. 372.

emerge early, the latter being viewed as a matter for the gods.[61] This distinction conveniently played into Maine's earlier observation and permitted him to avoid further discussion of 'sin' in this chapter.

In time, this undifferentiated notion of 'wrong' was divided into civil wrongs (*delicta*) and criminal wrongs (*crimina*). It is to the development of these two categories that we now turn. Maine regarded the former as the older of the two. In his view, the development of criminal law was predicated on the eventual existence of a State that could prosecute crimes on behalf of its citizens through organs such as a prosecution service and a system of criminal courts. Since these were not yet present in the earliest phases of ancient law, individuals used civil procedure to redress 'wrongs' committed against them. The State did not emerge fully formed from the social compact. Rather, it developed gradually. It is this development process from the private redress of 'wrongs' using civil procedure to prosecuting crime by the State on which Maine focused in the remainder of this chapter.

He identified two examples where, in early Roman law, the State behaved like an individual – presumably a head of a household – to preserve the logic of Maine's comments about the dominance of the family in ancient law.[62] These played an essential role in his narrative. As long as the State behaved like an individual, it did not yet assume the role it would later adopt in punishing crimes as the State. Accordingly, this kind of behaviour would impede the growth of criminal law. The first instance relates to an issue of classification. Unlike in civil law, where legal rules could be developed further by analogy, in Roman criminal law, when a new crime was identified, a new statute had to be enacted in which an ad hoc tribunal and a procedure were set up to prosecute the crime. This led to a proliferation of individual crimes, the prosecution of which was regulated by specific statutes. Since the route whereby a statute was enacted for a new crime through the popular assembly was identical to that used by an individual proposing a new statute under civil law, this shows the state behaving like an individual.

Another example is visible in the earliest forms of Roman civil procedure. In the actions-at-law system, the default procedure to raise an action was the *legis actio* involving a wager (*sacramentum*).[63] The procedure's nature and the wager's existence were significant to Maine. Within the ritualised nature of the procedure, Maine saw 'the origin of justice', as he called it: '[t]wo armed men

[61] Strachan-Davidson, *Problems of the Roman Criminal Law*, I, 25, noted that the early separation between law and religion, posited by Maine, was subsequently accepted and elaborated on by Mommsen and Girard. Gibbon and Fernández-Armesto, *The History of the Decline and Fall of the Roman Empire. Vol. 5, Justinian and the Roman Law*, 296, states: 'A sin, a vice, a crime, are the objects of theology, ethics, and jurisprudence. Whenever their judgments agree, they corroborate each other; but as often as they differ, a prudent legislator appreciates the guilt and punishment according to the measure of social injury.' This is likely the source of Maine's view on this matter.

[62] Maine, *Ancient Law*, 373–8.

[63] Pollock and Maine, *Introduction and Notes*, 57–9, for a survey, with a specific focus on Maine's use of the Homeric trial scene.

are wrangling about some disputed property. The Praetor, *vir pietate gravis*, happens to be going by, and interposes to stop the contest.'[64]

Initially, mentioning 'disputed property' here might seem strange to anyone wishing to understand Roman law's history of 'wrongs'. This is because Maine focused his discussion of this action-at-law on the example presented in Gaius's Institutes, which concerned a dispute over ownership.[65] He used this discussion of the *legis actio sacramento* in general to make a point about the function of penalties. In Roman law, the wager was forfeited to the State by the losing party. In a sense, it represented the financial value equivalent to the time and effort expended by the State, acting as an individual, in resolving the dispute as a referee.[66] This, too, added support to Maine's argument concerning the early behaviour of the State.

The origin of allowing claims for multiples of the value of the object stolen or destroyed in Roman law also supported Maine's discussion of examples of the State behaving as an individual in the early stages of ancient law. Here, the focus is on how financial penalties are calculated. He phrased it as follows:

> In settling the damages to be awarded, they [the earliest administrators of justice] took as their guide the measure of vengeance likely to be extracted by an aggrieved person under the circumstances of the case. This is the true explanation of the very different penalties imposed by ancient law on offenders caught in the act or soon after it, and on offenders detected after considerable delay.[67]

This statement and Maine's subsequent discussion of the differing penalties for manifest or non-manifest theft also permitted him to surmise that in ancient law, proof of guilt was likely determined in a much more straightforward manner than in later law.

The remainder of the chapter focuses not so much on the specifics of delict as a branch of civil law but on the emergence of crime/criminal law as a legal category distinct from 'delict'. Like the discussion on *nexum* in the contract chapter, Maine's point is that the original undifferentiated notion of 'wrong' is eventually subdivided into delict and crime. This development went hand in hand with the growth of the State itself. One of Maine's central points, already mentioned above, is that in the earliest phases of ancient law, 'wrongs' were punished by the State in a manner analogous to the behaviour of an individual: '[t]he state conceived itself to be wronged and the popular assembly struck straight at the offender with the same movement which accompanied its legislative action.'[68]

It was only when the State began to behave as a State (and not as an individual) in prosecuting crimes that criminal law, in the proper sense, began to develop.

64 Maine, *Ancient Law*, 376.

65 Inst.Gai.4.16; Maine, *Ancient Law*, 376–7.

66 Maine, *Ancient Law*, 378. Diamond, *Primitive Law*, 196, criticises Maine's position that private arbitration, as a general rule, precedes the development of courts in ancient law in the abstract.

67 Maine, *Ancient Law*, 378.

68 Ibid. 381.

This statement permitted Maine to set out a brief overview of the growth of Roman criminal law.[69] As Strachan-Davidson later pointed out, Maine's account here was likely inspired by a book concerning the history of the Roman criminal process by the German jurist Karl Gustav Geib (1808–1864), published in Leipzig in 1842.[70] This seems plausible since Geib's narrative is a historical account of the development of the criminal process in Roman law from the earliest phases of Roman law. Maine's account consisted of the following broad narrative. The earliest form of the criminal process was the so-called *iudicia populi*, originally presided over by the king and later by the *comitia*. Maine describes these as 'solemn trials of great offenders under legislative forms'.[71] In other words, each prosecution was preceded by enacting individual pieces of legislation to deal with specific criminal offences. While these pieces of legislation initially envisaged the *comitia* dealing with the prosecution of offenders, in time, the matter was delegated to an ad hoc commission, a *quaestio*, to deal with the prosecution of individuals. At first, these temporary commissions ceased functioning when the trial concluded. The next phase was to appoint individuals who could be deployed as members when a new *quaestio* had to be formed. Maine phrased it as follows: 'Instead of being appointed when and as state-offences were committed, they had a general, though a temporary jurisdiction over such as might be perpetrated.'[72] The final step involved the transformation of these standing commissions from temporary to 'permanent benches or chambers' with staff elected to deal with a broad spectrum of criminal offences.

The underlying message of Maine's treatment of the growth of Roman criminal law is clear. In the tradition of Historical Jurisprudence, he argued in favour of a gradual rise of institutions through which the notion of criminal law and the punishment of crime developed. The crux of his account was the movement from ad hoc commissions to standing courts and the simultaneous growth of the concept of crime. While much of Maine's account could be substantiated with historical information, such as the enactment of the *Lex Calpurnia de Repetundis* in 149 BCE, which created a standing court to try persons for corruption, or the legislative reforms of Sulla and later Augustus of the criminal law, the picture remained incomplete.[73] At the same time, such a high-level treatment of the topic was bound to elicit criticism. The first point of criticism related to Maine's view that criminal law, in ancient law, developed as an exception to the standard procedure of dealing with 'wrongs'. He phrased it as follows:

> And this is the earliest conception of a *crimen* or crime – an act involving such high issues that the state, instead of leaving its cognisance to the civil tribunal or the reli-

[69] Ibid. 385–6. Compare Gibbon and Fernández-Armesto, *The History of the Decline and Fall of the Roman Empire. Vol. 5, Justinian and the Roman Law*, 292–3.

[70] Geib, *Geschichte des Römischen Criminalprocesses bis zum Tode Justinians*; Strachan-Davidson, *Problems of the Roman Criminal Law*, II, 16.

[71] Maine, *Ancient Law*, 382.

[72] Ibid. 383–4.

[73] Gibbon and Fernández-Armesto, *The History of the Decline and Fall of the Roman Empire. Vol. 5, Justinian and the Roman Law*, 295–6.

> gious court, directed a special law or *privilegium* against the perpetrator. Every indictment therefore took the form of a bill of pains and penalties . . . The procedure was identical with the forms of passing an ordinary statute: it was set in motion by the same persons and conducted with precisely the same solemnities.[74]

Strachan-Davidson would later observe that this account, while 'seductive in its simplicity', was problematic when viewed in the context of the origins of criminal law in archaic Rome. The crux of his criticism of Maine's position was twofold. First, he objected to the inference that any member of the community could take the initiative to initiate a criminal prosecution.[75] In his view, only the magistrates could initiate this process; thus, the community acted through the magistrates. 'There is no trace in the authorized version of Roman history at any time of a process answering to a bill of pains and penalties', he added. The second point of criticism he raised relates to Maine's equation of the criminal process with the procedure required for the promulgation of a statute. He noted: '[t]he details of Maine's identification of judgement with legislation will not bear close inspection: neither as regards the "persons", not as regards the "solemnities" is his statement exact.'

Another element of Maine's account of the development of the *quaestiones* that came under criticism was his position on their power as delegated committees of the *comitia* and its implications for appeal. Strachan-Davidson summarised it as follows:

> If the jurors [as members of the *quaestio*] had been indeed delegates exercising the power of the People in their stead, it would have followed according to all principles of Roman jurisprudence that there should have been an appeal from the delegate to the delegator. Again, there is absolutely nothing in the procedure of the standing *quaestiones* which can suggest that they were armed, as the People's deputies, with the People's powers, legislative or otherwise.[76]

As these two points of criticism show, Maine's desire to produce a narrative of gradual development should be viewed critically and sceptically in the spirit of Historical Jurisprudence. It is legitimate to ask to what extent Strachan-Davidson's criticisms of Maine's account undermine the book's general narrative. This is a complex and ultimately unanswerable question. In the development of Roman criminal law, Maine saw a general trend (or cycle) from ad hoc prosecution to standing courts applying general rules of law. The description of this trend was the main aim of this chapter. If, as Strachan-Davidson pointed out, Maine's speculations concerning the power of the *quaestiones* and the importance of statute law and its processes of promulgation in the development of Roman criminal law are less than credible, such criticisms are not fatal to his larger argument. Instead, all

[74] Ibid. 372–3.

[75] Strachan-Davidson, *Problems of the Roman Criminal Law*, I, 132–33.

[76] Ibid. II, 16–17.

that they highlight is precisely the point made by Maine concerning the difficulty in tracing the development of the State.

A topic related to Maine's views on the power of the *quaestiones* was their apparent inability to pronounce the death penalty on a person convicted of a crime. As Maine pointed out, this disappearance of the death penalty from Roman criminal law was discussed with significant effect by scholars of the eighteenth century when making more prominent points about 'the Roman character or . . . modern social economy'.[77] The intellectual inspiration for this statement likely came from Gibbon's chapter, which interpreted the enactment of various statutory reforms in criminal law as part of the progress of 'the manners of Rome'. In Maine's view, this development was far from accidental and had little to do with these more significant claims. Instead, it was the logical consequence of viewing the standing *quaestiones* as derivations of the *comitia tributa*. This body did not have the power to pronounce the death penalty as part of its powers and thus had little to do with the moral progress of the Romans in matters relating to capital punishment. Strachan-Davidson, writing roughly fifty years later, questioned Maine's interpretation of this matter, mainly owing to the lack of proof. In his view, the disappearance of the death penalty in Republican criminal law should be sought elsewhere. It lay 'solely to the facilities for flight allowed to the criminal'.[78] Whether one accepts Maine's view or the one proposed later by Strachan-Davidson, both show that the eighteenth-century perspective, which attributed the matter to the Roman moral character, cannot be supported.

While ostensibly still about the development of Roman criminal law, the final part of this chapter critiques the limitations of statute law more generally. Maine's focus here is on the state of Roman criminal law in the aftermath of the reforms of Sulla and later Augustus. The focus of Maine's critique is twofold. First, despite the opportunity afforded by these statutory changes to reform Roman criminal law comprehensively, they did not reform the system of courts, thus perpetuating a problem already visible in Republican Roman law, whereby many tribunals existed to deal with similar matters. Second, the statutory reforms did not alter the nature and classification of criminal law. Maine expresses it as follows: '[t]he statutes of Sylla and Augustus were the foundation of the penal jurisprudence of the Empire, and nothing can be more extraordinary than some of the classifications which they bequeathed to it.'[79]

His point is that the crimes created during the Republic often overlapped in content and that, despite the opportunity offered by the statutory reforms in the late Republic and early Empire to rationalise them, no attempt was made. Additionally, the relationship between existing civil law penalties and criminal law offences, despite some overlap, was not clarified. This spoke to his scepticism about classification as a solution to all problems. It is difficult not to see these

77 Maine, *Ancient Law*, 387.

78 Strachan-Davidson, *Problems of the Roman Criminal Law*, II, 18–19.

79 Maine, *Ancient Law*, 393.

final comments as a more general critique of legislation as an 'instrumentality' of legal change. Maine's more significant point was clear. Any branch of law was the product of a long history of development. Even when statutory intervention occurs, they do not always address some of the more fundamental issues created by this history.[80]

4. CONCLUSIONS

Contract, delict and crime play different roles in Maine's narrative. Collectively, they form the end of the narrative arc of *Ancient Law*, but individually, their functions within the narrative are distinct. The contract chapter critiques natural law scholarship's 'state of nature' debate. More specifically, it is a criticism of the ahistorical nature of this debate, rooted in musings on the social compact. Maine's primary aim with this chapter was to show that, historically speaking, contract did not play a significant role in ancient law, due to the nature of ancient society and the focus of ancient law on the collective rather than the individual. This chapter also served another purpose. Once Maine had shown that contract did not play an expansive role in ancient law, he could use this insight to comment on morality. In natural law scholarship, discussions of the social compact had become intertwined with those concerning morality – specifically through the 'golden age' fallacy. Thus, people of the past were judged to have had a higher morality, which has since been lost. Maine objected to this ahistorical interpretation. Instead, he argued, using historical examples, that morality was contingent and could only be assessed in its historical context. One could not apply contemporary morality to those of the past.

Nowhere are the different functions served by the legal institutions mentioned above more evident in Maine's work than when his treatment of contract and delict is compared. In his analysis, the law of 'wrongs' – a much more expansive concept than delict – played an extensive role in ancient law. It is essential to point out why Maine settled on a broad idea of 'wrong' here. First, it permitted him to make a point about the differentiation between spiritual and secular wrongs. Second, it allowed him to present an argument regarding the relationship between delict and crime. Since the latter, in Roman law, was heavily based on statute law, it could then be used to make various points about the limits of statute law. As such, it closed the narrative arc concerning 'legal instrumentalities' that began at the start of the book.

[80] Ibid. 305–6, for a similar point.

Conclusions

> The vain titles of the victories of Justinian are crumbled into dust; but the name of the legislator is inscribed on a fair and everlasting monument. Under his reign, and by his care, the civil jurisprudence was digested in the immortal works of the Code, the Pandects, and the Institutes: the public reason of the Romans has been silently or studiously transfused into the domestic institutions of Europe, and the laws of Justinian still command the respect or obedience of independent nations.[1]

It seems appropriate to end this monograph by quoting a passage from Gibbon's famous chapter on Roman law in his *Decline and Fall*. Both its narrative and method profoundly impacted Maine's intellectual development, and the sentiment expressed here effectively summarises the purpose of his book. *Ancient Law* is a book about Roman law. It was written as a series of lectures to make the case for studying and teaching Roman law in England and to showcase what it could offer students embarking on studying law at Cambridge or Middle Temple. This was its fundamental purpose. At the same time, as Cocks has argued, the final book that emerged from these lectures was designed to appeal to a broader audience. In keeping with its Humanist aims, Maine constructed its narrative to engage, albeit subtly, with several geo-political issues of his day, such as the state of English law and the British colonial presence in India.

This monograph was motivated by two journal articles published in the past twenty-five years concerning the intellectual concept of ancient law. The first article, by O'brien in 2005, specifically focused on Maine's book and argued that it should be interpreted as part of a European intellectual tradition of Humanism that dates back to the early modern period.[2] The subsequent article by Westbrook in 2010 contended that the study of ancient law as an intellectual phenomenon should be undertaken within the framework of European legal discussions concerning natural law and the Enlightenment.[3] The two articles presented a persuasive argument for the re-evaluation and contextualisation of Maine's work.

Ancient Law is a complex piece of rhetorical prose in which Maine marshalled his primary interest, Roman law, to persuade his audience of the intellectual importance of the subject. It was deeply rooted in his study of classics at Cambridge. The style and content of the book align fully with the European tradition of Humanism.

[1] Gibbon and Fernández-Armesto, *The History of the Decline and Fall of the Roman Empire. Vol. 5, Justinian and the Roman Law*, 249.

[2] O'brien, '"Something Older than Law Itself"'.

[3] Westbrook, 'The Early History of Law'. See also now, Humfress, *Ancient Law*, 598–614.

Unfortunately, critics in the roughly fifty years following the book's publication minimised this aspect of Maine's contribution. The reasons for this are complex and relate to Maine's perceived lack of understanding of Roman law and the legal positivist critique of Humanism and its aims. This dismissal significantly reduced subsequent scholarly engagement with the book. To fully understand Maine's message in this book, one must revisit his examination of 'progress'. In the book, he adeptly deconstructs the Victorian notion of progress as a universal, unidirectional force destined to result in improvement. Maine contended that this understanding of the term was historically incorrect. He was also deeply sceptical of its underlying intellectual assumptions and their pervasive impact on modernity. Instead, he championed an awareness of an older sense of the term rooted in Greek philosophy. This necessitated narrowing the scope of 'progress' to a select few legal systems, particularly Roman law.

Roman law was central to the narrative of *Ancient Law*. Maine saw it as the prime example of how a historical legal system adapted to change. He believed it could serve as a model to indirectly analyse contemporaneous problems surrounding teaching English law. His analysis of Roman law differed from the typical textbooks of the mid-nineteenth century. Instead of focusing on a detailed analysis of legal doctrine, he used Roman law to identify legal phenomena (or early jural conceptions, as he called them) and trace their development, often drawing insights from past and present legal systems in instances where information was lacking. This approach allowed him to examine fundamental issues of his own time, such as the relationship between law, religion and morality. It also enabled him to engage critically with the ideas of renowned legal scholars from the past, like Rousseau, Montesquieu and Bentham, on these issues. While Maine's approach differed from the traditional emphasis on legal doctrine found in Roman law scholarship of the time, it was neither incompatible with it nor presented as an alternative. As he later pointed out in his address to students at the University of Calcutta, legal doctrine is an essential component of law teaching. Still, it had to be tempered by 'common sense'.

Maine's exploration of phenomena in Roman law primarily sought to reveal how a legal system adapts to change. This focus is crucial to his work for those studying this field. His analysis provided valuable insights into Roman law and was thoughtfully crafted to deliver a comprehensive critique. The latter portion of Maine's book explores case studies that examine specific aspects of Roman law to trace the development of these legal phenomena. An often overlooked but vital element in his analysis is the absence of a linear progression from 'primitive' to 'sophisticated' or worse to better, aligning with the book's central theme as a critique of the universality and unidirectionality of Victorian notions of 'progress'. Instead, Maine's examination showcases cycles of change, illustrating how older and newer ideas vied for predominance as Roman law adapted to new circumstances.

His exploration of Roman law has a distinct starting and ending point. He commences with the enactment of the Twelve Tables and concludes with the

Justinianic project, aligning with his cyclical perspective of legal change. While he briefly touches on the emergence of law in 'prehistory', Maine appears uninterested in the topic. As this monograph has shown, there are specific intellectual reasons for this. He believed that little could be learned about this notion from his available sources. It is essential to remember that while Roman law was valuable to Maine's project, it did not always offer complete evidence due to a lack of information or because, in his view, subsequent interpretations by legal scholars in the natural law tradition had distorted the contemporaneous understanding of Roman law. Hence, Maine incorporated insights from comparator systems to create speculative earlier and later stages of these phenomena.

I do not intend to provide a systematic overview of Maine's insights regarding each area of Roman law. Instead, I will limit myself to three of the most significant conclusions.

The central theme of *Ancient Law* revolves around the gradual decline of the legal significance of the family, as well as the growing importance of individual members in various areas of the law. It is essential to note that the family in Maine's narrative never entirely disappears; rather, it only loses some of its legal significance. Maine intended to convey the opposite of the nineteenth-century notion of universal and unidirectional 'progress'. In discussing the patriarchal family, he emphasises its foundation on a power structure. While Roman law presented evidence of this power at a certain point in its trajectory, it also illustrated that such authority was bound to atrophy when it became inconvenient. The subsequent history of European legal development revealed that power tended to resurface in family relationships, as seen in the marital authority of the husband over the wife. As a result, 'progress' represented an unending cycle of fluctuating power within the family and among its members.

The second conclusion pertains to property. Maine examines succession and property as distinct yet intellectually linked areas of law, as evidenced in his analysis of Roman law. His crucial observation revolves around how subsequent natural law scholarship has muddled contemporaneous understanding of the original Roman law. This is particularly noticeable in his discussion on certain aspects of the law of succession and property and their relationship to natural law. In his discussion on the law of succession, Maine critiques the use of Roman law at a specific point in its historical development to exaggerate the resemblance between Roman law and modern law. Once again, as his discussion in this chapter shows, he favours a cyclical perspective on legal change. There is an interplay between the testator's freedom to distribute their assets and the entitlement of family members to a share of the inheritance. A similar thread runs through the discussion of property law. Maine's scepticism of the intellectual baggage associated with some modes of ownership acquisition in later periods of European legal scholarship due to their association with natural law is especially incisive.

The final conclusion focuses on legal obligations. Maine discusses contract, delict and crime and makes two essential points. The first concerns the historically contingent nature of contract law. The Victorian intellectual discourse on this branch of law developed a close association between individual will and contract formation. Maine used his analysis of the development of contract law in Roman law to demonstrate the historical contingency of this position, emphasising that it should not be retroactively applied to the past. Although his treatment of the cyclical nature of legal change is less prominent in this chapter, it is present. Later scholarly investigations into the more recent history of contract in European legal thought have similarly questioned a linear or unidirectional development in this branch of law. The second point concerns the interplay between protecting the citizens' interests and the growth of the State. Delict in Roman law originated in a form of the State that had yet to fully develop its institutions to protect the interests of its citizens. As time passes and the State grows through institutions, other options, such as those afforded by criminal law, come to protect the interests of citizens.

* * *

The later historiography of *Ancient Law* and its influence across several academic disciplines is complex. Having surveyed the nearly two centuries of scholarship the book has generated, it is possible to outline a tentative general narrative showcasing its influence. While this is not the primary aim of this monograph, a few general comments are warranted. By the end of the nineteenth century, Historical Jurisprudence had fallen out of fashion in Britain for several reasons. As Cocks demonstrated in his 1988 book, one of the main points of criticism raised against it was its intellectual breadth and its association with various ideologies of the nineteenth century.[4] To this may be added the ever-closer association between the Indo-European discourse and the rise of 'scientific racism' by the end of the nineteenth century.[5] Subsequent criticisms of Maine's book should be understood within this context. A notable critique of Maine's book was its lack of a 'synthesis of legal and philosophical inquiries'.[6] There is some truth to this. Maine never set out to produce an abstract theory of legal change that could be applied predictively. He did not aim to create an abstract conception of 'ancient law' even if some later commentators interpreted his work that way. As this monograph has shown, such criticism is based on a misunderstanding of the nature and purpose of Maine's work.

Regardless of these points of critique, the ever-growing volume of scholarship on *Ancient Law* shows that it has contributed significantly to various debates in different subject areas during the nineteenth and twentieth centuries.[7] Besides the evident impact of Maine's work on the revival of Roman law in England, it

4 Cocks, *Sir Henry Maine*, 143–5.

5 Hock, 'Did Indo-European Linguistics Prepare the Ground for Nazism?', generally; Sayce, *The Primitive Home of the Aryans*, generally.

6 Cocks, *Sir Henry Maine*, 145.

7 Stein, *Legal Evolution*, 99–115.

also influenced subsequent discussions about English legal history and its scope.[8] Additionally, it played a significant role in debates concerning legal positivism and its place in English law.[9]

Maine's impact varied in other scientific fields that developed in the nineteenth century. His impact on sociology was comparatively short-lived due to the nature of his investigation and the sources used.[10] His focus on law as a social construct that must adapt to change through specific mechanisms was insightful, but he did not attempt to create a predictive model that could be applied to other legal systems. This limited his usefulness for subsequent investigations into the relationship between law and societal change. Furthermore, his methodology was not based on collecting and interpreting empirical data; its claims to 'scientific' rigour notwithstanding. It is also fair to say that his lack of focus on the broader context in which law exists and the growth of its institutions limited the book's utility to scholars of sociology.[11] Maine's influence on the emerging field of anthropology is noteworthy, if controversial.[12] His work forms part of a broader historiography of nineteenth-century anthropology that focused on debates concerning race, the origins of man and the differences between 'barbarism' and 'civilisation'.[13] He attempted to avoid the more controversial aspects of 'prehistory' and the emergence of law in *Ancient Law*. Still, his academic work was inevitably drawn into these debates. Maine's contribution to these debates is more nuanced than some of his Victorian contemporaries, but its European exceptionalism and colonial undertone are clear for all to see.[14]

What, then, is the significance of Maine's *Ancient Law* in today's context? The answer to this question is threefold. First, as this monograph has shown, the book's message has become obscured in the later assessments of Maine's works and legacy. More focus should be placed on Maine's use of Roman law and his knowledge of the subject. Once this is addressed, the book's message and purpose become clear. This message, in turn, deserves critical interrogation in light of its subsequent historiography.

Second, Maine's book demonstrates why Roman law remains an important foundational subject for law students in the Anglophone world. By dismissing a significant part of the book's content as unreliable, subsequent scholarship has failed to fully engage with Maine's complex arguments. It is, ultimately, not fatal

[8] Cocks, *Sir Henry Maine*, 146–54; Stein, *Legal Evolution*, 106–10, for an account of the criticism levelled against his work by scholars of the history of English law.

[9] O'brien, '"Something Older than Law Itself"'; Postema, 'The British Tradition of Legal Positivism', for a survey.

[10] Cocks, *Sir Henry Maine*, 155–9; Goldman, 'A Peculiarity of the English?'; Steinmetz, 'The Imperial Entanglements of Sociology in the United States, Britain, and France Since the Nineteenth Century', generally.

[11] Thomas, *Legal Artifices*, 1–6.

[12] Cocks, *Sir Henry Maine*, 159–69; Stein, *Legal Evolution*, 101–6.

[13] Kuper, 'Civilization, Culture, and Race', for a survey.

[14] Mantena, 'Law and "Tradition"', for a survey.

to the intellectual legacy of the book that later generations of Roman law scholars criticised or disagreed with Maine's views on Roman law. After all, his was a nineteenth-century perspective derived from the sources he had to hand. As legal scholars know only too well, perspectives on the law change over time. This holds true even for Roman law. More importantly, works like Maine's show the perils of accepting the speculative insights of early modern natural law scholarship on Roman law. There is nothing 'natural' about the developmental trajectory of Roman law. Its unique history has significantly influenced the legal and intellectual growth in ideas in Europe and beyond. This alone justifies its continued presence in law teaching in the Anglophone world.

Finally, and more significant intellectually, is the ongoing relevance of Maine's 'method', particularly when applied to current debates concerning the emerging methodologies of global and comparative legal history.[15] Legal history requires an investigation into and interpretation of actual historical facts.[16] It cannot be based solely on high-level, speculative narratives created a priori. These become self-reinforcing, much like natural law scholarship in the eighteenth century and beyond. Such narratives also inevitably import dangerous intellectual baggage into contemporary law. 'Progress' as betterment is an excellent example. To defeat such speculations, actual historical research, often with a global or comparative element, is required.[17] At the same time, as Maine's work shows, interpreting historical facts can never be entirely objective. His comments on religion and morality clearly illustrate this point.

Dubber has shown that the historical and comparative dimensions of (new) Historical Jurisprudence are essential for analysing the nature of law.[18] This type of exercise invariably has its constraints. Maine was acutely aware that some form of demarcation was required. Of course, every legal system can be compared to another, past and present, but such comparisons would hardly have produced the narrative Maine wanted to construct in his book. It was necessary, therefore, to build an underlying intellectual link that facilitated comparison. To him, this could be found in specific legal systems' shared Indo-European linguistic heritage. It also permitted him to focus only on one past legal system, Roman law, as the archetypal example of ancient law. It is crucial, however, to reflect on Maine's use of comparator legal systems from the past and the present in *Ancient Law*. His focus throughout the book is firmly on Roman law. The comparative observations are designed to inform his reconstruction of Roman law. He used them to postulate earlier and later points, albeit conjecturally, on the trajectory of the development of specific legal phenomena. There is no indication that his aim was

15 Yale, 'Further Thoughts on Maine's Historical Jurisprudence'; Eldridge, 'Gone and Forgotten', generally.

16 Lobban, 'The Varieties of Legal History', generally.

17 *Pace* Posner, 'A Theory of Primitive Society, with Special Reference to Law'. This work appears to advocate for a new conception of natural law grounded in economic insights.

18 Dubber, 'New Historical Jurisprudence'; Ibbetson, 'Comparative Legal History'; Ibbetson, 'The Challenges of Comparative Legal History', generally.

ever to fully reconstruct these systems in detail. He did not have the knowledge required for an undertaking of this kind, nor was it necessary for his endeavour. At the same time, though, as subsequent scholarship showed, the desire to find comparable phenomena led to interpretive errors.

Maine did not attempt to create an abstract notion of 'ancient law' distilled from commonly occurring legal rules or concepts identified in the legal systems he chose to investigate. The title of Maine's book has misled subsequent readers into making this incorrect assumption regarding its content. Undoubtedly, scholars' attempts towards the end of the nineteenth century to create such a conception of 'ancient law' has contributed to the confusion. *Ancient Law* is not a philosophical treatise in the natural law tradition. It is a critique of this very idea. Maine held speculative abstractions, often rooted in ambiguous interpretations of earlier natural law, in contempt, viewing them as detrimental to his scholarly pursuits. His work is fundamentally based on Roman law. It aimed to show how this legal order had adapted to social change across various historical periods. Roman law served as the scientific foundation for Maine's analysis, providing the bedrock upon which all other concepts and arguments presented in the book were built.

Bibliography

Abrahams, R. 'Ancient Law and Modern Field Work'. In *The Victorian Achievement of Sir Henry Maine: A Centennial Reappraisal*, 185–92. Cambridge: Cambridge University Press, 1991.

Adcock, R. K. *Liberalism, Progress, and Comparative Inquiry: Trans-Atlantic Exchanges and the Making of the American Science of Politics*. Ann Arbor: ProQuest Dissertations Publishing, 2007.

Agnani, S. 'The Reception of Edmund Burke's Imperial Ideas Relating to India, or Burke, the Brahmin and the Hot-House'. In *The Reception of Edmund Burke in Europe*, 171–90. New York: Bloomsbury, 2017.

Ahmad, I. 'Aristotle's Natural Theory of the Origin of the State'. *The Indian Journal of Political Science* 3, no. 1 (1941): 1–12.

Amunátegui Perelló, C. F. *Origen de los poderes del paterfamilias: el pater familias y la patria potestas*. Madrid: Dykinson, 2009.

Ando, C. 'Fact, Fiction, and Social Reality in Roman Law'. In *Legal Fictions in Theory and Practice*, 295–324. Cham: Springer, 2015.

Annas, J. 'The Stoics: Human Nature and the Point of View of the Universe'. In *The Morality of Happiness*, 159–79. Oxford: Oxford University Press, 1995.

Ashley, M., W. J. Ashley and N. D. Fustel de Coulanges. *The Origin of Property in Land*. London: Sonnenschein, 1891.

Austin, J. *The Province of Jurisprudence Determined*. London: Murray, 1832.

Atiyah, P. S. *The Rise and Fall of Freedom of Contract*. Oxford: Clarendon Press, 2003.

Baker, J. *750 Years of Law at Cambridge*. Cambridge: Printing Services, 1996.

Batzel, V. M. 'Sir Henry James Sumner Maine: A Study in Naturalistic Law'. PhD thesis, University of Iowa, 1968.

Bayly, C. A. *The New Cambridge History of India II.1, Indian Society and the Making of the British Empire*. Cambridge: Cambridge University Press, 2008.

Bayly, C. A. 'Maine and Change in Nineteenth-Century India'. In *The Victorian Achievement of Sir Henry Maine: A Centennial Reappraisal*, 389–97. Cambridge: Cambridge University Press, 1991.

Bayly, S. *Caste, Society and Politics in India from the Eighteenth Century to the Modern Age*. Cambridge: Cambridge University Press, 1999.

Becchi, P. 'German Legal Science: The Crisis of Natural Law Theory, the Historicisms, and "Conceptual Jurisprudence"'. In *A Treatise of Legal Philosophy and General Jurisprudence volume 9*, 185–224. Dordrecht: Springer, 2009.

Becker, J. D. 'A Preliminary Comparison of the Political Thought of Locke and Filmer'. PhD thesis, University of Houston, 1979.

Beiser, F. C. *The German Historicist Tradition*. Oxford: Oxford University Press, 2015.

Bell, D. 'Empire'. In *Historicism and the Human Sciences in Victorian Britain*, 211–36. Cambridge: Cambridge University Press, 2017.

Beltrão, C. '*Sacra Privata Perpetua Manento*. A Reading of Cicero's *De Legibus*'. In *Roman Identity: Between Ideal and Performance*, 313–34. Brepols: Turnhout, 2022.

Beneduzi, R. *Equity in the Civil Law Tradition*. Cham: Springer, 2021.

Bentham, J., E. Dumont and R. Hildreth. *Theory of Legislation*. Boston: Weeks, Jordan, 1840.

Benvenisti, E. 'The Origins of the Concept of Belligerent Occupation'. *Law and History Review* 26, no. 3 (2008): 621–48.

Benvenisti, E. *The International Law of Occupation*. 2nd ed. Oxford: Oxford University Press, 2012.

Berman, H. J. 'The Origins of Historical Jurisprudence: Coke, Selden, Hale'. *Yale Law Journal* 103, no. 7 (1994): 1651–738.

Bevir, M. 'Historicism and the Human Sciences in Victorian Britain'. In *Historicism and the Human Sciences in Victorian Britain*, 1–20. Cambridge: Cambridge University Press, 2017.

Blackstone, W. *Commentaries on the Laws of England. Book II, Of the Rights of Things*. Edited by S. Stern and W. R. Prest. Oxford: Oxford University Press, 2016.

Bock, K. E. 'Comparison of Histories: The Contribution of Henry Maine'. *Comparative Studies in Society and History* 16, no. 2 (1974): 232–62.

Bock, K. E. 'The Moral Philosophy of Sir Henry Summer Maine'. *Journal of the History of Ideas* 37, no. 1 (1976): 147–54.

Bordoni, C. *Hubris and Progress: A Future Born of Presumption*. Translated by Wendy Doherty. London: Routledge, Taylor & Francis Group, 2019.

Bryce, J. *The Academical Study of the Civil Law: An Inaugural Lecture, Delivered at Oxford, February 25, 1871*. London: Macmillan, 1871.

Bryce, J. *The Ancient Roman Empire and the British Empire in India: The Diffusion of Roman and English Law throughout the World; Two Historical Studies*. London: Milford, 1914.

Buckland, W. W. *Equity in Roman Law: Lectures Delivered in the University of London, at the Request of the Faculty of Laws*. London: University of London Press, 1911.

Burke, E. *An Appeal from the New to the Old Whigs, in Consequence of Some Late Discussions in Parliament, Etc*. Dublin: M. Mills, 1791.

Burrow, J. W. *Evolution and Society: A Study in Victorian Social Theory*. London: Cambridge University Press, 1966.

Burrow, J. W. 'Henry Maine and Mid-Victorian Ideas of Progress'. In *The Victorian Achievement of Sir Henry Maine: A Centennial Reappraisal*, 55–69. Cambridge: Cambridge University Press, 1991.

Cairns, J. W. 'Slavery without a Code Noir: Scotland 1700–78'. In *Lawyers, the Law and History*, 148–78. Ireland: Four Courts Press, 2013.

Cairns, J. W., and P. J. du Plessis, eds. 'Introduction'. In *The Creation of the Ius Commune*, 1–6. Edinburgh: Edinburgh University Press, 2022.

Canale, D. 'The Many Faces of the Codification of Law in Modern Continental Europe'. In *A Treatise of Legal Philosophy and General Jurisprudence volume 9*, 135–83. Dordrecht: Springer, 2009.

Capogrossi Colognesi, L. *Modelli di stato e di famiglia nella storiografia dell'800*. 2nd ed. Roma: La Sapienza, 1994.

Capogrossi Colognesi, L. *Dalla storia di Roma alle origini della società civile: un dibattito ottocentesco*. Bologna: Il mulino, 2008.

Capogrossi Colognesi, L. *Law and Power in the Making of the Roman Commonwealth*. Translated by Laura Kopp. Cambridge: Cambridge University Press, 2014.

Capogrossi Colognesi, L. *La costruzione del diritto privato romano*. Bologna: Il mulino, 2016.

Capogrossi Colognesi, L. 'Niebuhr and Bachofen: New Forms of Evidence on Roman History'. In *Roman Law before the Twelve Tables*, 155–70. Edinburgh: Edinburgh University Press, 2022.

Carbonneau, T. E. 'The Implicit Teaching of Utopian Speculations: Rousseau's Contribution to The Natural Law Tradition'. *Seattle University Law Review* 3, no. 1 (1979): 123–58.

Carrithers, D. 'Montesquieu's Philosophy of History'. *Journal of the History of Ideas* 47, no. 1 (1986): 61–80.

Carroll, C. 'Humanism and English Literature in the Fifteenth and Sixteenth Centuries'. In *The Cambridge Companion to Renaissance Humanism*, 246–68. Cambridge: Cambridge University Press, 1996.

Carter, W. M. 'The Abolition of Slavery in the United States'. In *The Legal Understanding of Slavery*, 177–96. Oxford: Oxford University Press, 2012.

Cassani, A. *Diritto, antropologia e storia: studi su Henry Sumner Maine*. Bologna: CLUEB, 2002.

Cassirer, E. *The Philosophy of the Enlightenment: Updated Edition*. Princeton: Princeton University Press, 2009.

Cecil, E. *Primogeniture: A Short History of Its Development in Various Countries and Its Practical Effects*. London: Murray, 1895.

Champs, E. de. 'Utility, Morality, and Reform: Bentham and Eighteenth-Century Continental Jurisprudence'. In *Bentham's Theory of Law and Public Opinion*, 184–207. Cambridge: Cambridge University Press, 2014.

Churchill, J. B. '*Ex Qua Quod Vellent Facerent*: Roman Magistrates' Authority over *Praeda* and *Manubiae*'. *Transactions of the American Philological Association (1974-)* 129 (1999): 85–116.

Clark, E. C. *Practical Jurisprudence: A Comment on Austin by E. C. Clark*. Cambridge: Cambridge University Press, 1883.

Cobb, T. R. R. *An Inquiry into the Law of Negro Slavery in the United States of America: To Which Is Prefixed an Historical Sketch of Slavery*. Philadelphia: Johnson, 1858.

Cocks, R. 'Maine, Progress and Theory'. In *The Victorian Achievement of Sir Henry Maine: A Centennial Reappraisal*, 70–5. Cambridge: Cambridge University Press, 1991.

Cocks, R. *Sir Henry Maine: A Study in Victorian Jurisprudence*. Cambridge: Cambridge University Press, 1988.

Cocks, R. 'Maine, Henry Sumner'. In *Encyclopedia of the Philosophy of Law and Social Philosophy*, 203–208. Dordrecht: Springer, 2020. https://doi.org/10.1007/978-94-007-6730-0_780-1.

Collini, S. 'Democracy and Excitement: Maine's Political Pessimism'. In *The Victorian Achievement of Sir Henry Maine: A Centennial Reappraisal*, 88–96. Cambridge: Cambridge University Press, 1991.

Collini, S. *Liberalism and Sociology: L.T. Hobhouse and Political Argument in England 1880–1914*. Cambridge: Cambridge University Press, 2009.

Comte, A. *The Positive Philosophy of Auguste Comte*. Translated by Harriet Martineau. New York: D. Appleton & Co., 1854.

Conlin, J. *Evolution and the Victorians: Science, Culture and Politics in Darwin's Britain*. London: Bloomsbury Academic, 2014.

Conniff, J. *The Useful Cobbler: Edmund Burke and the Politics of Progress*. Albany: State University of New York Press, 1994.

Conway, S. 'Bentham and the Nineteenth-Century Revolution in Government'. In *Victorian Liberalism: Nineteenth-Century Political Thought and Practice*, 71–90. London: Routledge, 1990.

Cornell, T. *The Beginnings of Rome: Italy and Rome from the Bronze Age to the Punic Wars (c. 1000-264 BC)*. London: Routledge, 1995.

Cornish, W. R. et al., eds. *Law and Society in England, 1750-1950*. 2nd ed. Oxford: Hart, 2019.

Cotterrell, R. *The Politics of Jurisprudence: A Critical Introduction to Legal Philosophy*. 2nd ed. London: LexisNexis UK, 2003.

Council of Legal Education. *A Century of Law Reform: Twelve Lectures on the Changes in the Law of England during the Nineteenth Century: Delivered at the Request of the Council of Legal Education in the Old Hall, Lincoln's Inn, during Michaelmas Term 1900 and Hilary Term 1901*. London: Macmillan, 1901.

Coxall, W. N. '"The Use and Misuse of Internal Evidence in Authorship Attributions": Some Further Thoughts'. *Victorian Periodicals Review* 20, no. 3 (1987): 93–102.

Crone, P. *Pre-Industrial Societies: Anatomy of the Pre-Modern World*. ACLS Humanities E-Book. London: Oneworld, 2015.

Crow, M. 'A Melvillean Moment: Law, History, and Empire from Gibbon to Melville'. *Leviathan* 22, no. 2 (2020): 24–37.

Davenport, E. 'Liberalism's Perverse Pleasures: Coercive Contract in Strange Case of Dr. Jekyll and Mr. Hyde'. *Victorian Studies* 63, no. 1 (2020): 9–33.

Davidson, J. *Montesquieu: Persian Letters*. Broadway Translations. London: Routledge, 1892.

Del Mar, M. 'Legal Fictions and Legal Change'. *International Journal of Law in Context* 9, no. 4 (2013): 442–65.

Del Mar, M. 'Legal Fictions and Legal Change in the Common Law Tradition'. In *Legal Fictions in Theory and Practice*, 225–53. Cham: Springer, 2015.

Dēmētriou, K. N., ed. *Brill's Companion to George Grote and the Classical Tradition*. Vol. 1. Leiden: Brill, 2014.

Demoule, J.-P. 'The Canonical Indo-European Model and Its Underlying Assumptions'. *Faits de Langues* 47, no. 1 (2016): 165–75.

Demoule, J-P. *The Indo-Europeans: Archaeology, Language, Race, and the Search for the Origins of the West*. Translated by Rhoda Cronin-Allanic. New York: Oxford University Press, 2023.

Derrett, D. *Sir Henry Maine and Law in India, 1858-1958*. Edinburgh: Green, 1959.

Desautels-Stein, J. *The Right to Exclude: A Critical Race Approach to Sovereignty, Borders, and International Law*. Oxford: Oxford University Press, 2023.

Deslauriers, M., P. Destrée, P. Pellegrin and E. Filotas. 'Natural Slavery'. In *The Cambridge Companion to Aristotle's Politics*, 92–116. Cambridge: Cambridge University Press, 2013.

Dewey, C. 'The Influence of Sir Henry Maine on Agrarian Policy in India'. In *The Victorian Achievement of Sir Henry Maine: A Centennial Reappraisal*, 353–75. Cambridge: Cambridge University Press, 1991.

Diamond, A. 'Fictions, Equity and Legislation: Maine's Three Agencies of Legal Change'. In *The Victorian Achievement of Sir Henry Maine: A Centennial Reappraisal*, 242–55. Cambridge: Cambridge University Press, 1991.

Diamond, A. S. *Primitive Law*. London: Longmans, 1935.

DiMatteo, L. A. 'Unframing Legal Reasoning: A Cyclical Theory of Legal Evolution'. *Southern California Interdisciplinary Law Journal* 27, no. 3 (2018): 483–548.

Di Robilant, A. *The Making of Modern Property: Reinventing Roman Law in Europe and Its Peripheries 1789–1950*. Cambridge: Cambridge University Press, 2023.

Dubber, M. D. 'New Historical Jurisprudence: Legal History as Critical Analysis of Law'. *Critical Analysis of Law: An International & Interdisciplinary Law Review* 2, no. 1 (2015): 1–18.

Duve, T. 'What Is Global Legal History?' *Comparative Legal History* 8, no. 2 (2020): 73–115.

Eberl, O. *Naturzustand Und Barbarei: Begründung Und Kritik Staatlicher Ordnung Im Zeichen Des Kolonialismus*. Hamburg: Hamburger Edition, 2023.

Eldridge, L. 'Gone and Forgotten: Vinogradoff's Historical Jurisprudence'. *Legal Studies (Society of Legal Scholars)* 41, no. 2 (2021): 194–213.

Elphinstone, M. *The History of India*. London: Murray, 1841.

Evans, M. O. *Theories and Criticisms of Sir Henry Maine*. London: Stevens, 1896.

Evans-Pritchard, E. E. *A History of Anthropological Thought; Edited by André Singer; with an Introduction by Ernest Gellner*. London: Faber, 1981.

Fassbender, B., A. Peters, S. Peter and D. Högger, eds. *The Oxford Handbook of the History of International Law*. Oxford: Oxford University Press, 2012.

Feaver, G. *From Status to Contract: A Biography of Sir Henry Maine, 1822–1888*. London: Longmans, 1969.

Feaver, G. 'The Victorian Values of Sir Henry Maine'. In *The Victorian Achievement of Sir Henry Maine: A Centennial Reappraisal*, 28–52. Cambridge: Cambridge University Press, 1991.

Ferguson, A. *The History of the Progress and Termination of the Roman Republic by Adam Ferguson, LL.D. Professor of Moral Philosophy in the University of Edinburgh. In Three Volumes. Illustrated with Maps*. London: printed for W. Strahan; T. Cadell, in the Strand; and W. Creech, in Edinburgh, 1783.

Field, D. D., ed. *Codification of the Common Law: Letter of Jeremy Bentham, and Report of Judges Story, Metcalf and Others*. New York: Polhemus, 1882.

Finkelman, P. 'Slavery in the United States'. In *The Legal Understanding of Slavery*, 105–34. Oxford: Oxford University Press, 2012.

Fitzmaurice, A. 'Discovery, Conquest, and Occupation of Territory'. In *The Oxford Handbook of the History of International Law*, 840–61. Oxford: Oxford University Press, 2012.

Fitzmaurice, A. *Sovereignty, Property and Empire, 1500–2000*. Cambridge: Cambridge University Press, 2014.

Freund, E. 'Historical Jurisprudence in Germany'. *Political Science Quarterly* 5, no. 3 (1890): 468–86.

Fuller, L. L. *Legal Fictions*. Stanford: Stanford University Press, 1967.

Gallagher, C. 'History/Historicism'. In *The Routledge Companion to Victorian Literature*, 248–59. New York: Routledge, 2020.

Garnsey, P. *Thinking about Property: From Antiquity to the Age of Revolution*. Cambridge; New York: Cambridge University Press, 2007.

Gaukroger, S. 'The Shaping of Character: The Classics as a Remedy for Cultural Despair in Victorian England'. *Critical Quarterly* 66, no. 2 (2024): 4–17.

Geib, G. *Geschichte des Römischen Criminalprocesses bis zum Tode Justinians*. Leipzig: Weidmann, 1842.

Geroulanos, S. *The Invention of Prehistory: Empire, Violence, and Our Obsession with Human Origins*. New York: Liveright/Norton, 2024.

Gibbins, J. R. 'J.S. Mill, Liberalism, and Progress'. In *Victorian Liberalism: Nineteenth-Century Political Thought and Practice*, 91–109. London: Routledge, 1990.

Gibbins, J. R. 'George Grote and Natural Religion'. In *Brill's Companion to George Grote and the Classical Tradition*, 85–116. Leiden: Brill, 2014.

Gibbon, E., and F. Fernández-Armesto. *The History of the Decline and Fall of the Roman Empire. Vol. 5, Justinian and the Roman Law*. London: Folio Society, 1987.

Goëtzmann, M. 'La "Comparative Jurisprudence" de Henry Sumner Maine, Entre École Analytique et École Historique'. Master's dissertation. Paris: Sorbonne, 2014.

Goëtzmann, M. 'La Comparative Jurisprudence de Henry Sumner Maine, Entre Critique et Approfondissement de La Théorie Impérativiste Du Droit'. *Droit & Philosophie* 12 (2020): 31–59.

Goldman, L. 'A Peculiarity of the English? The Social Science Association and the Absence of Sociology in Nineteenth-Century Britain'. *Past & Present* 114, no. 1 (1987): 133–71.

Gooch, G. P. *History and Historians in the Nineteenth Century*. 2nd ed. London: Longmans, Green, 1952.

Goodlad, L. 'Moral Character'. In *Historicism and the Human Sciences in Victorian Britain*, 128–53. Cambridge: Cambridge University Press, 2017.

Göttner-Abendroth, H. *Matriarchal Societies: Studies on Indigenous Cultures across the Globe*. New York: Peter Lang, 2013.

Grant Duff, M. E. *Sir Henry Maine: A Brief Memoir of His Life by Sir M.E. Grant Duff with Some of His Indian Speeches and Minutes Selected and Edited by Whitley Stokes*. London: Murray, 1892.

Grimshawe, T. S. *An Earnest Appeal to British Humanity in Behalf of Hindoo Widows: In Which the Abolition of the Barbarous Rite of Burning Alive Is Proved to Be Safe and Practicable*. London: Hatchard and Son, Seeley and Son, 1825.

Grossi, P. *An Alternative to Private Property: Collective Property in the Juridical Consciousness of the Nineteenth Century*. Translated by Lydia G. Cochrane. Chicago: University of Chicago Press, 1981.

Grote, G. *A History of Greece*. London: Murray, 1846. (Cambridge: Cambridge University Press, 2010).

Grotius, H. *Grotius on the Rights of War and Peace: An Abridged Translation by William Whewell*. Cambridge: Cambridge University Press, 1853.

Hadjigeorgiou, A. 'The Legacy of Sir Henry Maine in the 21st Century'. *Noesis*, 34 (2020): 159–92.

Hägerström, A. 'Rights, Obligations and the Binding Force of Contracts in Roman Law and in Natural Law Theory'. *Grotiana (1980)* 43, no. 2 (2022): 309–93.

Hall, E., and H. Stead, eds. *People's History of Classics: Class and Greco-Roman Antiquity in Britain and Ireland 1689 to 1939*. Abingdon: Taylor & Francis, 2020.

Harries, J. 'The Law in Cicero's Writings'. In *The Cambridge Companion to Cicero*, 107–21. Cambridge: Cambridge University Press, 2013.

Harris, J. A. 'Treatises of Government and Treatises of Anarchy: Locke versus Filmer Revisited'. *Locke Studies* 19, no. 1 (2020): 1–32.

Harris, J. A. 'Of the Origin of Government: The Afterlives of Locke and Filmer in an Eighteenth-Century British Debate'. *Intellectual History Review* 33, no. 1 (2023): 33–55.

Harrison, F. *On Jurisprudence and the Conflict of Laws*. Oxford: Clarendon Press, 1919.

Hart, H. L. A. *Essays on Bentham: Studies on Jurisprudence and Political Theory*. Oxford: Clarendon Press, 1982.

Haxthausen, A. *The Russian Empire: Its People, Institutions and Resources; Translated by Robert Farie*. London: Chapman and Hall, 1856.

Heineccius, J. G. *A Methodical System of Universal Law: Or The Laws of Nature and Nations: With Supplements and a Discourse by George Turnbull*. Indianapolis: Liberty Fund, 2008.

Helmholz, R. H. 'The Law of Slavery and the European *Ius Commune*'. In *The Legal Understanding of Slavery*, 17–39. Oxford: Oxford University Press, 2012.

Hendrickson, R. 'Ordinary Passions and Philosophic Morality: On the Uniqueness of Montesquieu's Commercial Republic'. *Perspectives on Political Science* 43, no. 1 (2014): 1–11.

Hock, H. H. 'Did Indo-European Linguistics Prepare the Ground for Nazism? Lessons From the Past for the Present and the Future'. In *Language in Time and Space: A Festschrift for Werner Winter on the Occasion of his 80th Birthday*, 167–188. Berlin; Boston: De Gruyter, 2011.

Hoeflich, M. H. 'John Austin and Joseph Story: Two Nineteenth-Century Perspectives on the Utility of the Civil Law for the Common Lawyer'. *American Journal of Legal History* 29, no. 1 (1985): 36–77.

Hoeflich, M. H. 'The Americanization of British Legal Education in the Nineteenth Century'. *Journal of Legal History* 8, no. 3 (1987): 244–59.

Hoeflich, M. H. 'Savigny and His Anglo-American Disciples'. *American Journal of Comparative Law* 37, no. 1 (1989): 17–37.

Hoeflich, M. H. 'Edward Gibbon, Roman Lawyer'. *American Journal of Comparative Law* 39, no. 4 (1991): 803–18.

Hoeflich, M. H. *Roman and Civil Law and the Development of Anglo-American Jurisprudence in the Nineteenth Century*. Athens, GA: University of Georgia Press, 1997.

Hofmann, H. 'From Jhering to Radbruch: On the Logic of Traditional Legal Concepts to the Social Theories of Law to the Renewal of Legal Idealism'. In *A Treatise of Legal Philosophy and General Jurisprudence*. Vol. 9. 301–54. Dordrecht: Springer, 2009.

Honoré, A. 'The Nature of Slavery'. In *The Legal Understanding of Slavery*, 9–16. Oxford: Oxford University Press, 2012.

Howarth, J. 'Gender, Domesticity, and Sexual Politics'. In *The Nineteenth Century*, 163–94. Oxford: Oxford University Press, 2000.

Huebner, S. R., and G. S. Nathan, eds. *Mediterranean Families in Antiquity: Households, Extended Families, and Domestic Space*. Chichester: Wiley-Blackwell, 2017.

Humfress, C., 'Natural Law and Casuistic Reasoning in Roman Jurisprudence'. In *State and Nature: Studies in Ancient and Medieval Philosophy*, 247–66, Berlin; Boston: De Gruyter, 2021.

Humfress, C., D. Ibbetson and P. Olivelle, eds. *The Cambridge Comparative History of Ancient Law*. Cambridge: Cambridge University Press, 2024.

Hunter, W. A., J. Ashton Cross and Gaius. *A Systematic and Historical Exposition of Roman Law in the Order of a Code*. 2nd ed. revised and enlarged. London: Maxwell, 1885.

Ibbetson, D. *A Historical Introduction to the Law of Obligations*. Oxford: Oxford University Press, 2001.

Ibbetson, D. 'Comparative Legal History'. In *Making Legal History*, 131–45. Cambridge: Cambridge University Press, 2011.

Ibbetson, D. 'The Challenges of Comparative Legal History'. *Comparative Legal History* 1, no. 1 (2013): 1–11.

Iurlaro, F. *The Invention of Custom: Natural Law and the Law of Nations, ca. 1550–1750*. Oxford: Oxford University Press, 2021.

Jackson, B. S. 'Law and Language: A Metaphor in Maine, a Model for His Successors?' In *The Victorian Achievement of Sir Henry Maine: A Centennial Reappraisal*, 256–93. Cambridge: Cambridge University Press, 1991.

Jain, M. P. 'Custom as a Source of Law in India'. In *Folk Law: Essays in the Theory and Practice of Lex Non Scripta*, 1:49–82. Madison: The University of Wisconsin Press, 1994.

James, D. *Property and its Forms in Classical German Philosophy*. Cambridge: Cambridge University Press, 2023.

Jamoussi, Z. *Primogeniture and Entail in England: A Survey of Their History and Representation in Literature*. Newcastle upon Tyne: Cambridge Scholars Publishing, 2011.

Jarvis, D. E. 'The Family as the Foundation of Political Rule in Western Philosophy: A Comparative Analysis of Aristotle's Politics and Hegel's Philosophy of Right'. *Journal of Family History* 36, no. 4 (2011): 440–63.

Jenkyns, R. *The Victorians and Ancient Greece*. Oxford: Blackwell, 1980.

Jhering, R. von. *Vorgeschichte der Indoeuropäer*. Leipzig: Breitkopf & Härtel, 1894.

Johnson, G. 'India and Henry Maine'. In *The Victorian Achievement of Sir Henry Maine: A Centennial Reappraisal*, 376–88. Cambridge: Cambridge University Press, 1991.

Jolly, R. 'Robert Louis Stevenson, Henry Maine, and the Anthropology of Comparative Law'. *Journal of British Studies* 45, no. 3 (2006): 556–80.

Jones, H. S. 'The Early Utilitarians, Race, and Empire: The State of the Argument'. In *Utilitarianism and Empire*, 179–87. Lanham: Lexington Books/Fortress Academic, 2005.

Kantor, G., T. B. Lambert and H. Skoda, eds. *Legalism: Property and Ownership*. Oxford: Oxford University Press, 2017.

Kelley, D. R. *Faces of History: Historical Inquiry from Herodotus to Herder*. New Haven: Yale University Press, 1998.

Kemble, J. M. *The Saxons in England: A History of the English Commonwealth till the Period of the Norman Conquest*. London: Longman, Brown, Green, & Longmans, 1849.

Kennedy, D. 'A Sense of Place: Rome, History, and Empire Revisited'. In *Roman Presences: Receptions of Rome in European Culture, 1789–1945*, 19–34. Cambridge: Cambridge University Press, 1999.

Kennedy, D. 'Savigny's Family/Patrimony Distinction and Its Place in the Global Genealogy of Classical Legal Thought'. *American Journal of Comparative Law* 58, no. 4 (2010): 811–41.

Kennedy, S. P. *Reforming the Law of Nature: The Secularisation of Political Thought, 1532–1689*. Edinburgh: Edinburgh University Press, 2023.

Kinzer, B. 'George Grote, The Philosophic Radical and Politician'. In *Brill's Companion to George Grote and the Classical Tradition*, 16–46. Leiden: Brill, 2014.

Kirkby, C. 'Law Evolves: the Uses of Primitive Law in Anglo-American Concepts of Modern Law, 1861-1961'. *American Journal of Legal History* 58, no. 4 (2018): 535–63.

Kletzer, C. 'Custom and Positivity: An Examination of the Philosophic Ground of the Hegel–Savigny Controversy'. In *The Nature of Customary Law*, 125–48. Cambridge: Cambridge University Press, 2007.

Kodama, S. 'Bentham's Distinction between Law and Morality and its Contemporary Significance'. *Revue d'études benthamiennes* no. 16 (2019). https://doi.org/10.4000/etudes-benthamiennes.6378.

Kraemer, C. J. 'The Influence of the Classics on English Literature'. *The Classical Journal* 22, no. 7 (1927): 485–97.

Krause, S. R. 'History and the Human Soul in Montesquieu'. *History of Political Thought* 24, no. 2 (2003): 235–61.

Kumar, K. 'Maine and the Theory of Progress'. In *The Victorian Achievement of Sir Henry Maine: A Centennial Reappraisal*, 76–87. Cambridge: Cambridge University Press, 1991.

Kumar, K. 'Greece and Rome in the British Empire: Contrasting Role Models'. *Journal of British Studies* 51, no. 1 (2012): 76–101.

Kuper, A. 'Ancestors: Henry Maine and the Constitution of Primitive Society'. *History and Anthropology* 1, no. 2 (1985): 265–86.

Kuper, A. 'The Rise and Fall of Maine's Patriarchal Society'. In *The Victorian Achievement of Sir Henry Maine: A Centennial Reappraisal*, 99–110. Cambridge: Cambridge University Press, 1991.

Kuper, A. *The Reinvention of Primitive Society: Transformations of a Myth*. London: Routledge, 2017.

Kuper, A. 'Civilization, Culture, and Race: Anthropology in the Nineteenth Century'. In *The Cambridge History of Modern European Thought: Volume 1: The Nineteenth Century*. 1:398–421. Cambridge: Cambridge University Press, 2019.

Kustermans, J. 'Henry Maine and the Modern Invention of Peace'. *Journal of the History of International Law = Revue d'histoire Du Droit International*, 20, no. 1 (2018): 57–88.

Laboulaye, É. *Essai sur les lois criminelles des Romains concernant la responsabilité des magistrats: mémoire couronné par l'académie des inscriptions et belles-lettres dans la séance du 11 aout 1843*. Paris: Durand, 1845.

Landauer, C. 'From Status to Treaty: Henry Sumner Maine's International Law'. *Canadian Journal of Law and Jurisprudence* 15, no. 2 (2002): 219–54.

Landauer, C. 'Henry Sumner Maine's Grand Tour: Roman Law in Ancient Law'. In *Law and History volume* 6, 135–57. Oxford: University Press, 2004.

Landman, J. H. 'Primitive Law, Evolution, and Sir Henry Sumner Maine'. *Michigan Law Review* 28, no. 4 (1930): 404–25.

Larrère, C., and W. Ning Seah. 'Montesquieu and the Classical World'. In *The Cambridge Companion to Montesquieu*, 76–93. Cambridge: Cambridge University Press, 2023.

Lee, D. 'Private Law Models for Public Law Concepts: The Roman Law Theory of *Dominium* in the Monarchomach Doctrine of Popular Sovereignty'. *Review of Politics* 70, no. 3 (2008): 370–99.

Lerminier, E. *Introduction générale à l'histoire du droit*. Paris: Mesnier, 1829.

Levy, J. T. 'Constitutional History'. In *The Cambridge Companion to Montesquieu*, 248–65. Cambridge: Cambridge University Press, 2023.

Liddel, P. 'The Comparative Approach in Grote's History of Greece'. In *Brill's Companion to George Grote and the Classical Tradition*, 211–54. Leiden: Brill, 2014.

Lippincott, B. E. *Victorian Critics of Democracy: Carlyle, Ruskin, Arnold, Stephen, Maine, Lecky*. London; Minneapolis: Oxford University Press; University of Minnesota Press, 1938.

Lira Gonzalez, A., and A. Martin. 'Henry S. Maine: History and Antiquity in Law'. *Nepantla* 3, no. 2 (2002): 407–22.

Lobban, M. 'Legal Fictions before the Age of Reform'. In *Legal Fictions in Theory and Practice*, 199–223. Cham: Springer, 2015.

Lobban, M. 'The Varieties of Legal History'. *Clio@Themis* 5, no. 5 (2021). https://doi.org/10.35562/cliothemis.1727.

Lovelass, P. *The Law's Disposal of a Person's Estate Who Dies without Will or Testament: Shewing in a Clear, Plain, Easy, and Familiar Manner, How a Man's Family or Relations Will Be Entitled to His Real and Personal Estate, by the Laws of England, and Customs of the City of London and Province of York. : To Which Is Added the Disposal of a Person's Estate, by Will and Testament ; Containing an Explanation of the Mortmain-Act, with Instructions and Necessary Forms for Every Person to Make, Alter, and Republish His Own Will : Likewise Directions for Executors How to Act after the Testator's Death* . . . The 6th ed., with Additions. London: Printed for the author, 1790.

Lyons, J. 'Linguistics and Law: The Legacy of Sir Henry Maine'. In *The Victorian Achievement of Sir Henry Maine: A Centennial Reappraisal*, 294–350. Cambridge: Cambridge University Press, 1991.

MacDonald, S. 'Problems with Principles: Montesquieu's Theory of Natural Justice'. *History of Political Thought* 24, no. 1 (2003): 109–30.

Macfarlane, A. D. J. 'Some Contributions of Maine to History and Anthropology'. In *The Victorian Achievement of Sir Henry Maine: A Centennial Reappraisal*, 111–42. Cambridge: Cambridge University Press, 1991.

Mack, P. 'Humanism and the Classical Tradition'. In *The Oxford History of the Renaissance*, 10–47. Oxford: Oxford University Press, 2023.

Mackeldey, F., and M. A. Dropsie. *Handbook of the Roman Law . . . Translated and Edited by M.A. Dropsie from the Fourteenth German Edition*. Philadelphia: Johnson, 1883.

Mackenzie, T. *Studies in Roman Law: With Comparative Views of the Laws of France, England, and Scotland.* Edinburgh: Blackwood, 1862.

Macnaghten, F.W. *Considerations on the Hindoo Law, as It Is Current in Bengal.* Serampore: Mission Press, 1824.

Macrae, D. '"The Laws of the Rites and the Priests": Varro and Late Republican Roman Sacral Jurisprudence'. *Bulletin of the Institute of Classical Studies* 60, no. 2 (2017): 34–48.

Maine, H. S. *Ancient Law: Its Connection with the Early History of Society, and Its Relation to Modern Ideas. By Henry Sumner Maine, Reader on Jurisprudence and the Civil Law at the Middle Temple, and Formerly Regius Professor of the Civil Law in the University of Cambridge.* London: Murray, 1861.

Maine, H. S. *The Early History of the Property of Married Women, as Collected from Roman and Hindoo Law; a Lecture, Delivered . . . 1873 . . .* Manchester: Ireland, 1873.

Maine, H. S. *Lectures on the Early History of Institutions by Sir Henry Sumner Maine.* London: Murray, 1875.

Maine, H. S. *Dissertations on Early Law and Custom: Chiefly Selected from Lectures Delivered at Oxford by Sir Henry Sumner Maine.* London: Murray, 1883.

Maine, H. S. *Popular Government.* 2nd ed. London: Murray, 1886.

Maine, H. S. *Village Communities in the East and West.* New ed. London: Murray, 1890.

Maine, H. S. *Ancient Law, Its Connection with the Early History of Society and Its Relation to Modern Ideas. Edited by Frederick Pollock.* London: Murray, 1907.

Maine, H. S., and G. Capellán de Miguel. *El gobierno popular.* Cívitas (CEPC). Madrid: Centro de Estudios Políticos y Constitucionales, 2016.

Majeed, J. 'Comparativism and References to Rome in British Imperial Attitudes to India'. In *Roman Presences: Receptions of Rome in European Culture, 1789-1945*, 88–109. Cambridge: Cambridge University Press, 1999.

Majeed, J. 'Bathos, Architecture and Knowing India: E. M. Forster's A Passage to India and Nineteenth-Century British Ethnology and the Romance Quest'. *Journal of Commonwealth Literature* 40, no. 1 (2005): 21–36.

Majeed, J., B. Schultz and G. Varouxakis. 'James Mill's The History of British India: The Question of Utilitarianism and Empire'. In *Utilitarianism and Empire*, 93–105. Lanham: Lexington Books/Fortress Academic, 2005.

Mantena, K. 'Law and "Tradition": Henry Maine and the Theoretical Origins of Indirect Rule'. In *Law and History volume* 6, 159–88. Oxford: Oxford University Press, 2004.

Mantena, K. *Alibis of Empire: Henry Maine and the Ends of Liberal Imperialism.* Princeton; Oxford: Princeton University Press, 2010.

Manu. *The Law Code of Manu – a New Translation Based on the Critical Edition by Patrick Olivelle.* Oxford: Oxford University Press, 2004.

Marcos, M. H. 'Conceptual Aspects of Legal Enlightenment in Europe'. In *A Treatise of Legal Philosophy and General Jurisprudence.* Vol. 9. 69–134. Dordrecht: Springer, 2009.

Martin, R. H. 'The Golden Age and the ΚΥΚΛΟΣ ΓΕΝΕΣΕΩΝ (Cyclical Theory) in Greek and Latin Literature'. *Greece & Rome* 12, no. 35–6 (1943): 62–71.

Mayne, J. D. *A Treatise on the Hindu Law and Usage*. London: Stevens, 1878.

McDonagh, J. 'Towards a Genealogy of the Village in the Nineteenth-Century British Colonial World: Mary Russell Mitford and Henry Sumner Maine'. In *Commodities and Culture in the Colonial World*, 145–59. London: Routledge, 2018.

McGowen, R. 'The Image of Justice and Reform of the Criminal Law in Early Nineteenth-Century England'. *Buffalo Law Review* 32, no. 1 (1983): 89–125.

McMahon, D. *Equality. The History of an Elusive Idea*. Ithaka/Bonnier: London, 2024.

Momigliano, A. 'From Mommsen to Max Weber'. *History and Theory* 21, no. 4 (1982): 16–32.

Montesquieu, Charles de Secondat et al., *The Spirit of the Laws*. Edited by A. M. Cohler, B. C. Miller and H. S. Stone. Cambridge: Cambridge University Press, 1989.

Muirhead, J. *Historical Introduction to the Private Law of Rome by James Muirhead; Revised and Edited by Henry Goudy. The Third Edition Revised and Edited by Alexander Grant*. London: Black, 1916.

Müller, F. M. *Three Lectures on the Science of Language and Its Place in General Education: Delivered at the Oxford University Extension Meeting 1889, with a Supplement 'My Predecessors', an Essay on the Genesis of the Idea of the Identity of Thought and Language in the History of Philosophy*. Chicago: Open Court, 1890.

Murphy, J. B. 'A Commentary on the *Comment*: Jeremy Bentham's Theory of Custom'. In *The Philosophy of Customary Law*, 59–88. New York: Oxford University Press, 2014.

Murphy, J. B. 'Habit and Convention at the Foundation of Custom'. In *The Philosophy of Customary Law*, 1–22. New York: Oxford University Press, 2014.

Nanz, K-P. *Die Entstehung des allgemeinen Vertragsbegriffs im 16. bis 18. Jahrhundert*. Munich: Schweitzer, 1985.

Nelson, R. A. *An Analysis of 'Ancient Law' with Notes Explanatory and Critical for the Use of Students*. Madras: Varadachari, 1899.

Newman, K. S. *Law and Economic Organization: A Comparative Study of Preindustrial Societies*. Cambridge: Cambridge: University Press, 1983.

Niebuhr, B. G. *Niebuhr's History of Rome Epitomised from the Larger Work and Adapted to the Use of Schools and Colleges by Travers Twiss, with Chronological Tables and an Appendix*. Oxford: Talboys, 1845.

Nielsen, D. A. *The Sociological Theories of Sir Henry Maine: Societal Transformation, Cultural Modernization and Civilization in Sociocultural Perspective*. Ann Arbor: ProQuest Dissertations Publishing, 1972.

Noone, J. B. 'Rousseau's Theory of Natural Law as Conditional'. *Journal of the History of Ideas* 33, no. 1 (1972): 23–42.

O'brien, N. '"Something Older than Law Itself": Sir Henry Maine, Niebuhr, and "the Path Not Chosen"'. *Journal of Legal History* 26, no. 3 (2005): 229–51.

O'brien, N. '"In Vino Veritas": Truth and Method in Vinogradoff's Historical Jurisprudence'. *Journal of Legal History* 29, no. 1 (2008): 39–61.

O'Neill, D. I. 'Rethinking Burke and India'. *History of Political Thought* 30, no. 3 (2009): 492–523.

Oldham, J. B. *Analysis of Maine's 'Ancient Law' with Notes*. 2nd ed. Oxford: Blackwell, 1922.

Orenstein, H. 'The Ethnological Theories of Henry Sumner Maine'. *American Anthropologist* 70, no. 2 (1968): 264–76.

Ortolan, J.-L.-E. *Explication historique des Instituts de l'empereur Justinien: avec le texte, la traduction en regard, et les explications sous chaque paragraphe, précédée d'une généralisation du droit romain, d'après les textes anciennement connus, ou plus récemment decouverts*. 4. éd. Paris: Joubert, 1847.

Ortolan, J.-L.-E., D. Nasmith and I. T. Prichard. *The History of Roman Law, from the Text of Ortolan's 'Histoire de La Législation Romaine et Généralisation Du Droit' (Edition of 1870). Translated . . . and Supplemented by a Chronometrical Chart of Roman History by I.T. Prichard and D. Nasmith*. London: Butterworths, 1871.

Palti, E. J. *Intellectual History and the Problem of Conceptual Change: Skinner, Pocock, Koselleck, Blumenberg, Foucault, and Rosanvallon*. Cambridge: Cambridge University Press, 2024.

Parker, I. K. 'A Critical Analysis of Filmer's and Locke's Use of Genesis in the Development of Their Political Philosophies'. PhD thesis, McMaster University, 1982.

Passmore, J. *The Perfectibility of Man*. 3rd ed. Indianapolis: Liberty Fund, 2000.

Peel, J. D. Y. 'Maine as an Ancestor of the Social Sciences'. In *The Victorian Achievement of Sir Henry Maine*, 179–84. Cambridge: Cambridge University Press, 1991.

Pereltsvaig, A. *The Indo-European Controversy: Facts and Fallacies in Historical Linguistics*. Paperback edition. Cambridge: Cambridge University Press, 2017.

Phillimore, G. G. 'Booty of War'. *Journal of the Society of Comparative Legislation* 3, no. 2 (1901): 214–30.

Piccinini, M. *Tra legge e contratto: una lettura di Ancient law di Henry S. Maine*. Milan: Giuffrè, 2003.

Pitts, J. 'Jeremy Bentham Legislator of the World?' In *Utilitarianism and Empire*, 57–91. Lanham: Lexington Books/Fortress Academic, 2005.

Pollock, F., and H. S. Maine. *Introduction and Notes to Sir Henry Maine's 'Ancient Law'*. 2nd ed. London: Murray, 1914.

Posner, R. A. 'A Theory of Primitive Society, with Special Reference to Law'. *Journal of Law & Economics* 23, no. 1 (1980): 1–53.

Postema, G. J. 'The British Tradition of Legal Positivism'. In *The Cambridge Companion to Legal Positivism*, 176–200. Cambridge: Cambridge University Press, 2021.

Pottage, A., A. Street and J. Copeman. 'Law after Anthropology: Object and Technique in Roman Law'. *Theory, Culture & Society* 31, no. 2–3 (2014): 147–66.

Prochaska, F. K. *Eminent Victorians on American Democracy: The View from Albion*. Oxford: Oxford University Press, 2012.

Psomiades, K. A. *Primitive Marriage: Victorian Anthropology, the Novel, and Sexual Modernity*. Oxford: Oxford University Press, 2023.

Rabban, D. M. 'From Maine to Maitland via America'. *Cambridge Law Journal* 68, no. 2 (2009): 410–35.

Rabban, D. M. 'Maitland: The Maturity of English Legal History'. In *Law's History: American Legal Thought and the Transatlantic Turn to History*, 383–422. Cambridge: Cambridge University Press, 2012.

Rahmatian, A. 'Friedrich Carl von Savigny's *Beruf* and *Volksgeistlehre*'. *Journal of Legal History* 28, no. 1 (2007): 1–29.

Reimann, M. 'Historical Jurisprudence'. In *The Oxford Handbook of Legal History*, 397–418. Oxford. Oxford University Press, 2018.

Reimann, M. 'Nineteenth Century German Legal Science'. *Boston College Law Review* 31, no. 4 (1990): 837–97.

Rey, S. *Manus: Une autre histoire de Rome*. Paris: Albin Michel, 2024.

Riley, P. 'Rousseau, Fénelon, and the Quarrel between the Ancients and the Moderns'. In *The Cambridge Companion to Rousseau*, 78–93. Cambridge: Cambridge University Press, 2001.

Roby, H. J. *Roman Private Law in the Times of Cicero and of the Antonines*. Cambridge: Cambridge University Press, 1902.

Rosen, F. 'Jeremy Bentham on Slavery and the Slave Trade'. In *Utilitarianism and Empire*, 33–56. Lanham: Lexington Books/Fortress Academic, 2005.

Rousseau, J.-J. *Basic Political Writings*. Edited by D. A. Cress. 2nd ed. Indianapolis: Hackett Publishing Company, 2011.

Rüfner, T. 'Testamentary Formalities in Roman Law'. In *Comparative Succession Law*, 1–26. Oxford: Oxford University Press, 2011.

Rumble, W. 'John Austin and His Nineteenth Century Critics: The Case of Sir Henry Sumner Maine'. *Northern Ireland Legal Quarterly* 39, no. 2 (1988): 119–49.

Rustigan, M. A. 'A Reinterpretation of Criminal Law Reform in Nineteenth-Century England'. *Journal of Criminal Justice* 8, no. 4 (1980): 205–19.

Sayce, A. H. *The Primitive Home of the Aryans [Northeastern Europe]*. Washington: Smithsonian Inst., 1891.

Savigny, F. C. von. *The History of the Roman Law during the Middle Ages Translated from the Original German of Carl von Savigny by E. Cathcart*. Vol. I. Edinburgh: Black, 1829.

Savigny, F. C. von. *Von Savigny's Treatise on Possession, or, The Jus Possessionis of the Civil Law Translated from the German by Sir Erskine Perry . . .* 6th ed. London: Sweet, 1848.

Savigny, F. C. von. *System of the Modern Roman Law, Translated from the German . . . by W. Holloway*. Vol. I. Madras: Higginbotham, 1867.

Savigny, F. C. von, and A. Hayward. *Of the Vocation of Our Age for Legislation and Jurisprudence, Translated from the German . . . by A. Hayward*. London: Littlewood, 1831.

Scala, D. J. 'Henry Sumner Maine's Ancient Law'. *Society (New Brunswick)* 39, no. 4 (2002): 46–54.

Scattola, M. '*Scientia Iuris* and *Ius Naturae*: The Jurisprudence of the Holy Roman Empire in the Seventeenth and Eighteenth Centuries'. In *A Treatise of Legal Philosophy and General Jurisprudence*. Vol. 9, 1–41. Dordrecht: Springer Netherlands, 2009.

Schauer, F. 'Legal Fictions Revisited'. In *Legal Fictions in Theory and Practice*, 113–19. Cham: Springer, 2015.

Schiavone, A. *The End of the Past: Ancient Rome and the Modern West*. Translated by Margery J. Schneider. Cambridge, Mass.: Harvard University Press, 2002.

Schiavone, A., and A. Goldstein. *What is Progress*, London: Europa, 2021.

Schmidt, K. 'Henry Maine's "Modern Law" From Status to Contract and Back Again?' *American Journal of Comparative Law* 65, no. 1 (2017): 145–86.

Schofield, P. 'Jeremy Bentham, the French Revolution and Political Radicalism'. *History of European Ideas* 30, no. 4 (2004): 381–401.

Schofield, P. 'Jeremy Bentham (1748–1832)'. In *The Oxford Handbook of Legal History*, 379–96. Oxford: Oxford University Press, 2018.

Sera-Shriar, E. 'Race'. In *Historicism and the Human Sciences in Victorian Britain*, 48–76. Cambridge: Cambridge University Press, 2017.

Shils, E. 'Henry Sumner Maine in the Tradition of the Analysis of Society'. In *The Victorian Achievement of Sir Henry Maine: A Centennial Reappraisal*, 143–78. Cambridge: Cambridge University Press, 1991.

Shmilovits, L. *Legal Fictions in Private Law*. Cambridge: Cambridge University Press, 2022.

Siedentop, L. *Inventing the Individual: The Origins of Western Liberalism*. Cambridge: Belknap Press of Harvard University Press, 2014.

Skinner, Q. 'Meaning and Understanding in the History of Ideas'. *History and Theory* 8, no. 1 (1969): 3–53.

Smellie, K. B. 'Sir Henry Maine'. *Economica*, no. 22 (1928): 64–94.

Smith, B. 'Maine's Concept of Progress'. *Journal of the History of Ideas* 24, no. 3 (1963): 407–12.

Smith, M. 'Four German Jurists. III'. *Political Science Quarterly* 12, no. 1 (1897): 21–62.

Smith, N. D. 'Aristotle's Theory of Natural Slavery'. *Phoenix* 37, no. 2 (1983): 109–22.

Somos, M. *American States of Nature: The Origins of Independence, 1761-1775*. New York: Oxford University Press, 2019.

Somos, M., and A. Peters, eds. *The State of Nature: Histories of an Idea*. Leiden: Brill, 2022.

Stein, P. G. *Legal Evolution: The Story of an Idea*. Cambridge: Cambridge University Press, 1980.

Stein, P. G. 'Maine and Legal Education'. In *The Victorian Achievement of Sir Henry Maine: A Centennial Reappraisal*, 195–208. Cambridge: Cambridge University Press, 1991.

Steinbach, S. *Understanding the Victorians. Politics, Culture, and Society in Nineteenth-Century Britain*. London: Routledge, 2016.

Steinmetz, G. 'The Imperial Entanglements of Sociology in the United States, Britain, and France Since the Nineteenth Century'. *Ab Imperio* 2009, no. 4 (2009): 23–79.

Stokes, E. *The English Utilitarians and India*. Oxford: Clarendon Press, 1959.

Strachan-Davidson, J. L. *Problems of the Roman Criminal Law*. Oxford: Clarendon Press, 1912.

Strange, T. A. L. *Elements of Hindu Law: Referable to British Judicature in India*. London: Payne and Foss, 1825.

Straumann, B., and B. Kingsbury. 'The State of Nature and Commercial Sociability in Early Modern International Legal Thought'. *Grotiana (1980)* 31, no. 1 (2010): 22–43.

Sturman, R. L. *The Government of Social Life in Colonial India: Liberalism, Religious Law, and Women's Rights*. Cambridge: Cambridge University Press, 2012.

Sverdlik, S. 'Bentham on Temptation and Deterrence'. *Utilitas* 31, no. 3 (2019): 246–61.

Swain, W. *The Law of Contract 1670–1870*. Cambridge: Cambridge University Press, 2015.

Taylor, J. *Elements of the Civil Law*. 4th ed. revised and corrected. London: Sweet, 1828.

Taylor, L. *Constructing the Family: Marriage and Work in Nineteenth-Century English Law*. Toronto: University of Toronto Press, 2023.

Tęgoborski, L. *Commentaries on the Productive Forces of Russia*. London: Longman, Brown, Green, and Longmans, 1855.

Thomas, Y. *Legal Artifices: Ten Essays on Roman Law in the Present Tense*. Edited by T. Zartaloudis and C. Francis. Translated by Anton Schütz and Chantal Schütz. Edinburgh: Edinburgh University Press, 2021.

Tomalin, M. 'Language'. In *Historicism and the Human Sciences in Victorian Britain*, 77–104. Cambridge: Cambridge University Press, 2017.

Tuori, K. *Lawyers and Savages: Ancient History and Legal Realism in the Making of Legal Anthropology*. Abingdon: Routledge, 2015.

Turner, F. M. 'Antiquity in Victorian Contexts'. *Browning Institute Studies* 10 (1982): 1–14.

Twining, W. 'Maine and Legal Education: A Comment'. In *The Victorian Achievement of Sir Henry Maine: A Centennial Reappraisal*, 209–16. Cambridge: Cambridge University Press, 1991.

Utz, S. G. 'Maine's *Ancient Law* and Legal Theory'. *Connecticut Law Review* 16, no. 4 (1984): 821–52.

Van Nuffelen, P., and L. Van Hoof. 'Posidonius and the Golden Age: A Note on Seneca, "Epistulae Morales" 90'. *Latomus* 72, no. 1 (2013): 186–95.

Varouxakis, G. 'Empire, Race, Euro-Centrism: John Stuart Mill and His Critics'. In *Utilitarianism and Empire*, 137–53. Lanham: Lexington Books/Fortress Academic, 2005.

Vesey-FitzGerald, S. G. 'Sir William Jones, the Jurist'. *Bulletin of the School of Oriental and African Studies, University of London* 11, no. 4 (1946): 807–17.

Viereck, P. *Conservative Thinkers: From John Adams to Winston Churchill*. New Brunswick, NJ: Transaction Publishers, 2006.

Vinogradoff, P. *The Teaching of Sir Henry Maine; an Inaugural Lecture Delivered in Corpus Christi College Hall on March 1, 1904*. London: Frowde, 1904.

Voigt, M., and K. Seeliger. *Das jus naturale, aequum et bonum, und jus gentium der Römer*. Leipzig: Voigt & Günther, 1856.

Waerdt, P. A. Vander. 'Philosophical Influence on Roman Jurisprudence? The Case of Stoicism and Natural Law'. In *Band 36/7. Teilband Philosophie, Wissenschaften, Technik. Philosophie (Systematische Themen; Indirekte Überlieferungen; Allgemeines; Nachträge)*, 4851–901. Berlin: De Gruyter, 2016.

Watson, A. *The Evolution of Law*. Baltimore: John Hopkins University Press, 1989.

Watson, A. *Slave Law in the Americas*. Athens, GA: University of Georgia Press, 2012.

Watson, P. *The French Mind: 400 Years of Romance, Revolution and Renewal*. London: Simon & Schuster UK Ltd., 2023.

Westbrook R. 'The Early History of Law: A Theoretical Essay'. *Zeitschrift der Savigny-Stiftung fur Rechtsgeschichte* 127 (2010): 1–13.

Weston, J. C. 'Edmund Burke's View of History'. *Review of Politics* 23, no. 2 (1961): 203–29.

Whatmore, R. *The End of Enlightenment: Empire, Commerce, Crisis*. London: Allen Lane, 2023.

Widerquist, K., and G. S. McCall. *The Prehistory of Private Property: Implications for Modern Political Theory*. Edinburgh: Edinburgh University Press, 2021.

Wood, E. M. *Liberty and Property: A Social History of Western Political Thought from Renaissance to Enlightenment*. London: Verso, 2012.

Woodard, C. 'A Wake (or Awakening?) For Historical Jurisprudence'. In *The Victorian Achievement of Sir Henry Maine: A Centennial Reappraisal*, 217–37. Cambridge: Cambridge University Press, 1991.

Yale, D. E. C. 'Further Thoughts on Maine's Historical Jurisprudence'. In *The Victorian Achievement of Sir Henry Maine: A Centennial Reappraisal*, 238–41. Cambridge: Cambridge University Press, 1991.

Zartaloudis, T. *The Birth of Nomos*. Edinburgh: Edinburgh University Press, 2018.

Zimmerman, C. C. *Family and Civilization*. New York: Harper, 1947.

Zumpt, A. W. *Das Criminalrecht der Römischen Republik*. Berlin: Dümmler, 1865.

Zwalve, W. J. 'The Equity of the Law: Law and Equity since Justinian'. In *Law & Equity: Approaches in Roman and Common Law*, 15–37. Leiden: Nijhoff, 2014.

Index

Introductory Note

References such as '178–9' indicate discussion of a topic across a range of pages. Wherever possible, in the case of topics with many references, these have either been divided into subtopics or only the most significant discussions are listed. Because the entire work is about 'Henry Maine', 'Victorian Humanism' and '*Ancient Law*', the use of these terms (and certain others which occur constantly throughout the book) as an entry point has been minimised. Information will be found under the corresponding detailed topics. Cross–references such as '*see also individual philosophers*' refer the reader to entries in a particular class (e.g. in this case 'Aristotle') rather than a specific 'individual philosophers' entry.